Pulp fictions of medieval England

Published in our
centenary year
〜 **2004** 〜
MANCHESTER
UNIVERSITY
PRESS

Pulp fictions of medieval England

Essays in popular romance

edited by
Nicola McDonald

Manchester University Press
Manchester and New York

distributed exclusively in the USA by Palgrave

Copyright © Manchester University Press 2004

While copyright in the volume as a whole is vested in Manchester University Press, copyright in individual chapters belongs to their respective authors, and no chapter may be reproduced wholly or in part without the express permission in writing of both author and publisher.

Published by Manchester University Press
Oxford Road, Manchester M13 9NR, UK
and Room 400, 175 Fifth Avenue, New York, NY 10010, USA
www.manchesteruniversitypress.co.uk

Distributed exclusively in the USA by
Palgrave, 175 Fifth Avenue, New York, NY 10010, USA

Distributed exclusively in Canada by
UBC Press, University of British Columbia, 2029 West Mall,
Vancouver, BC, Canada V6T 1Z2

British Library Cataloguing-in-Publication Data
A catalogue record for this book is available from the British Library

Library of Congress Cataloging-in-Publication Data applied for

ISBN 0 7190 6318 3   *hardback*
      0 7190 6319 1   *paperback*

First published 2004

11 10 09 08 07 06 05 04   10 9 8 7 6 5 4 3 2 1

Typeset in Bembo by
Koinonia, Manchester
Printed in Great Britain by
CPI, Bath

Contents

List of contributors

SUZANNE CONKLIN AKBARI, Associate Professor of English and Medieval Studies, University of Toronto

ALCUIN BLAMIRES, Reader in English Literature, Goldsmith's College, University of London

SHEILA DELANY, Professor of English, Simon Fraser University

ARLYN DIAMOND, Professor of English, University of Massachusetts at Amherst

JANE GILBERT, Lecturer, Department of French, University College London

NICOLA MCDONALD, Lecturer, Department of English and Related Literature and the Centre for Medieval Studies, University of York

ELISA NARIN VAN COURT, Associate Professor of English, Colby College

AD PUTTER, Reader in English Literature and Director of the Centre for Medieval Studies, University of Bristol

FELICITY RIDDY, Professor of English, Department of English and Related Literature and the Centre for Medieval Studies, University of York

REBECCA WILCOX is completing her doctorate in medieval literature at the University of Texas at Austin

A polemical introduction

Nicola McDonald

The Middle English romances have been called the 'ugly ducklings of medieval English studies'.[1] In a discipline that contests even the most basic definition of the genre, romance's low prestige is one of the few critical certainties. Despite its status as medieval England's most popular secular genre (more than one hundred romances are extant), the origin of the modern novel (still the most significant literary form), the ancestor of almost all contemporary popular fiction (in print and on screen) and the most audacious and compendious testimony to the imaginary world of the Middle Ages, Middle English popular romance remains, with rare exceptions, under read and under studied. Popular romance is the pulp fiction of medieval England, the 'principal secular literature of entertainment' for an enormously diverse audience that endures for over two hundred and fifty years.[2] It is fast-paced and formulaic; it markets itself unabashedly as genre fiction; it is comparatively cheap and, in performance, ephemeral; it has a sensationalist taste for sex and violence; and it seems content to reproduce the easy certainties of sexist, racist and other bigoted ideologies. But this is not a reason to dismiss it. On the contrary, popular romance provides us with a unique opportunity to explore the complex workings of the medieval imaginary and the world outside the text that feeds and supports it.

The purpose of this collection of essays, all specially commissioned for this volume, is to demonstrate that popular romance not only merits and rewards serious critical attention, but that we ignore it to the detriment of our understanding of the complex and conflicted world of medieval England. Each essay concentrates on a single Middle English popular romance that has so far received little critical attention; together they exemplify, but by no means exhaust, both the richness of the primary material and the range of critical analysis that the genre invites. Contributors have been asked to provide relevant introductory material (including date of composition, extant manuscripts, and a plot summary) in order to make these neglected texts accessible to a non-specialist audience, but the focus of the essay is a sustained argument that demonstrates that the romances invite innovative, exacting and theoretically charged analysis. Readers will notice that the essays do not support a single, homogeneous reading of popular romance; in other words, this volume's authors work with assumptions and come to conclusions, about issues as fundamental as the genre's aesthetic codes, its political and cultural ideologies, its historical consciousness, that are different and sometimes opposed. This is a sign of healthy scholarship and of the vitality of the field of inquiry.

As an introduction to the ten essays that comprise this book, I provide neither a historical overview of the genre (authorship, audience, manuscripts) nor a survey of the different theoretical approaches that help elucidate the workings of popular culture; both of these have recently received admirable treatment elsewhere.[3] Instead, I offer a short polemical essay that confronts head-on the paradox that informs and ultimately circumscribes all of our thinking about Middle English popular romance. 'Popular' in its capacity to attract a large and heterogeneous medieval audience, as well as in its ability to provide that audience with enormous enjoyment, romance's popularity is likewise what excludes it from serious and sustained academic consideration: judged low-class, on account of its non-aristocratic audience, its reliance on stereotypes, formulae and conventional plot structures, and its particular brand of unadulterated good fun, criticism repeatedly dismisses these narratives as unworthy of the kind of close reading, as well as historically and theoretically informed analysis, that we regularly afford so-called elite medieval English art (in particular, but not limited to, Chaucer, Langland and the *Gawain*-poet). There are of course exceptions to the general trends I identify below; not all readers vilify popular romance, its readers or its aesthetic, but the tenacity with which the received denigration of romance, much of it traceable to outdated standards of aesthetic judgement and intellectual elitism, not only holds but continues to shape the field of inquiry, is nothing short of remarkable. The introduction is divided into two sections that tackle in turn what I think is at stake in our appreciation and enjoyment of these inescapably popular narratives: romance's status as a socially and aesthetically degenerate form of fiction and its capacity to generate textual pleasure. Not everyone will agree with it, but if it stimulates debate about popular romance it will have more than served its purpose.

Dangerous recreations

Medieval romance shares with other incendiary fictions a reputation for subverting social and moral order: indecent, unorthodox, criminal; and like these works its consumption has been policed. Romance, so its censors insist, perverts the mind; it incites illicit thought, obscene behaviour, and a propensity for violent action. Reviled by the medieval church as 'vayn carpynge', foolish and corrupting lies, and dismissed by men with literary pretensions (like Harry Bailey) as 'nat woorth a toord', romance becomes, in the centuries following its invention, the subject of energetic condemnation, a byword for moral degeneracy, religious heresy, political tyranny and everything that's bad about fiction.[4] John Florio (translating Montaigne) judges the whole corpus 'a wit-besotting trash of bookes', while the antiquarian Thomas Percy, at once apologist and bowdleriser, admits that they 'would do hurt' to 'common Readers'. Juan Luis Vives, the Spanish humanist and friend of Sir Thomas More, in a sweeping prohibition of romance, outlines its dangers more precisely: 'they make them [men and women] wylye and craftye, they kindle and styr up couetousnes, inflame angre, and all beastly and filthy desyre'. England's Roger Ascham likewise warns of social mayhem: 'a man by redinge [romance], shulde be led to none other ends, but only manslaughter and baudrye'. James Beattie concurs: 'Romances are a dangerous recreation', they 'corrupt the heart', 'stimulate the passions' and fill the mind with 'criminal propensities'.[5] These critics (medieval ecclesiast, early humanist, eighteenth-century antiquarian and beyond), whether moralists, educators or simply middle-class men determined on social advancement, are keen to protect readers from the kind of depravity that texts like *Guy of Warwick*, *Libeaus Desconus* or *Ipomadon* necessarily engender. The outrage and invective that romance inspires – from men who are bound neither by country nor century – is barely distinguishable from the rhetoric of interdiction that continues to characterise the pro-censorship lobby today.

The early critics of romance, insistent on the genre's disruptive potential, have been treated by modern scholarship with a mixture of disdain and humorous detachment.[6] Given its diminished modern status, we simply cannot believe that medieval romance bears worrying about; it no longer attracts enough attention to merit public disapprobation, be it moral, political or cultural, let alone to excite the censors. Relegated along with most other medieval English literature, by the relative obscurity of its language, to an almost exclusively academic audience, its consumption is policed only by critical fashion. And for a long time now, romance – at least Middle English popular romance – has been unfashionable. I recall romance's history of censorship not only because it testifies to the enormous popularity of these narratives, (whether in the original Middle English or in modernised and abridged versions) from the late Middle Ages to the nineteenth century, nor simply because it demonstrates their inherent unorthodoxy (a point to which I will return below), but because, despite differences in tone and rhetoric, it is animated by the same assumptions and anxieties that determine popular romance's degraded academic status.

Scholars long ago remarked that the objections voiced by the humanists, as well as eighteenth-century men of taste and others like them, are based primarily on romance's distance from the newly discovered and celebrated forms of classical poetry. As such they are more indicative of post-medieval prejudice, about everything from social class to Catholicism, than anything inherent in the medieval genre. And it is precisely these inherited distinctions that we, informed by the insights of post-structuralist thought, have learned to interrogate. Yet, popular romance has hardly benefited from the collapse of the traditional hierarchies of aesthetic (and with it academic) judgement. There must be many reasons why. The slowness with which medieval English studies has responded to developments in contemporary critical thought is undoubtedly a key factor; but, given that the recent surge in theoretically informed medieval research remains unmatched in romance scholarship, it cannot be the only one. I want to propose that the problem with popular romance is not, contrary to expectation, its opponents (whose invective invites rebuttal) but rather its friends.

Ad Putter and Jane Gilbert have already suggested that 'embarrassment' explains the 'predominance in romance studies of scholarship on manuscripts, editorial problems, and textual history'; this kind of work does not demand aesthetic judgement and so is never required to confront the texts' reputation as 'poetic disasters'.[7] Implicit in Putter and Gilbert's comment is the sense that, despite its evident industry, such scholarship has simultaneously done the genre a disservice. I think they're right; but I want to propose that romance scholarship is informed by something that is more damaging than a sin of omission.

From its inception, scholarship on the Middle English popular romances has been characterised by a thinly – if at all – veiled repugnance to the romances themselves, not only to their poetic form but their subject matter and the medieval audience who is imagined to enjoy them. As Arthur Johnston has demonstrated, it is in the middle of the eighteenth century, with the publication of the first modern editions, that the study of Middle English romance is born; more recent analysis by John Ganim, Nick Groom and David Matthews has exposed the ideologies latent in much of that early work and I build on their insights.[8] Thomas Percy, antiquarian and *arriviste*, and his spectacularly successful *Reliques of Ancient English Poetry*, published first in 1765, signals the start of modern abuses of romance. The 'seminal, epoch-making' work of English Romanticism, Percy's *Reliques* – along with his infamous Folio manuscript and the attention they both excited – has made an indelible mark on the way popular romance continues to be read.[9]

Four years after the publication of the *Reliques*, a three-volume work comprising mainly Middle English ballads and a set of four critical essays including one 'On the ancient metrical romances', Percy recorded on the inside cover of his Folio manuscript the following account of its discovery:

> Northumberland House, November 7th, 1769.
> This very curious Old Manuscript in its present mutilated state, but unbound and sadly torn &c., I rescued from destruction, and begged at the hands of my worthy friend Humphrey Pitt Esq. ... I saw it lying dirty on the floor under a Bureau in the Parlour: being used by the maids to light the fire. It was afterwards sent, most unfortunately, to an ignorant Bookbinder, who pared the margin, when I put it into Boards in order to lend it to Dr. Johnson. [10]

The son of a provincial grocer and born Thomas Piercy, the editor of the *Reliques*, armed with a self-fashioned aristocratic pedigree and the patronage of his wealthy namesake, was by 1769 well advanced in what was to be, thanks to the *Reliques'* popular success, a starry church career.[11] Whether or not Percy's narrative is true – it bears striking resemblance to a number of stories concerning the rescue of early manuscripts circulating at the time – is irrelevant; what is more significant is how, at a distance of more than ten years from its acquisition, he constructs his relationship to the source of his hard-earned success. The Folio, an artefact that Percy jealously guarded like a personal fetish, is mutilated and dirty, abused by serving women and damaged by a tradesman. Its physical and social dereliction opposes, and is used to confirm, Percy's own social and intellectual status, on a par with the titled Northumberlands (with whom he shares the estate) and the celebrated Dr Johnson (with whom he fraternises). Percy's embarrass-ment with his medieval relic and with the volumes of poetry that issued from it and the other dilapidated manuscripts he consulted, something he excuses in a later letter to John Pinkerton as the 'follies' of 'my youth',[12] was to become so intense that by the time he was confirmed as Lord Bishop of Dromore he refused to sign his name to the *Reliques*' fourth edition; a nephew, conveniently called Thomas Percy, stepped into the breach. What Percy's narratives (the stories he inscribes on his manuscript and in the trajectory of his own career) demonstrate is the tenacity with which the taint of the popular clings to these medieval texts: the brutish and illiterate medieval that is imagined to engender romance (Percy calls it 'gross and ignorant'[13]) is neatly replaced with a no less repugnant, but more reflective of eighteenth-century preoccupations, world of service, trade and dirt. Percy, like later romance *amateurs* (and later still professionals), is required to establish a distance between himself and the medieval texts in order not to be tarred with the same brush. Ironically, the very success of the *Reliques* with an ever-widening eighteenth-century audience reinforces its inherent vulgarity and simultaneously threatens Percy's social, and intellectual, integrity. When Vicesimus Knox congratulates Percy on rescuing this popular poetry 'from the hands of the vulgar' and obtaining for it 'a place in the collection of the man of taste', he means it literally:[14] Percy effectively snatches the Folio from the maids and enshrines it (the religious connotations of *Reliques* are doubtless purposeful) in the best way an eighteenth-century aspirant gentleman knows how. Percy's *Reliques*, packed full with the 'barbar-ous productions' of 'unpolished ages' as its Dedication promises, excites its editor and the public more because of its grotesque curiosi-ties than in spite of them.[15]

Certainly, I am being hard on Percy; he is neither unique, nor uniquely at fault. The *Reliques*, and with it Percy's ideas about romance, reflect its editor's personal anxieties and aspirations, but it is equally the product of an eighteenth-century antiquarian culture that exploits the past, as well as other peoples and cultures, as a confirmation of its own superiority and achievement. The printing and publication of the *Reliques*, a process that took three years and that saw Percy publish work on Chinese, runic and Hebrew poetry and fantasise about an international volume comprising, in addition, ancient Arabic, Indian, Peruvian, Lapp, Scottish and Greenland poetry,[16] is coincident both with England's emergence, at the end of the Seven Years' War, as Europe's dominant colonial and commercial power and with a domestic rage for primitive poetry that cannot be disinterested. Percy drew inspiration from, but also fuelled, English fascination with the primitive.[17] Along with men like Thomas Warton and Richard Hurd, both of whom read romance (although Hurd reads very little) as a function of their interest in Spenser, Percy promotes the Middle Ages as an age of romance, wild with imagination but, in perfect antithesis to his own eminently tasteful time, irredeemably barbarous; at the same time he promotes himself as someone able to know the difference. Where Percy encapsulates all of the ambivalence that distinguishes eighteenth-century readings of romance, his real importance for later scholarship – despite the fact he never completed his own proposed edition of the romances – lies in the longevity of his influence on those who continue to champion the genre.

Four editions of the *Reliques* were printed in Percy's lifetime, at least twenty-three in the nineteenth century, and the volumes continue to be reprinted (picked up by Everyman in 1906) well into the twentieth century.[18] But Percy's influence on the culture of reading Middle English romance is finally too amorphous to support any simple narrative of direct literary descent. Percy's judgements on romance, its authors and audiences, and the assumptions they entail – evident in his published work as well as his copious correspondence (Warton's opinion of romance, for instance, as espoused in his *History of English Poetry*, is enormously indebted to his exchanges with Percy) – are elaborated and modified by subsequent generations of readers in a web of intertextual relationships that cannot be rationalised. George Ellis' three-volume *Specimens of Early English Metrical Romances* – important for being the first published anthology of romance, a mix of prose summary and illustrative quotation – bears Percy's imprint everywhere, nowhere more so than in the invidious relationship between the reader and the romances that Ellis finds necessary, time and again, to reiterate.[19] He mocks their long-winded plots, ludicrous emotions and general absurdity, retelling romances like *Guy of Warwick* and *Amis and Amiloun*, with the kind of smug irony that is designed only to assert his, and his reader's, superiority over the imagined and denigrated medieval. Ellis, a comfortably off gentleman and sometime diplomat who fraternises with 'princes wits [and] fine ladies', has none of Percy's social anxiety;[20] he uses the romances instead as a butt for his wit, a testament to a kind of social elegance that is best expressed in droll conversation and barbed quips. When Southey remarks that there is 'something in his manners' that shows it is 'a condescension in him' to edit his *Specimens*, he inadvertently identifies an attitude that is characteristic of all conventional scholarship on the popular romances.[21]

Whether we are talking about the work of Walter Scott (whose recollection of reading Percy as a boy in the mid 1780s confirms the logic that identifies romance with childish intellects) or W. R. J. Barron (whose 1987 *English Medieval Romance*, a volume that treats English romance as derivative and finally second-rate, remains the most comprehensive modern analysis of these narratives), popular romance is invariably positioned against something that is judged to be superior; what that something is – epic, French romance or simply good taste – changes in accordance with prevailing prejudice and fashion, but the direction of comparison, whereby popular romance is denigrated, never varies. Scott, so often classed among romance's more persuasive advocates, posits in his essay on 'Romance', written for the first supplement to the *Encyclopaedia Britannica* (1824), that romance is precisely everything that epic – distinguished by its 'due proportion', 'force', 'precision', 'taste' and 'genius' as 'art' – is not: 'when a story languishes in tedious and minute details' and relies for its interest on 'wild excursions of unbridled fancy' rather than 'the skill of the poet', then its author is 'no more than a humble romancer'. Scott here mimics the rhetoric of neo-classical distinction, but his particular prejudice, inseparable from his social aspirations (like Percy he is a man on the make), comes into focus when he imagines the medieval audience 'circumscribed in knowledge' and 'limited in conversational powers': 'to prevent those pauses of discourse which sometimes fall heavily on a company', a poet-minstrel is employed, he argues, to supply 'an agreeable train of ideas to those guests who had few of their own'.[22] From Scott we learn less about medieval romance than about the imperative of polite conversation that exercises the nineteenth-century host, just as later we learn more from W. P. Ker about Victorian antipathies toward the world of manufacturing: 'hot, dusty and fatigued', romance has 'come through the mills' of men 'who know their business, and have an eye to their profits'.[23]

So far, I have demonstrated only that invidious distinction, reflective of an overt discomfort with the low social status of popular literature, real or imagined, is the hallmark of early (by which I mean pre-twentieth-century) scholarship on the popular romances. Men like Percy, Scott, and even Ker, who write in an idiom markedly different from our own, are easy targets for modern scholars keen to demonstrate the superiority of their own brand of criticism. But criticism, even when couched in the familiar terms of a shared profess-ional discourse, is of course never free of its authors' preoccupations and assumptions. What is so remarkable about the modern treatment of popular romance, especially in the work of the genre's putative (and influential) friends, is its duplication of the interests, and prejudices, of its antecedents. Pearsall's scathing denunciation of the romances – 'it is ... difficult to understand why poems that are so bad according to almost every criteria of literary value should have held such a central position in the literary culture of their own period'[24] – not only replicates eighteenth-century aesthetic assumptions about popular romance, but the social prejudice that fuels those assumptions. Aesthetic judgement is here indistinguishable from a preoccupation with social class and, finally, secondary to that preoccupation. Indeed, the logic of aesthetic distinction that Pearsall posits is explicitly predicated on the class affiliation of the original audience he assumes for each romance (and vice-versa). As the 'emergent bourgeoisie' (alternatively 'lower or lower-middle-class') – for whom the 'outright vulgarisation' of French romance is originally produced – becomes less emergent, the romances are likewise described as more sophisticated: 'witty, smooth, [and] enormously leisurely'. Aberrantly 'crude' products of this later period are attributed to 'the lowest classes of society' because, according to this scheme of things, they can belong nowhere else. The composer-poets are similarly stigmatised: while low-class romances are 'knock[ed] together' (the association with manual labour is inescapable), superior ones are said to issue from those with intimate knowledge of 'upper-class life'.[25] Pearsall, like Percy, is of course not alone; in fact, the identification of modern denigrations of romance with individual scholars erroneously suggests that the phenomenon is limited, and limitable, to a few key works or authors. Rather, it so pervades acade-mic discourse, whether in print or informal conversation, that the identification of 'the general run' of romance as 'rustic', 'primitive' or 'amateurish', the product of (and for) 'social aspirants' who 'lack understanding' of 'their social superiors', is commonplace.[26] Contem-porary (and widespread) assumptions that popular romance is a degraded and degenerate form of literature, the product of 'hacks' who 'ransack' aristocratic sources and treat them with 'outrageous violence' confirm Pierre Bourdieu's conviction that academic distinctions 'fulfil a social function of legitimating social differences'.[27] What the study of popular romance demonstrates is the extent to which contemporary medieval scholarship – whether as a result of its embattled status in the academy or simply because of the academic's inherent need to assert his or her own intellectual superiority – is threatened, whether consciously or not, by the 'great mass' (as Barron calls it[28]) who is able to enjoy popular romance.

blys, ioye *and* mykyll myrght*: the pleasures of romance*

If scholarship is distrustful of the assumed vulgarity of the Middle English popular romances – a function, as the term implies, of their low social status and denigrated aesthetic (factors that, I have argued, are indistinguishable) – it is equally discomforted by the way that medieval, as well as modern, audiences derive evident, and enormous, pleasure from these narratives. One of the ironies of English romance studies is that the genre's harshest critics are simultaneously those who have an enormous personal investment in the very popularity that they denounce. Percy, for all of his apologetics, patently enjoys popular romance – the 'levities' of his youth[29] – and he devotes considerable energy and intelligence to his scholarship. His repudiation of the romances, effected as an assertion of his own good taste and critical acumen, is simultaneously the response of a protestant clergyman ill at ease with such a public testimonial to his private pleasures. Percy's fear of censure from his 'graver brethren', alluded to in his private correspondence, is indicative of the kind of anxieties that persist today.[30] In her provocative essay on 'enjoying the Middle Ages', Louise Fradenberg posits that the preoccupation with 'utility' and 'necessity' in humanities departments (fuelled by the increasing pressure to justify the humanities as economically productive and publicly useful, as well as by the 'ambivalence about enjoyment' characteristic of influential critical schools – she focuses on the Marxist and feminist) is explicitly opposed to the enjoyment of medieval culture. Although medievalists know, she asserts, that 'the pleasure of knowledgeable discourses on pleasure' is what we 'deliver to our audiences', we have assumed as our 'ethical task' to 'discipline' enjoyment out of academic inquiry. In other words, medieval studies (as a modern academic discipline) has invested medieval culture with a seriousness (what Fradenberg calls 'an *ethos* of *pietas*') that marginalises or denies those aspects of the culture that are predominantly productive of enjoyment.[31] So far as popular romance is concerned (a genre Fradenberg does not consider directly), I think she is right.

Manuscript evidence – unmatched, in the sheer number of surviving texts, by any other secular genre – attests not only to the social
and geographical diversity of romance's medieval audience, but to the
genre's capacity to generate desire for its distinctive form of narrative
and with it the pleasure of gratification: romances written in the
thirteenth century continue to be copied into the fifteenth century,
while the persistent demand for yet more romance guarantees the
production of new texts well into the renaissance. Modern scholars are
likewise keen to confirm that Middle English romance flourishes
because of its capacity to 'delight' or 'entertain' – in other words to
provide enjoyment for – its audience.[32] Yet, it is precisely this popularity (the genre's capacity to be well liked) that impedes critical
appreciation not only of the romance aesthetic, but of its ideologies
and of the kinds of readings it can sustain. David Benson (writing
about the *Seege of Troye*) sums up dominant attitudes to the genre as a
whole: 'entertainment for the common folk', popular romance is
'disqualified from claiming the attention of any serious audience'.[33]
The kind of pleasure that is generated by Middle English romance is
constructed by modern scholarship as second-rate (both 'entertain'
and 'delight' are purposefully condescending) and it is set in opposition
to the apparently superior gratification derived from the 'supreme
products of [the] age'.[34] We need to remember, of course, that these
distinctions (between the enjoyment afforded by popular romance and
the sublimated gratification of so-called elite medieval art) are at least
as indicative of the need for academic self-legitimation and self-
perpetuation as of anything intrinsic to romance or its production of
pleasure. Academic communities have long been resistant to popular
art and to the kind of pleasure it produces; the denial of 'lower' forms
of enjoyment (musicals, Hollywood films, pulp fiction) is one of the
most important ways in which consumers and critics of high culture
(opera, art-house cinema, the post-modern novel) assert their cultural
credentials and intellectual credibility.[35] What then is something
endemic to academic study is today exacerbated and, despite growing
theoretical interest in popular culture, perpetuated by what Fradenberg identifies as the prevailing seriousness (or *ethos* of *pietas*) that
drives most modern research on the Middle Ages. Because popular
romance makes explicit its commitment to its audience's pleasure and
because it is structured to gratify that pleasure, it fails to attract the kind
of high profile attention (by academics and their publishers) that has
recently been accorded medieval texts (the *Book of Margery Kempe* or
Hoccleve's *Regiment of Princes*, for instance) that, once as little regarded

as popular romance, are now judged 'serious' because they more readily (or obviously) coincide with the agendas that propel academic study.

Key to modern scholarship's ambivalence about the kind of pleasure that popular romance generates is the assumption that it is passive, a pleasure that comes from the consumption, without thought or agency, of standardised products that espouse normative ideologies. Although critics are quick to disparage the aesthetics of popular romance as 'rustic' or 'primitive', a sign that it issues from the 'great mass' who is incapable of understanding or appreciating the aesthetics of the elite, its ideologies (of gender, social class, race, religion and so on) are assumed not to challenge but rather to mimic those of that same elite. Popular romance, in other words, loses on both counts – degenerate in form and style it has none of the disruptive potential that is commonly attributed to the degenerate – and its pleasure, by all accounts banal, is refigured as form of coercion: sated with the kind of gratification that the genre provides (usually in the form of wish fulfilment), the audience is contentedly complicit in its own oppression. The view that popular culture serves as an opiate is widely held by critics who otherwise adhere to divergent theoretical schools. Its broad appeal is in part attributable to the way in which it replicates the distinctions upon which academic inquiry is built: the critic knows an opiate when s/he sees one – the masses apparently don't – and the critical act is validated by its exposure (invariably expressed in terms of 'us' and 'them') of the ideologies that oppress the unwitting consumer.[36] Popular romance can and does replicate dominant ideologies; so-called elite art, despite what we imagine is its inherently radical potential, likewise does so all the time. Not all dominant ideologies, however, are equally opposed to the disparate interests of the popular audience: the audience of Middle English romance is at least as heterogeneous (in terms of age, gender, wealth, social rank, education and regional affiliation) as it is homogeneous. And indeed, the individual members of that audience are just as likely as we are to have complex wants and needs that they will seek to satisfy in different, and sometimes contradictory, ways. But more importantly, popular culture (and with it popular romance) is not simply, as its detractors would have us believe, an instrument of social control – popular romance is too diverse a genre to support such reductive analysis – and neither is its audience made up solely of dupes. Popular romance is rather a space, narrative as well as imaginary, in which cultural norms and divergences from those norms are negotiated and articulated.[37]

I want now to look more closely at the kind of pleasure – what the medieval poet designates 'blys', 'ioye' or 'mykyll myrght'[38] – that is produced by popular romance. More than any other medieval genre, the Middle English romances are exemplary of what modern narratologists call 'narrative desire'.[39] They are predominantly stories *about* desire: in the simplest terms, the protagonist's desire for something – for instance, a husband, wife or lover, wealth, property or status (expressed as a family or knightly identity) – and the satisfaction of that desire. The plot is regularly complicated by the proliferation of desires that are sometimes incompatible – unwanted amorous advances are repulsed; a couple's desire for an heir gives way to the heir's own desires; misplaced desire is redirected to more appropriate ends – and the protagonist usually discovers that the satisfaction of one desire (for a wife, for instance) guarantees the satisfaction of others (for material wealth, status, property). Just as importantly, however, they are also stories in which desire functions as what Peter Brooks calls the 'motor force' of narrative.[40] At the start of virtually every romance a desire is present, usually in a state of initial arousal, that is so intense (because thwarted or challenged) that action – some kind of forward narrative movement designed to bring about change – is demanded. Sexual desire (whether wanted, unwanted or feared) is one of the most common initiatory devices, but a desire for offspring, material wealth, a lost identity, political or religious dominion, or simply *aventure* are equally effective as a way of getting the story off the ground. This desire, like all desires, is structurally end-oriented. In other words, it gives to narrative the textual energy that propels the plot forward in search of satisfaction; it pushes the protagonist through or around the obstacles that delay the achievement of desire. Modern narrative is often distinguished by the way in which it frustrates the conventional trajectory of desire, pulls it up short and resists the closure that is otherwise, in narrative terms, inevitable. Our desires, such narratives contend, are not finally satisfiable; indeed, desire is a perpetual want whose very resistance to satisfaction exposes the inescapable fictionality of stories that do close with desire's gratification. Of course such resistance to closure is not limited to modern literature, far from it. But it is wholly at odds with what we find in the popular romances. The kind of desire that propels popular romance *always* finds satisfaction. *Aventure*, the essence we are told of romance, presumes in fact an unfolding of narrative that – because it is literally *advenire*, 'to arrive at' or 'to reach' – is inescapably mindful of its end. As the reworking of the Orpheus story demonstrates, Eurydice must – because Orpheus' desire for her is what animates the narrative – be reunited with her husband, even if the sources have to be changed to accommodate the new happy ending. The pleasure of romance is found then not simply in the gratification of desire (the desire of audience and protagonist may coincide, but it is not necessary), but in the way that desire is played out: in the way expectations are raised, challenged (by a series of apparently insurmountable obstacles), and then finally satisfied. The perfunctory nature of most romance conclusions (lovers are united, families reunited, status achieved, and wealth, property, dominion secured all in a few short lines) is indicative of their necessity (although short they cannot be omitted), but also of the fact that the narrative's energy, and with it its pleasure, is predominantly elsewhere.

The blatant artifice of the happy ending is one of the more obvious ways in which popular romance exposes the mechanics of its construction. Formulaic diction, stock motifs, repetition and recapitulation of key events and themes, intertextual dialogue (with other romances) and citation of bookish sources all serve to remind the audience that the romance is the product of a textually informed redactor, that this is a story and that someone has skilfully constructed it. The sharply demarcated ending – coincident with the gratification of desire and usually furnished with an *explicit* (for instance, 'here endeth', 'Amen') that simultaneously underscores the text's allegiance to other forms of fiction ('lay', 'rime', 'song' etc.) – is paired with an equally artificial beginning that likewise serves to promote the narrative as a romance, that is, as a story that adheres to, and makes sense within, established fictional codes. The prominence of references to oral performance, the subject of so many debates about the transmission and reception of the romances, indicates most importantly the way in which the text establishes its relationship with its audience as a purposefully shaped narrative driven by the story-teller's 'I'.[41] Part of romance pleasure is, undoubtedly, derived from the genre's status as a collective fiction: the audience participates in a shared imaginative experience that both presupposes a community of listeners (whether that community is a real, aural one or a disparate group of readers does not matter) and grants access to that community through a mutual familiarity with the codes that shape and give meaning to the romance story. But the way in which popular romance flaunts its status as fiction points to another kind of pleasure. And that is the pleasure *of* fiction.

Fiction, however imperfectly, takes its audience outside of the norms and conventions that structure everyday life; this may simply be a liberation from real-time and real-space, but equally it provides an opportunity for the radical formation of new times and spaces.

Fictional worlds necessarily have limits – the limits of what is (for audience and author) possible – but, generally speaking, the more flagrantly a text promotes itself as fiction, the greater are its opportunities to test precisely those limits. The otherworlds of medieval romance have long been recognised as a distinctive feature of the genre and indeed they are often credited with its popular appeal. The world of faerie – replete with its magic rings, fairy mistresses and love potions – and the forest – home to dragons, giants and other monstrous creatures – are commonly identified as archetypal romance spaces, but equally, if not more, typical of romance is the imaginary space it generates simply by insisting that it is a fiction. Within the circumscribed space of the narrative, both author and audience are freed from the exigencies of daily life not just so that they can escape the world they know (magic operates only in a minority of the Middle English popular romances and likewise forests are not obligatory), but so that they can explore – to test, to defy, to confirm – the principles by which it operates. Although invariably located in an elite aristocratic milieu (from whence neither author not audience is likely to issue), these narratives treat of subjects like courtship and marriage, domestic violence, political and social authority, ethical conduct, national identity and religious faith that are germane sometimes to daily life, sometimes to the fantasies and anxieties of that life *in extremis*. And they treat of them in ways that, because the text is rigidly structured to gratify narrative desire (because it constantly assures us it is a fiction), are all the more provocative, all the more conducive to our discovery of the limits – both where they are and where they aren't – of the world in which we live. What so distinguishes popular romance as a genre is the way in which it forges its meanings out of the clash between the marvellous and the mundane. Because the narrative necessarily achieves satisfaction (the knight wins the lady, the Christian wins victory) and because satisfaction is always, for an audience who knows how romance works, a foregone conclusion, there are few limits to what can take place en route to satisfaction: nuns are raped, virgins stripped naked and whipped, mothers are mutilated by their sons, apes abduct small boys and knights feed with dogs, infants are slaughtered by their parents, Christians eat Saracens, the list goes on. But because that satisfaction is so self-consciously, so overtly fictional, the narrative, with all of its extraordinary twists and turns, can never finally be reduced to the simple certainties (young girls *will* escape their incestuous fathers, the rightful heir *will* inherit unjustly lost property) that its end embodies. In other words, the structure of romance is too rigid to contain the complexities and effusions of its narrative; and that is why we enjoy it so much.

Popular Middle English romance locates itself precisely at the juncture that Barthes identifies as the ultimate site of textual pleasure or what he calls *jouissance* (a term whose meaning encompasses enjoyment, bliss and sexual pleasure):[42] between conformity and rebellion, between the kind of narrative order that finds resolution in the inviolable happy ending and the chaos that is threatened by the giants and rapists, incubi, cannibals and necrophiliacs, to say nothing of the abusive parents and their wild offspring, who roam the romance landscape. Narrative pleasure is produced by, and in, the gap that exists between the conventions that structure romance (the use of stock characters, formulaic language as well, of course, as the social and cultural norms that are omnipresent) and the transgressions that its narrative produces. The prevalence of convention in romance is integral to the kind of pleasure it achieves; without convention (without a system of norms and expectations that can be transgressed), the effect of transgression is lost. And it is in this *effect* that pleasure is located. It is only when romance establishes, for instance, the importance of female chastity that there is any stake in trying to defend it; but once the import of chastity is established, then the narrative can get on with the business of violating it. The pleasure of this kind of narrative is primarily located not in the final preservation of chastity (which, if it occurs, is always treated perfunctorily and with blatant artifice), but in the interplay, or more violently in the collision, of transgression (rape, incest, or other sexual perversions) and convention (female chastity).

Narrative order might well be able to achieve textual resolution, to forge normative solutions out of the capacious desires that animate popular romance, but it can never efface the transgressions that ultimately generate the narrative and the pleasure that the audience finds in it. Popular romance is (despite its predilection for the happy endings that seem to confirm social norms and dominant ideologies) an imaginary space – I would argue *the* pre-eminent imaginary space in medieval English literature – in which the transgression of cultural boundaries is both embodied and explored; this transgression is sometimes punished, sometimes rehabilitated, and sometimes accommodated, but it is never repressed. And it is with this in mind that I want to return for a moment to the anxieties that exercised romance's early detractors: popular romance, put simply, is a dangerous recreation. Despite the gulf that inevitably separates us from these medieval narratives, they retain the power to shock us, to unsettle our assumptions about, among other things, gender and sexuality, race, religion, political formations, social class, ethics, morality and aesthetic distinctions. As scholarship's ongoing discomfort with popular romance – its audience, its aesthetic and its pleasures – demonstrates, we cannot dismiss these texts as crude, second-rate narratives that unquestioningly reproduce established ideologies. Popular romance remains a collection of 'dirty books', where 'dirty' signifies not simply sexually explicit, obscene or morally repugnant, although romance can be all of these things, but that which is essential to all provocative literature, the interrogation of the norms that order and regulate our lives.

Notes

I am grateful to Alastair Minnis, Felicity Riddy, Hélène Tronc and the Press's readers for advice and critique and for their unfailing support for *Pulp fictions*.

1 Stephen Knight, 'The social function of the Middle English romances', in D. Aers (ed.), *Medieval Literature: Criticism, Ideology and History* (New York, 1986), pp. 99–122 (p. 99).

2 Derek Pearsall, 'Middle English romance and its audiences', in Mary-Jo Arn and Hanneke Wirtjes (eds), *Historical and Editorial Studies in Medieval and Early Modern English for Johan Gerritsen* (Groningen, 1985), pp. 37–47 (p. 42).

3 See Ad Putter and Jane Gilbert (eds), *The Spirit of Medieval English Popular Romance* (Harlow, 2000), pp. 1–38.

4 William of Nassington, *Speculum Vitae*, cited in G. R. Owst, *Literature and Pulpit in Medieval England* (Oxford, 1961), p. 13; Geoffrey Chaucer, *Riverside Chaucer*, ed. Larry D. Benson *et al.* (Oxford, 1988), *Canterbury Tales* VII, 930.

5 *The Essayes of Michael Lord of Montaigne*, 2 vols, trans. John Florio (London, 1603), vol. 2, ch. 25; *The Correspondence of Thomas Percy and Richard Farmer*, ed. C. Brooks (Baton Rouge, LA, 1946), p. 7; *The office and duetie of an husband made by the excellent philosopher Lodouicus Viues*, trans. T. Paynell (London, 1546); Roger Ascham , 'Toxophilus', in *English Works*, ed. W. A. Wright (Cambridge, 1904), p. xiv; James Beattie, 'On fable and romance', *Dissertations Moral and Critical*, 2 vols (Dublin, 1783), vol. 2, p. 320.

6 See for instance, C. S. Lewis, *English Literature in the Sixteenth Century Excluding Drama* (Oxford, 1954), pp. 28–9. Robert P. Adams, '"Bold bawdry and open manslaughter": the English new humanist attack on medieval romance', *Huntington Library Quarterly* 23 (1959), 33–48 makes a rare attempt to place the humanist condemnation of romance in its social and political context.

7 Putter and Gilbert, *The Spirit of Medieval English Popular Romance*, p. vii.

8 Arthur Johnston, *Enchanted Ground: The Study of Medieval Romance in the*

Eighteenth Century (London, 1964); John Ganim, 'The myth of medieval romance', in H. Bloch and S. G. Nichols (eds), *Medievalism and the Modernist Temper* (Baltimore, 1996), pp. 148–66; Nick Groom, *The Making of Percy's Reliques* (Oxford, 1999); David Matthews, *The Making of Middle English, 1765–1910* (Minneapolis, 1999).

9 Thomas Percy's three-volume *Reliques of Ancient English Poetry* was first published by James Dodsley on 14 February 1765 after a two-and-a half years in the print shop; during this time Percy made ongoing changes to the contents of the volume and secured the Duchess of Northumberland as his dedicatee. The *Reliques* was an enormous and immediate success, attracting most famously the attention of Coleridge, Wordsworth and Sir Walter Scott; it ran to four editions in Percy's lifetime and more than fifty have been published since his death in 1811. Groom's assessment of it as 'epoch-making' (*The Making of Percy's Reliques*, p. 3) is standard; J. M. P. Donatelli, 'Old barons in new robes: Percy's use of the metrical romances in the *Reliques of Ancient English Poetry*', in P. J. Gallacher and H. Damico (eds), *Hermeneutics and Medieval Culture* (Albany, 1989), pp. 225–35 likewise urges that 'it changed the course of English literature' (p. 225). In addition to editing his 'reliques', Percy writes four essays, including one 'On the ancient and metrical romances' and a second 'On the ancient minstrels'; the former is the first piece of critical scholarship on the romances and contains the first bibliography of extant texts. Percy's inspiration for the *Reliques* was his acquisition c. 1753 of the so-called Folio MS (now London, British Library, MS Additional 27879), a seventeenth-century commonplace book with an eclectic collection of romances, ballads and songs, most late medieval but almost all imperfect or corrupt. The contents of the manuscript have been edited by J. W. Hales and F. J. Furnivall, *Bishop Percy's Folio MS*, 4 vols (London, 1867–68); the most recent account of the manuscript is G. Rogers, 'The Percy folio manuscript revisited', in M. Mills *et al.* (eds), *Romance in Medieval England* (Cambridge, 1991), pp. 39–64. Percy's judgement of romance is not, of course, wholly original; his observations are in part anticipated by Thomas Warton, *Observations on the Faerie Queene* (1764) and before that men like Richard Blackmore ('Essay on epic poetry', 1716) and Richard Hurd (*Letters on Chivalry and Romance*, 1762). What distinguishes Percy, apart from his unmatched popularity, and why I focus on him here is his reputation as an influential advocate of medieval popular romance; what I want to demonstrate is the extent to which such advocacy is, in the history of romance scholarship, invariably compromised.

10 Percy's inscription is printed in Hales and Furnivall, *Bishop Percy's Folio Manuscript*, vol. 1, p. lxxiv.

11 Chaplain to the Northumberlands and author of their family history (a position he secured on the back of the *Reliques'* popular success), Percy was appointed in 1769 one of the King's Chaplains en route, via a deanship, to the bishopric of Dromore, Ireland.

12 *The Correspondence of Thomas Percy and John Pinkerton*, ed. Harriet Harvey Wood (New Haven, 1985), p. 10.

13 Thomas Percy, *The Reliques of Ancient English Poetry*, 3 vol (London, 1765), vol. 3, p. iii.

14 Vicesimus Knox, *Essays Moral and Literary*, 2 vol (London, 1782), vol. 2, p. 214.

15 Percy, *Reliques of Ancient English Poetry*, vol. 1, p. vi. Groom, *The Making of Percy's Reliques*, pp. 40–60 makes an energetic case for Percy's purposeful inclusion of violent, grotesque and salacious material. The *Reliques* 'welters in gore: the bloodiness of death and dismemberment incarnadines the entire three volumes, and if occasionally watered by humour or levity, it is more often deepened by a colossal amorality'; it is 'about eating, drinking, fornicating, singing, and killing' (pp. 45, 59).

16 *The Correspondence of Thomas Percy and Evan Evans*, ed. A. Lewis (New Haven, 1957), pp. 30–1.

17 For a short account of the eighteenth-century vogue for primitivism and its social and political context see F. Stafford, 'Primitivism and the "primitive" poet: a cultural context for Macpherson's Ossian', in T. Brown (ed.) *Celticism* (Amsterdam, 1996), pp. 79–96.

18 For an account of the nineteenth-century editions of the *Reliques*, I am indebted to Nick Groom's introduction to the facsimile edition of *Reliques of Ancient English Poetry*, 3 vols (Routledge, 1996), vol. 1, p. 54.

19 George Ellis, *Specimens of Early English Metrical Romances* (London, 1805).

20 *The Letters of Sir Walter Scott*, ed. H. J. C. Grierson, 12 vol (London, 1932–37), vol. 3, p. 60.

21 Southey's letter is cited in J. W. Robberds, *Memoir of William Taylor*, 2 vols (London, 1843), vol. 2, p. 31.

22 *The Miscellaneous Prose Works of Sir Walter Scott*, 6 vols (Edinburgh, 1827), vol. 6, pp. 164–5, 186.

23 W. P. Ker, *Epic and Romance: Essays on Medieval Literature* (London, 1897), p. 371.

24 Derek Pearsall, 'Understanding Middle English romance', *Review* 2 (1980), 105–25 (p.105).

25 Derek Pearsall, 'The development of Middle English romance', *Mediaeval Studies* 27 (1965), 91–116 (pp. 91–2, 104, 114).

26 John Burrow, 'The uses of incognito: *Ipomadon* A', in C. Meale (ed.), *Readings in Medieval English Romance* (Cambridge, 1994), pp. 25–34 (p. 34); Valerie Krishna, *Five Middle English Arthurian Romances* (New York, 1991), p. 24; Rogers, 'The Percy Folio manuscript revisited', p. 55; John Finlayson, 'Definitions of Middle English romance', *Chaucer Review* 15 (1980), 44–62, 168–81 (pp. 59, 178). Donald B. Sands, *Middle English Verse Romances* (Exeter, 1986), one of the most widely used student editions of the romances, provides a salutary reminder of how difficult it is for seasoned, let alone new, readers to escape the prejudicial judgements of past scholarship. Sands consistently characterises the Middle English

romances he edits as 'pedestrian' and 'naïve', 'grop[ing]' narratives that read 'much better the first time around than ... on the second or third'; at best 'one is hard put to say much against [them]', at worst, they exhibit 'the wrong-headed logic often attributed to children' (pp. 2, 5, 130, 350, 233).

27 Derek Pearsall and I. C. Cunningham (eds), *The Auchinleck Manuscript* (London, 1977), p. ix; Dorothy Everett, *Essays on Middle English Literature* (Oxford, 1955), p. 12; Andrew Taylor, 'Fragmentation, corruption, and minstrel narration: the question of the Middle English romances', *YES* 22 (1992), 38–62 (p. 58). Pierre Bourdieu, *Distinction: A Social Critique of Taste*, trans. R. Nice (London, 1984), persuasively demonstrates the extent to which social hierarchies, and the ideologies that support and reproduce them, lie behind the aesthetic distinction between 'high' and 'low' art (the citation is from p. 7).

28 W. R. J. Barron, *English Medieval Romance* (London, 1989), p. 51.

29 *The Correspondence of Percy and Pinkerton*, p. 10.

30 *The Correspondence of Percy and Evans*, p. 102.

31 Louise Fradenberg, '"So that we may speak of them": enjoying the Middle Ages', *New Literary History* 28 (1997), 205–30 (pp. 207–9).

32 See, for instance, Pearsall, 'Middle English romance and its audiences', p. 42 and Sands, *Middle English Verse Romances*, pp. viii, 1. Rosalind Field, 'Romance in England' in D. Wallace (ed.), *The Cambridge History of Medieval English Literature* (Cambridge, 1999), pp. 152–76 cites Pearsall and argues that, given the contested nature of the genre, the only thing we can be sure about is 'the essentially recreational function of romance': '[i]t is entertainment for an audience; ... a successful romance is one which gives pleasure, whether or not accompanied by information or instruction' (pp. 152–3).

33 C. D. Benson, *The History of Troy in Middle English Literature* (Woodbridge, 1980), p. 134.

34 Sands, *Middle English Verse Romances*, p. vii.

35 Bourdieu argues that '[t]he denial of lower, coarse, vulgar, venal, servile – in a word, natural – enjoyment, which constitutes the sacred sphere of culture, implies an affirmation of the superiority of those who can be satisfied with the sublimated, refined, disinterested, gratuitous, distinguished pleasures forever closed to the profane', *Distinction*, p. 7. See especially his chapters 'The aristocracy of culture' and 'Postscript' (pp. 12–96, 485–500).

36 Conscious of the complexity of both popular culture and the audience's agency in producing meaning from it, many modern theorists are increasingly uncomfortable with analysis that seeks to 'liberate' consumers from their own false consciousness; the stance of 'enlightenment', reproductive of the social and intellectual distinctions that have for so long marginalised the study of popular culture and stigmatised its audiences, is finally disabling. See, for instance, Jokes Hermes' introductory remarks to *Reading Women's Magazines: An Analysis of Everyday Media Use* (Cambridge, 1995) and Janice Radway's revised introduction to the second

edition of *Reading Romance: Women, Patriarchy and Popular Literature* (Chapel Hill, 1991).

37 Indebted to the work of Italian Marxist Antonio Gramsci – in particular his proposition that political hegemony is achieved by means of negotiation, whereby so-called dominant ideologies are not only in constant flux but are the product of a complex process of give-and take between dominant and subordinate groups – many cultural theorists have come to see popular culture as a site of contestation that is marked as much by resistance as incorporation. The virtue of what has come to be called Neo-Gramsci studies is that it acknowledges both the complexity of both popular culture and its consumers. For Gramsci's account of hegemony and how it works see 'Hegemony, Intellectuals and the State', anthologised in John Storey (ed.), *Cultural Theory and Popular Culture; A Reader*, 2nd edn (Harlow, 1998), pp. 210-16.

38 See for instance, *Syr Tryamowre* in *Of Love and Chivalry: An Anthology of Middle English Romance*, ed. J. Fellows (London, 1993), line 3; *Sir Eglamour of Artois*, ed. F. E. Richardson, EETS o.s. 256 (London, 1965), line 4; *Emaré* in *The Middle English Breton Lays*, eds A. Laskaya and E. Salisbury (Kalamazoo, 1995), line 20.

39 For his provocative analysis of narrative desire and its mechanics, I am indebted to Peter Brooks, *Reading for the Plot: Design and Intention in Narrative* (Cambridge, MA, 1992; first pub. New York, 1984), especially pp. 37–61.

40 Brooks, *Reading for the Plot*, p. 48.

41 Although Andrew Taylor has done much to debunk the romantic myth of the roaming minstrel who orally composes his romances and performs them to brutish illiterates in taverns and great halls ('The myth of the minstrel manuscript', *Speculum* 66 (1992), 43–73; 'Fragmentation, corruption, and minstrel narration: the question of the Middle English romances', *YES* 22 (1992), 38–62), some of the most innovative recent scholarship makes an informed case for renewed attention to romance's distinctively performative aesthetic. See, for instance, Nancy Mason Bradbury, *Writing Aloud: Storytelling in Late Medieval England* (Urbana, 1998) and the work of performer-scholar Linda Marie Zaerr.

42 Barthes distinguishes between the text of *jouissance* (which 'unsettles the reader's historical, cultural, psychological assumptions') and the text of *plaisir* (which 'comes from culture and does not break with it'), but the distinction is neither rigid nor consistent. I want to propose instead that the two kinds of pleasure can be found in the same text and are not incompatible; in other words, we can enjoy the pleasure of happy endings while simultaneously challenging the assumptions that underpin those endings. See Roland Barthes, *The Pleasure of the Text*, trans. R. Miller (Oxford, 1990; English trans. first pub. New York, 1975), especially pp. 3–14; the distinction between *jouissance* and *plaisir* is made most explicitly on p. 14.

Incorporation in the
Siege of Melayne

Suzanne Conklin Akbari

In the debate concerning precisely what constitutes a medieval 'romance' the *Siege of Melayne* occupies a special position. As a number of readers have noted, this poem participates in the conventions both of romance (understood as a genre fundamentally concerned with the deeds of knights) and of hagiography. The focus of such cross-generic readings is usually the character of Archbishop Turpin who, as Barron puts it, has 'as much of the saint as of the soldier in his nature'.[1] The cross-generic status of the *Siege of Melayne* is also in evidence in the dramatic scene which takes place in the chamber of the sultan Arabas, when a crucifix is cast by the Saracens into a great fire and, miraculously, does not burn. Elsewhere in the poem, too, as I will illustrate below, religious and even eucharistic imagery plays a vital role in the unfolding of the narrative. Yet I do not wish to argue that the generic distinctions of romance and hagiography are collapsed in the *Siege of Melayne*, or for that matter in any other medieval romance, for such efforts have not met with success. Diana Childress has suggested that the overlap between romance and hagiography can be best understood by defining a new category of 'secular legend': 'From romance the secular legend borrows settings, style, and many story motifs … But instead of enter-taining their audiences … the authors of the secular legends aim to teach moral lessons.'[2] Andrea Hopkins has found, however, that this is not the case in a group of texts which she identifies as 'penitential romances.' Like Childress's 'secular legends', these romances feature a hero who 'does penance for his sinfulness or who may patiently undergo physical hardship and deprivation and who is rescued or rescues others by divine miracles'.[3] Yet Hopkins concludes that these romances were not thought 'to constitute a fundamentally different kind of literature from other romances which do not deal with predominantly religious or didactic subject-matter'. The penitential romances are also found in conjunction with didactic penitential manuals, which 'suggests that the two types of composition were not seen as incompatible with each other, but instead answered different needs in their medieval readers'.[4] The shared manuscript context of penitential manual and penitential romance illustrates the interdependence of two genres that, in modern scholarship, have too long been considered separately. Instead, as Jocelyn Wogan-Browne suggests, the overlap both of content and of audience in romance and hagiography should impel us not to dismiss these categories entirely, but rather to move 'beyond the modern literary-critical model of romance priority to a refocusing of romance and hagiography in their shared medieval contexts'.[5] Such an effort requires that we look at the manuscripts in which these texts appear in order to find out how medieval writers and compilers identify the works, and to consider what such identification tells us about reading practices.

In the following pages, I will explicate the religious content of the *Siege of Melayne*, exploring how hagiographic, devotional, and eucharistic themes are used to depict a Christian community characterised by strength in the face of adversity, and wholeness in the face of efforts to fragment the community. The body of Turpin, the image of the crucified Christ, and the Host each represent the *Corpus Christi*, the body of Christ which stands for the community of Christian souls.[6] What is peculiar about the *Siege of Melayne*, however, is that this community is not merely unified, but so full that it cannot accept any more members: here, incorporation in the body of Christ has a finite limit. In the poem, the wholeness of the body signifies both inclusion (of the Christians who are already its members) and exclusion (of the Saracen converts who might seek to join). Having outlined the religious content of the *Siege of Melayne*, I will suggest that it can be seen as representative of what one might call 'devotional romance' (that is, a chivalric narrative with pronounced spiritual or theological content), and will briefly compare some examples. While the category of 'devotional romance' may be useful to modern readers, it is nonetheless crucial to note that the manuscript context shows the extent to which medieval readers were unfettered by generic constraints. The combination and juxtaposition of texts within medieval manuscript collections illustrate the interpenetration of genres more than their distinct identity. As Paul Strohm has observed, while 'a concept of *romaunce* was generally shared and the term was used to classify and describe actual narratives', nonetheless 'the term is used in some strange ways', that is, used to identify texts which modern readers would not call 'romance'.[7] I will conclude by showing that the *Siege of Melayne*, along with other texts in the same manuscript, illustrates the fluidity and variability of genre, which functions less as a consistent category than as an interpretive tool. Genre is, at least to some extent, not given by the writer but imposed by the reader, established not in a single creative moment but repeatedly, in a series of interpretive acts.[8]

The *Siege of Melayne* survives in a single manuscript dated to the mid-fifteenth century, known as the London Thornton manuscript (British Library, MS Additional 31042). John Thompson has given an exhaustive account of the manuscript's physical makeup and probable mode of production, with commentary on the significance of the combination and interrelation of texts in the manuscript.[9] Since the *Siege of Melayne* survives in this single witness, and is not alluded to or cited elsewhere,[10] the poem itself is almost impossible to date. A lost Anglo-Norman original was posited by the text's first editor, Sidney Herrtage, at the suggestion of Gaston Paris. Though subsequent editors have repeated this assertion, no evidence of such an original has appeared. Herrtage dated the poem to the late fourteenth century, presumably on the basis of its relationship to the group of Ferumbras romances which he had also edited.[11] Though the *Siege of Melayne* does not include the figure of Ferumbras, a converted Saracen of great physical and chivalric stature, Charlemagne appears in both works as the emperor at the head of the Christian army. The poem's more recent editors have dated the poem with comparable uncertainty: Mills and Shepherd c. 1400, Lupack, like Herrtage and Thompson, the second half of the fourteenth century.[12] The poem's focus on the eucharist as a symbol not only of the Christian community but of the military host, and its emphasis on the inherence of the blood within the eucharistic host, supports a comparatively late date for the poem, when the debate regarding the simultaneous presence of both body and blood within the transubstantiated wafer was of increasing interest to lay readers – enough to merit clerical condemnation of the denial of concomitance in 1415 at the Council of Constance.

The religious context of the *Siege of Melayne* has long been noted. Childress observes that, in Archbishop Turpin, we find a hero who is more 'like a saint who endures prodigious physical torture'.[13] The poem's latest editor, Shepherd, has drawn attention to a deeper level of theological engagement within the poem, agreeing with Barron that Turpin is 'something of a Christ figure' in the poem, and suggesting that the description of the desolate battlefield where Christian soldiers resort to drinking standing water stained with their own blood may 'reflect the imagery of the Crucifixion and the Eucharist'.[14] For the purposes of this discussion, I will schematise the religious content of the *Siege of Melayne* as follows: the hagiographic, seen in the character of Turpin; the devotional, illustrated in the dramatic scene in the Sultan's chamber in which the crucifix, tortured by fire, miraculously refuses to burn; and the eucharistic, seen both directly, in the scene in which Turpin celebrates Mass for the weary troops before yet another battle, and indirectly, in the description of the bloodied (military) host itself. The wounds of Turpin, which increasingly become the focus of attention both within the narrative (for Charlemagne) and without (for the reader), serve to unify these disparate strands of religious content, so that the reader, like Charlemagne, becomes absorbed in the longed-for visual experience of Turpin's hidden wounds.

On one level, Turpin's depiction in the *Siege of Melayne* can be characterised as hagiographical; on another level, however, he appears to be both more than a saint and less. In keeping with earlier descriptions of Turpin (most famously in the *Chanson de Roland*), the Archbishop is a *miles Christi* in the fullest sense of the term: he throws himself into the heat of battle more passionately than any knight. While other nobles lead delegations of knights and soldiers, Turpin gathers around himself an army of priests; he has permission from the pope, says Turpin, to let them fight 'Bothe with schelde and spere' (619). Turpin seeks and receives permission to lead the vanguard, 'Assemble[d] undire my banere' (924). Turpin expresses his pastoral function in conventional terms, offering the sacrifice of the Mass on behalf of the disheartened troops (881–910), but he also acts as a rather aggressive shepherd in urging the troops to action. He does not hesitate to apply the pastoral rod even to Charlemagne himself, when the emperor's resolve appears less than firm. Turpin accuses the hesitant emperor of heresy (673), and cries out, 'here I curse the, thou kynge! / Because thou lyffes in eresye / Thou ne dare noghte fyghte one Goddes enemy' (688–90). If the emperor does not apply himself wholeheartedly to the fight against the Saracens, declares Turpin, 'I sall stroye the, / Bryne and breke downn thi cité' (752–3). Threatened with utter destruction, both spiritual and physical, Charles gives in. The relentless devotion to God's will displayed by Turpin, together with his patient endurance of the wounds he repeatedly suffers in battle, contribute to the picture of Turpin as a warrior-saint. As Barron and Shepherd have observed, however, the specific nature of Turpin's wounds seem to hint at an even more exalted role: not merely warrior-saint, but figure of Christ. It might be argued that all saints are, in some sense, figures of Christ: what, after all, are the stigmata mysteriously acquired by some saints but the signs of the perfection of the saint's ability to mirror Jesus' suffering in the Crucifixion? Yet Turpin's wounds seem to point to a more specific identification:

> The bischoppe es so woundede that tyde,
> With a spere thoroweowte the syde,
> That one his ribbis gan rese.
> Thurgh the schelde and the browne bare,
> A schaftemonde of his flesche he schare:
> Lordynnges, this es no lese. (1301–6)

Turpin himself compares his own wound to Christ's; though I suffer 'A glafe thorowte my syde', says Turpin, 'Criste for me sufferde mare; / He askede no salve to his sare' (1345–7; cf. 701–2). Turpin refuses not only salve for his wounds, but also food, drink, and even rest: 'I sall never ette ne drynke, / Ne with myn eghe slepe a wynke, / ... / To yone cité yolden bee' (1349–52). Turpin's protracted suffering is extended over 'dayes three' (1579), evoking the period between the Crucifixion and the Resurrection.

One peculiarity of Turpin's behaviour detracts from the hagiographical motif so prominent in the general characterisation of the Archbishop: that is, the abuse he heaps upon the Virgin Mary. Following the news of the initial Christian defeat at Milan, Turpin throws down his staff and mitre, and rebukes the Mother of Jesus: 'A! Mary mylde, whare was thi myght, / That thou lete thi men thus to dede be dighte? / ... / Had thou noghte, Marye, yitt bene borne, / Ne had noghte oure gud men thus bene lorne: / The wyte is all in the' (548–9, 554–6). The blame is all on you; strong words to apply to the Virgin, especially coming from a warrior-saint. On the one hand, Turpin's rebuke of Mary can be seen as simply a manifestation of the same zeal which causes Turpin to disregard secular authority (as opposed to the Virgin's divine authority) when he chastises Charles for cowardice and 'heresy'. On the other hand, as Mills has pointed out, Turpin's behaviour toward Mary associates him less with other heroic figures in the *chansons de geste* or medieval romances than with the enemy: the verbal rebuke of pagan gods, and even the physical destruction of their images, is a common scene in those texts.[15] As Mills puts it, 'here it is very difficult to avoid the feeling that he is being presented as a pagan'.[16] It is important not to overemphasise the significance of Turpin's action toward Mary since, as Patrick Geary has shown, 'abuse' of the saints – such as lowering an image in order to elicit more effective intercession on the part of the saint – was not an uncommon practice during the Middle Ages.[17] Yet it is undeniable that Turpin stands out among other figures both in the *Siege of Melayne* and in comparable texts by virtue of the violence with which he pursues his single-minded devotion to the cause of God.[18]

The poem's most recent editor, Shepherd, has taken note of the 'crusading element' present in the work, that is, 'the militant Christianity, the belief in aggressive martial support for the Faith'. He points out that chronicles of the First Crusade feature men such as Peter Bartholomew, whose ecstatic visions served to fire up the spirits of the knights at Antioch.[19] Even more strikingly similar to Turpin, however, is the behaviour of the priests attending their crusader flock at Antioch during the siege of 1098. The earliest chroniclers of the First Crusade – Fulcher of Chartres, Peter Tudebode, Raymond d'Aguilers, and the anonymous author of the *Gesta Francorum* – recount how the crusaders, tortured 'by cruel hunger' and simultaneously 'paralyzed by fear of the Turks', embarked upon 'three days of fasting' during which they purified themselves 'by confessing their sins ... by absolution, and by faithfully receiving communion of the body and blood of Christ'.[20] In his account, Raymond d'Aguilers emphasises how these acts of devotion lifted up the spirits of the half-starved crusaders: 'So dejected were the Christians that father and son, brother and brother, exchanged neither salvation [greeting] nor glances as they passed on the streets. With the sudden change in spirit one could see the Christians go out as spirited horses, rattle their arms, wave their spears, and boisterously celebrate with acts and speeches.'[21] In his account of the siege of Antioch, written before 1185 on the eve of the fall of Acre to Saladin during the Third Crusade, William of Tyre amplifies Raymond's account to accentuate both the devastating hunger of the crusaders and the devotion of the clergy attending them: 'the bodies of beasts which had died of suffocation or disease were dug up and devoured. Such were the foods by which they tried to quell the cravings of hunger and to prolong their miserable lives.' The famished people are heartened, however, first by the discovery of a miraculous relic and, second, by the ministrations of the priests who 'celebrated divine service in the churches and offered the sacrifice. They then invited the people ... to fortify themselves against the perils of the world by the body and blood of Christ.' William draws attention to the role of the clergy, who mingle with the troops 'clad in their sacerdotal robes and bearing in their hands the cross and the images of the saints', and singles out the Bishop of Puy who, in pressing the battle forward, 'was continually offering himself as a sacrifice for the Lord'.[22] The Bishop, in William's account, both offers sacrifice (in the Mass) and *is* the sacrifice (in the battle). This is a double role that Turpin will also play in the *Siege of Melayne*.

The crusade chronicles also provide a rich background for the second aspect of the religious content of the poem, that is, the devotional. After the initial fall of Milan but before the aggressive assault on the city by Charlemagne's troops, a group of Christian knights, including Roland and Oliver, are captured and led to the chamber of the Sultan Arabas. There, they are privy to a miracle: the Sultan commands his men to 'feche one of theire goddis in, / And if he in this fire will byrne, / Alle other sett att noghte' (422–4). The crucifix is cast into the fire, heaped with 'bromstone' and 'pykke and terre' (458–9), yet it does not burn. In part, this miracle is a testimony to the devotion of Roland, who not only refuses the tempting offer of conversion made to him by Arabas (who mistakes Roland for Charlemagne himself), but bears witness to the Christian faith he fights for:

> Goddis forbode and the holy Trynytee,
> That ever Fraunce hethen were for mee,
> And lese our Crysten laye!
> For sothe, thou sowdane, trowe thou moste
> One the Fader and the Sone and the Holy Goste,
> Thire thre are alle in one. (406–11)

As if in fulfilment of this testimony, the crucifix does not burn, but 'laye still ay as it were colde' (447); at last, the fire goes out, the crucifix emits a loud 'crake' (467), and 'A fire than fro the crosse gane frusche, / And in the Sarazene eghne it gaffe a dosche, / … / That thay stode still als any stone' (470–3). The tormented crucifix becomes the tormentor, immobilising the Saracens so that 'Hanndis nore fete myghte thay stirre none' (474), making them vulnerable to the knights who then 'tuke the grete lordes with ire / And brynte tham in that bale fire' (488–9). In the test of fire, the Saracens lose every time.

Once again, comparable episodes are found in the earliest chronicles of the First Crusade, where the ordeal of fire is used by the Christians to test the veracity of Peter Bartholomew, who claims to have discovered a relic of the lance which was used to pierce Christ's side on the Cross. Raymond d'Aguilers recounts how Peter Bartholomew willingly walked through flames, carrying the lance, and emerged almost totally unscathed; for Raymond, this is proof of the relic's authenticity.[23] Like the 'faire rode' (427) in the *Siege of Melayne*, the lance does not burn. A rather different manifestation of the ordeal of fire appears in Tudebode's account of the Crusade. He tells how the Christian knight Rainald is taken prisoner by the Saracen emir, who offers Rainald his life if he will only convert: 'Deny your God, whom you worship and believe, and accept Mohammed and our other gods. If you do so, we shall give you all that you desire.' Rainald refuses, falls on his knees, and bears witness to the authority of the Christian Trinity. So far, his story adumbrates that of Roland in the *Siege of Melayne*. But while in the latter text, Roland merely looks on as the crucifix is tested in the fire, Rainald pays for his faith with his life. The emir, 'in a towering rage because he could not make Rainald turn apostate', causes all the Christians within his grasp in Antioch to be stripped naked and bound together in a circle:

> He then had chaff, firewood, and hay piled around them, and … ordered them put to the torch. The Christians, those knights of Christ, shrieked and screamed so that their voices resounded in heaven to God for whose love their flesh and bones were cremated.[24]

In the *Siege of Melayne*, the appearance of the 'still' and 'colde' form of the crucifix (447) in place of the burning flesh of the faithful crusaders transforms what is (in Tudebode's account) a spiritual victory alone into a victory which is both spiritual and military. In the later text, it is the Saracen lords and not the Christian knights who are immobilised, 'still als any stone' (473), and burned in 'that bale fire' (489).

The treatment of the crucifix in the *Siege of Melayne* is peculiar in that the ordeal suffered by the object – remaining untouched in spite of being surrounded by burning brimstone and pitch – is less characteristic of the testing of images than it is of the testing of saints. Hagiographic texts repeatedly offer accounts of saints whose bodies, when subjected to torture, remain whole; which, when subjected to the flames, do not burn.[25] The anthropomorphisation of the crucifix in the *Siege of Melayne* may be, in part, a consequence of its relationship to the account of the torment and death of the Christians in Antioch described by Tudebode. But, more importantly, the anthropomorphisation of the crucifix is part of a wider tendency in late medieval literature to emphasise the immanence of Christ's humanity, in devotional objects such as the crucifix and, especially, in the relic of

Christ *par excellence*: that is, the eucharistic host. In this context, it is striking to note the resemblance of the behaviour of the crucifix in the *Siege of Melayne* to that of the host in the fifteenth-century Croxton *Play of the Sacrament*: like the crucifix in the earlier poem, the eucharist in the drama moves from being victim to tormentor. When the unscrupulous Jew Jonathas stabs the consecrated host, it bleeds, illustrating the reality of the transubstantiation the bread has undergone. The play thus dramatises the bleeding host miracles which were common in the later Middle Ages.[26] Yet the bleeding host rapidly switches from victim to aggressor: when the panicking Jonathas tries to cast the host into a bubbling pot of oil, the host stubbornly sticks to his hand. Overcome by 'woodnesse', Jonathas attempts to drown himself and the host together; his fellows restrain him, and are compelled to cut the arm off in order to separate Jonathas from the host. When hand and host together are plunged into the boiling cauldron, 'All thys oyle waxyth redde as blood.' When in desperation the Jews finally seal the host in a hot oven, the oven itself bursts; blood streams out, and the image of the crucified Christ emerges to address the terrified sinner.[27]

The violence with which the host turns upon its tormentor in the Croxton *Play of the Sacrament* bears affinities to the destructive power which is deceptively latent in the 'still' and 'colde' crucifix in the *Siege of Melayne*. The violent 'crake' emitted by the rood, which renders its persecutors helpless, is echoed in the sound of 'the ovyn rave asunder and all tobrast' of the Croxton *Play of the Sacrament*.[28] Yet the fate of the tormentor in each case is dramatically different: in the Croxton play, Jonathas and his fellows are moved by the sight of Christ, emerging from the sacrament itself, to convert to Christianity; in the *Siege of Melayne*, the sultan Arabas and his lords are utterly destroyed in body and in spirit. The difference between these two texts runs far deeper than generic distinctions. In the play, the content of the narrative is not merely didactic but also mimetic: the audience is impelled to undergo a kind of conversion analogous to that experienced by Jonathas. While they do not move from Judaism to Christianity, as Jonathas does, they too are led to turn towards Christ, and especially towards his actual bodily presence in the eucharist. In the siege poem, conversely, conversion is a non-issue. The sultan Arabas and his men are not accepted or even invited into the Christian community: their lot is death. Yet the sultan maintains a kind of immortality; not a personal immortality, but what might be called a categorical immortality. Arabas is dead, but 'the Sultan' continues to rule the Saracens and harry the Christians, for as soon as Arabas' death is known, 'the Sarazenes crouned sir Garsy'

(491). Without missing a beat, the interminable conflict of pagan wrong and Christian right marches on.

The exclusion of conversion in the *Siege of Melayne* distinguishes it sharply from the other Charlemagne romances conventionally associated with it. In texts of the Ferumbras group, following the model of the Old French *Fierabras*, the eponymous hero is the son of a Saracen ruler. Distinguished by his great stature and his feats of arms, Ferumbras presents himself as an eminently desirable recruit for the Christian side. He is led to convert by a combination of religious conviction and admiration for the Christian knights' chivalric accomplishments. In the *Sowdone of Babylone*, for example, an early fifteenth-century manifestation of the Ferumbras group, the Saracen champion bends to the authority of the sword as much as that of the Cross:

> Hoo, Olyvere, I yelde me to the,
> And here I become thy man.
> I am so hurte I may not stonde;
> I put me alle in thy grace.
> My goddis ben false by water and londe;
> I reneye hem alle here in this place.
> Baptised nowe wole I be.
> To Jhesu Crist I wole me take –
> That Charles the Kinge shal sene –
> And alle my goddes forsake.[29]

The juxtaposition of divine and feudal authority evident here – Ferumbras bowing down before Jesus Christ in the sight of 'Charles the Kinge' – is even more evident in *Otuel and Roland*, an early fourteenth-century example of the Charlemagne romances. There, the Saracen knight Otuel couches his conversion in terms which even more vigorously conflate the divine and the feudal: when a white dove, embodiment of the Holy Spirit, alights upon him, Otuel declares, 'Mahoun and Iouyn, y wyl for-sake, / and to Jhesu crist y wyl me take, / to bene hys knyght.'[30] Ferumbras declares that he is henceforth Oliver's 'man', while Otuel pledges that he is Jesus' 'knyght'; in each case, however, the assumption of Christian identity is simultaneous with the acquisition of a place within the feudal system in which man owes loyalty to man.

Not so in the *Siege of Melayne*. Conversion appears at the outset of the narrative, only to be flatly rejected: the Sultan repeatedly requests that Charlemagne and his men 'torne and hethyn bee' (50; cf. 49–84, 390–408, 1033–56). It is unsurprising that conversion from the Christian law to Saracen law is not an option; what is surprising, however, is that conversion from Saracen law to Christian law is also excluded. Such conversion is featured prominently in romances such as the *Sowdone of Babylone* and *Otuel and Roland*, as noted above, as well as in texts further afield, such as the early fourteenth-century *King of Tars*.[31] The unusual exclusion of conversion in the *Siege of Melayne* is the consequence of how the community is constituted within the text: the men led by Charlemagne (with helpful prodding by Turpin) are united by both religious and chivalric bonds. They are a military host ('oste', 1592) brought together by the eucharistic host ('oste', 891), and while other romances emphasise the eagerness of the body of the Church to incorporate new members, in the *Siege of Melayne*, the boat is full. This community is full to overflowing; there is no room for anyone else.

This fullness is very much in evidence in the pivotal scene in which Turpin, in his priestly role, celebrates Mass for the assembled troops. It is clear that this eucharistic sacrifice is especially touched by grace, for Turpin finds the gifts of God upon the altar:

> He blyssede the awtere with his hande,
> And a fayre oste of brede therappon he fande,
> That ever he sawe with syghte.
> His chalesse was so full of wyne
> There myghte no more hafe gone therin,
> It come fro heven on highte. (890–5)

Turpin shares his knowledge regarding the sacred origin of these gifts, telling 'the hoste with lowde steven / How brede and wyne was sent fro heven' (902–3). This experience energises Turpin who, full of 'egernesse', laughs out loud (913). The troops, too, are revivified by the Mass, following a pattern established in the chronicles of the First Crusade, as noted earlier. As priest, Turpin draws the community together through the sacrifice of the Mass;[32] as warrior, Turpin draws them together by offering himself up as a sacrifice upon the battlefield, like such priestly heroes as the Bishop of Puy described by William of Tyre. The wounds he sustains are visible signs of the damage inflicted upon the crusaders by the Saracen enemy.

Yet Turpin's wounds are not simply a sign of vulnerability: like the bleeding wafer in the Croxton *Play of the Sacrament* that turns on its tormentor, like the crucifix surrounded by flames that destroys its persecutors in the earlier scene in the chamber of the sultan Arabas, the wounded body of Turpin proves to be the locus of an awful power. In the steadfastness with which he endures his wounds, refusing 'salve', 'mete' and 'drynke' (1188–90; cf. 1347–9), Turpin acts as an exemplar to the Christian troops who are also afflicted with grievous wounds, so much so that the entire field is covered with blood:

> Bot one the morne the Cristen stode
> A thowsande over theire fete in theire blode,
> Of their awenn wondes wanne.
> Othere refreschynge noghte many hade
> Bot blody water of a slade,
> That thurghe the oste ran. (1202–7)

This passage is resonant in two respects, evoking both the deprivation suffered by the knights of the First Crusade and the symbolic framework of the eucharist which provides the model for community formation. The anonymous author of the *Gesta Francorum* recounts how the crusaders at the castle of Xerigordo suffered from the lack of clean water:

> Our men were therefore so terribly afflicted by thirst that they bled their horses and asses and drank the blood; others let down belts and clothes into a sewer and squeezed out the liquid into their mouths; others passed water into one another's cupped hands and drank; others dug up damp earth and lay down on their backs, piling the earth upon their chests because they were so dry with thirst.[33]

The abjection experienced by the crusaders at Xerigordo, driven to extreme uncleanliness and even a kind of self-interment, is transmuted in the *Siege of Melayne* into a moment of eucharistic union. Instead of the blood of unclean animals, the knights at Milan drink their own blood, which colours the stream bright red. The blood flowing through the military host mirrors the blood flowing through the eucharistic host in the sacrifice of the Mass. It is not abject but uplifting, a sign not of military vulnerability but of redemptive suffering.

At first glance, it may seem peculiar to find the eucharistic host characterised in terms of blood rather than bread. After all, in the words of the Fourth Lateran Council, Christ's 'body and blood are truly contained in the sacrament of the altar in the forms of the bread and the wine, the bread being transubstantiated into the body and the wine into the blood'.[34] Yet even at the time of the Council in 1215, theologians were engaged in defining the host as both blood and body of Christ. These speculations would become church doctrine exactly two hundred years later, when the Council of Constance declared that both body and blood were concomitant – that is, simultaneously present – in the host: 'let it be most firmly believed, without any doubt, that the whole body of Christ is truly contained in the form of the bread, as also in the form of the wine'.[35] With this declaration of the real presence of both body and blood in each of the two manifestations of the sacrament, there could be no room to object that each communicant must partake of both bread and wine. The practice of withholding the chalice from the laity, which had begun in the twelfth century in response to concerns regarding the danger that the consecrated wine might be spilled, had by 1415 acquired the authority of infallible doctrine.[36] As the chalice was withheld, the wafer was accorded greater symbolic significance: it increasingly became the object of devotion, so that even the sight of the consecrated host was believed to afford spiritual benefits.[37]

Yet this is not to suggest that Christ's blood, previously understood to appear in the form of the wine, had come to be of lesser importance. Far from it: the late Middle Ages saw a flowering of devotion to the Passion which included, as a crucial element of the supplicant's affective response, a special focus on the blood flowing from the wounds of Christ. The early fourteenth-century mystic Richard Rolle, for example, uses the blood of Christ as a kind of repeated refrain to focus his contemplation:

> Swet Jhesu, I thank the with al my hert for al that blode that thou so plenteuously bled in thy coronynge before al folke, when thy swet face was al on blode … Here, swete Jhesu, I beseche the, weshe my soule with that blode, and enoynt and depeynt my soule and my mynd with that preciouse blode.[38]

Rolle is representative of a widespread emphasis in late medieval piety on compassion, that is, literally sharing the passion of Christ. As Richard Kieckhefer puts it, such a response 'closed the distance' between the worshipper and God: 'identifying oneself with him, one suffered along with him and strove to partake in his sufferings'.[39] Whether mediated through words or through images, the blood of Christ served as the means through which the individual soul could be united with God. Miracles of bleeding hosts served to remind the worshipper of the real presence of Jesus' body and blood, and hence to underline the importance of both communion and the mere sight of the sacrament. Eamon Duffy quotes a popular lyric which plays on the liveliness of the host, the blood pulsing just below the surface:

> Hyt semes quite, and is red
> Hyt is quike, and seemes dede:
> Hyt is flesche and seemes brede
> Hyt is one and semes too;
> Hyt is God body and no more.[40]

The blood running through the host, invisible except in special moments of revelation, was a powerful reminder of the immanence of Christ, his hidden but immediate presence. Just so, in the *Siege of Melayne*, the bloody water which runs through the battlefield both witnesses to the suffering of the Christian knights and promises that their suffering will be redemptive, in imitation of the suffering of Christ himself. While the early twelfth-century chronicles of the First Crusade recount how the crusaders were stirred to action by the discovery of a sacred relic, the lance discovered by Peter Bartholo-mew, the troops at Milan are energised by something else: the very body of Christ, present in the eucharistic host of the Mass celebrated by Turpin; in the military host, spread out on a field flowing with their own blood mixed with water; and in the wounded body of Turpin, pierced in the side in imitation of his Saviour.

The wounds of Turpin become the focus of attention in the *Siege of Melayne*, as Charlemagne repeatedly begs him to remove the clothing which hides them. After the first injury, 'the kynge prayede the bischoppe fre / His wonde that he wolde late hym see, / That he hade tane in that fighte' (1184–6). Turpin refuses; after the next wound, Charles again asks, 'Fadir for Goddes are, / Thy woundes that thou walde late me see; / If any surgeoun myghte helpe thee, / My com-forthe ware the mare' (1339–42). Finally, the only surviving manu-script of the poem breaks off just a few lines after Charlemagne, brought to tears by the sight of the suffering Turpin, laments 'the floure of presthode' who 'will no man his wondes late see' (1584, 1589). Turpin's withholding of the sight of his wounds serves two functions. Firstly, the refusal to uncover is also a refusal of medicine ('salve', 1188, 1347) that might heal the wounds, and hence part of the overall vow of fasting that Turpin has undertaken. Secondly, the refusal to uncover keeps Charles and his knights in a state of tension: I will not eat or sleep, Turpin declares, until 'yone cité yolden bee, / Or ells therfore in batelle dye, / The sothe is noghte to hyde' (1352–4). Paradoxically, the hidden wounds of Turpin are a testimony to precisely that which is not hidden, and cannot be hidden: that is, 'the sothe'. It is the very hidden nature of the wounds that guarantees their veracity, and their efficacy.

Charlemagne's desire to see the wounds of Turpin mimics the desire to see the wounds of Christ which appears in late medieval devotional texts such as *The Prickynge of Love*. There, the wound in Christ's side is the focus of tremendous longing, a breast to be sucked and a womb to be entered: the devout worshipper desires to be the very lance which entered Christ's body, rendered holy by its contact with the suffering flesh of the redeemer.[41] This moment of seeing the wounds was enacted liturgically in the elevation of the host, the crucial moment in the sequence of the Mass when the community of the faithful could look on and adore the newly transubstantiated sacrament. This practice, which began early in the twelfth century, became the focus of theological debate because it required that theologians specify precisely when the bread and wine were transubstantiated. Elevate the host a moment too early, and you incite the flock to idolatry; elevate it at the right moment, and you offer them the clearest sight of Christ they can hope for in this life.[42] It is for this reason that the host is kept hidden until the words 'Hoc est corpus meum' are pronounced; the same suspense surrounds the body of Turpin in the *Siege of Melayne*. Like the consecrated eucharist, Turpin's body simultaneously displays and conceals the wounds of Christ.[43]

Miri Rubin has recently demonstrated that the symbol of the eucharist can function not just to include members of the community, generating a collective body, but also to exclude. Host desecration stories in particular, she argues, serve to delineate the boundaries which exclude Jews from the salvation of the New Law.[44] This dynamic is very much in action in the *Siege of Melayne* which, unlike related romances of the Charlemagne group, forecloses the possibility of conversion and assimilation. This text is not about crossing boundaries but preserving them, both on the level of the individual body and on the level of the Christian community. Turpin vows to maintain the integrity of his body, abstaining from food, drink, salve and sleep; the Christian knights keep close watch on the besieged city of Milan, so that 'no Sarazene solde come owte' (1514). In order to prevent them from 'isschuynge owte of the cité, / Kynge Charles with his menyé / Helde his batelle still' (1523–5). For the community as for the individual, nothing in and nothing out.

Other medieval romances, while very different from the *Siege of Melayne*, also draw upon theological concepts in order to define the nature of the community depicted within the text; these can be loosely categorised as 'devotional romances'. In *Otuel and Roland*, for example, the Saracen Otuel is moved to convert not simply by the chivalric might of his opponent, Oliver, but by the hand of God: a white dove, symbol of the Holy Spirit, descends upon him, demonstrating in no hidden way the workings of providence in the course of the battle between pagan and Christian. The descent of the dove is, to Otuel, a sign to convert; to the Christian knights who are at war with the Saracens, it is a sign to accept Otuel as one of themselves. A theologically based notion of community is at work also in *Richard Coer de Lion*, where the king takes very seriously his role as head of the nation. His consumption of the flesh of dead Saracens is a grotesque parody of the priest's sacerdotal role: like the priest, Richard consumes body and blood on behalf of his community. Just as the sacrifice of the Mass, in the crusade accounts as in the *Siege of Melayne*, restores courage and aggression to the Christian knights, feasting on the Saracens restores Richard to his old leonine self and inspires his troops to destroy their enemy.[45]

Versions of both *Otuel and Roland* and *Richard Coer de Lion* are among those texts included, along with the unique copy of the *Siege of Melayne*, in the London Thornton manuscript. But this fact should not lead us to imagine that the similarities among these three texts that I have briefly sketched out above are the consequence of their presence in this compilation, that Robert Thornton is somehow responsible for skewing otherwise 'pure' romances toward a more didactic, explicitly Christian orientation. On the contrary, the presence of these poems in the London Thornton manuscript is a witness to the common nature of texts which may appear very dissimilar to us, both with regard to genre and with regard to subject matter. Modern readers persist in applying the name 'romance' to texts which prove to be too slippery to be confined by such generic constraints. This can be illustrated by reference to the London Thornton manuscript which, as Thompson has shown, contains a wide variety of material that can be classified as entertaining or didactic, lyric or romance. Modern readers typically identify 'four romances in this manuscript, *The Siege of Jerusalem*, *The Sege of Melayne*, *The Romance of Duke Rowland and of Sir Ottuell of Spayne*, and *The Romance of Kyng Richard the Conqueroure*'.[46] Yet the manuscript's medieval compiler would not (and did not) classify his texts in that way: Thornton does refer to *Richard Coer de Lion* and

Rowland and Ottuell as romances, but he also titles an apocryphal account of the childhood of Jesus *The Romance of Ypokrephum*. When Finlayson, for example, notes the juxtaposition of *Richard* and the *Ypokrephum* in the London Thornton manuscript, he concludes that this simply 'suggest[s] that *Richard* was regarded as an edifying narrative'.[47] More interestingly, I think, it suggests that, for the compiler, romance was a category that was not necessarily restricted to the deeds of knights.

What, then, could the compiler have intended by juxtaposing these two 'romances', one national in scope, one spiritual? In his analysis of the manuscript, Thompson notes that the incipit which calls the *Ypokrephum* a romance appears to have been added later by Thornton, and therefore may represent 'a determined effort … to create in his reader's mind some limited sense of continuity, despite the unlikely pairing of the blood-thirsty Richard with a story about the childhood of Christ'.[48] But, as we have seen, this pairing is far from unlikely, for the model of community formation based on the presence of Christ's body in the sacrifice of the Mass serves as the model for community formation in devotional romances such as *Richard Coer de Lion* and the *Siege of Melayne*. Although it may seem strange to a modern reader to label an account of Christ's childhood a romance, evidently it was not strange to medieval readers. Further, it is worth noting that Thornton, unlike modern readers, does not identify the *Siege of Melayne* as a romance; like the *Siege of Jerusalem*, which appears immediately before it in the manuscript, it is identified as a 'sege'.[49] This might lead us to conclude that siege poems constitute a genre distinct from romance, or perhaps a sub-genre of romance: while, as Diane Speed has suggested, romances focus on the role of the hero as the focal point of his community or nation,[50] siege poems stress instead the factors that threaten to tear the community apart. Shepherd has pointed out the affinities between the *Siege of Melayne* and the sixteenth-century *Capystranus*, both of which depict the pressures brought to bear on the Christian nation by the threat of pagan – in the *Capystranus*, Turkish – domination.[51] In his study of Middle English siege poems, Malcolm Hebron argues that these works 'illustrate disasters of a magnitude which reveals the shape of history'. The siege is 'a purging experience, a painful rite of passage in which a great cultural or spiritual change is effected'.[52]

Yet I think it would be a mistake to label these sieges a separate genre, to create yet another category with which to divide and classify Middle English texts. Like Childress's 'secular legend', like Hopkins's 'penitential romance', the siege poem is useful only as a provisional means of understanding how people in the Middle Ages organised their reading. If Thornton places the *Siege of Jerusalem* and the *Siege of Melayne* side by side, we ought to think about them in that way too; if Thornton pairs the 'romances' of *Richard* and *Ypokrephum*, we ought to do so as well, remembering that each collection of texts is itself an interpretive act.[53] When, for example, the manuscript Harley 3954 juxtaposes the *Ypokrephum* with *Mandeville's Travels*,[54] our response ought not to be 'What an unlikely combination!' Instead, we must ask what these texts might mean together: in this case, surely the solemn retracing of Jesus' steps, which is the very heart of the first half of *Mandeville's Travels*, is the link to the story of *Ypokrephum*, a narrative walk through Jesus' childhood.[55]

Now, it is certainly true that some 'unlikely combinations' are simply the result of happenstance: the compiler happens to have space in a manuscript booklet to accommodate a work of a certain length, and therefore includes it. Yet we need not assume that such is always the case. The manuscripts prepared by Robert Thornton are a remarkable example of late medieval compilation and reading practices that we are just beginning to understand. It is not the case, as has been said, that 'identifying the genre takes the first step toward a more complete understanding of these works';[56] rather, the first step is to recognise the fluidity of genre, its dependence upon manuscript context.[57] Whether understood as romance or siege, hagiography or secular legend, the *Siege of Melayne* partakes of all these categories. Each context represents a different point of view; since the *Siege of Melayne* survives only in a single exemplar, it offers us the rare opportunity to see with the single eye.

Notes

Thanks to David Klausner and Fiona Somerset for their comments on an earlier draft of this essay.

1 W. R. J. Barron, *English Medieval Romance* (London, 1987), p. 97; on genre, see also pp. 1–10, 48–62. Mehl classifies the *Siege of Melayne* among the 'homiletic' romances, which 'occupy a position exactly in the middle between these two genres' of romance and hagiography (Dieter Mehl, *The Middle English Romances of the Thirteenth and Fourteenth Centuries* (London, 1969), p. 121). Shepherd identifies it as a 'generic "hybrid"' in which 'the heroic and the hagiographic are combined' (Stephen H. A. Shepherd, '"This grete journee": the *Sege of Melayne*', in Maldwyn Mills,

Jennifer Fellows, and Carol M. Meale (eds), *Romance in Medieval England* (Cambridge, 1991), pp. 113–31; quotations from pp. 114, 116). See also Diana T. Childress, 'Between romance and legend: "secular hagiography" in Middle English literature', *Philological Quarterly*, 57 (1978), 311–22, esp. p. 316.

2 Childress, 'Between romance and legend', p. 319.

3 *Ibid.*, p. 320.

4 Andrea Hopkins, *The Sinful Knights: A Study of Middle English Penitential Romances* (Oxford, 1990), p. 198.

5 Jocelyn Wogan-Browne, '"Bet ... to ... rede ... on holy seyntes lyves ...": romance and hagiography again', in Carol M. Meale (ed.), *Readings in Middle English Romance* (Cambridge, 1994), pp. 83–97; quotation from p. 96.

6 On the body of Christ as symbol of community, see the seminal article of Mervyn James, 'Ritual, drama and social body in the late medieval English town', *Past and Present*, 98 (1983), 3–29; Miri Rubin, 'Small groups: identity and solidarity in the late Middle Ages', in Jennifer Kermode (ed.), *Enterprise and Individuals in Fifteenth-Century England* (Stroud, 1991), pp. 132–50; Miri Rubin, *Charity and Community in Medieval Cambridge* (Cambridge, 1987), 'Introduction'.

7 Paul Strohm, 'The origin and meaning of Middle English *romaunce*', *Genre*, 10 (1977), 1–28 (pp. 12–13). See also Finlayson's effort to establish a 'suggested paradigm' of romance to which, however, 'many Middle English romances conform only imperfectly': John Finlayson, 'Definitions of Middle English romance', *Chaucer Review*, 15 (1980), 168–81 (p. 179).

8 I owe this insight to Andrew Cole and Fiona Somerset.

9 John J. Thompson, *Robert Thornton and the London Thornton Manuscript: British Library MS Additional 31042* (Cambridge, 1987). For more on Thornton, see also John J. Thompson, 'Collecting Middle English romances and some related book-production activities in the later Middle Ages', in Mills, Fellows, and Meale (eds), *Romance in Medieval England*, pp. 17–38.

10 Shepherd notes a sixteenth-century allusion ('Journee', p. 113 n. 4).

11 *The Sege of Melayne, and the Romance of Duke Rowland and Sir Ottuell of Spayne, ... with ... the Song of Roland*, ed. Sidney J. Herrtage, EETS e.s. 35 (London, 1880, repr. Millwood, NY, 1975), pp. x, xiii.

12 *Six Middle English Romances*, ed. Maldwyn Mills, 2nd edn (London, 1992), p. ix, n. 3; *Middle English Romances*, ed. Stephen H. A. Shepherd (New York and London, 1995), p. 268n; *Three Middle English Charlemagne Romances: The Sultan of Babylon, The Siege of Milan, and The Tale of Ralph the Collier*, ed. Alan Lupack (Kalamazoo, 1990), p. 105. None of the modern editions differ from Herrtage's edition in any significant way; line numbers and punctuation differ slightly. Quotations from the *Siege of Melayne* are based on Mills's edition and are cited parenthetically in the text.

13 Childress, 'Between romance and legend', p. 316.

14 Shepherd, 'Journee', pp. 128, 129.

15 Suzanne Conklin Akbari, 'Imagining Islam: the role of images in medi-
    eval depictions of Muslims', *Scripta Mediterranea*, 19–20 (1998–99), 9–27.

16 *Six Middle English Romances*, ed. Mills, p. xiii.

17 Patrick Geary, 'Humiliation of saints', in Stephen Wilson (ed.), *Saints and
    their Cults: Studies in Religious Sociology, Folklore, and History* (Cambridge,
    1983), pp. 123–40. Hardman similarly notes the resemblance of Turpin's
    rebuke of Mary and that seen in certain miracles of the Virgin; yet, as
    Hardman herself acknowledges, the *Siege of Melayne* differs from such
    texts in that the romance 'defers the satisfaction until later', that is, beyond
    the extant end of the romance. See Phillipa Hardman, 'The *Sege of Melayne*:
    a fifteenth-century reading', in Rosalind Field (ed.), *Tradition and Trans-
    formation in Medieval Romance* (Cambridge, 1999), pp. 71–86 (p. 82).

18 It is possible that the treatment of Mary in the text may also suggest a
    comparatively late date for the poem. Her intercessory role is referred to
    only in a negative sense, in Turpin's condemnation, which may reflect
    attitudes toward mediation (whether through images or through saints)
    during the last decade of the fourteenth century. (Here I disagree with
    Hardman's argument that the poem displays 'a devotion to the Virgin'
    ('Sege', p. 79).) Nicholas Watson has argued that the short text of Julian
    of Norwich's *Revelation of Divine Love* should be assigned a date after 1400
    based on its reflection of contemporary attitudes toward images. See 'The
    composition of Julian of Norwich's *Revelation of Divine Love*', *Speculum*,
    68 (1993), 637–83, esp. pp. 657–66.

19 Shepherd, 'Journee', pp. 123, 126.

20 Peter Tudebode, *Historia de Hierosolymitano Itinere*, ed. and trans. John
    Hugh Hill and Laurita Hill (Philadelphia, 1974), p. 85. See also *Gesta
    Francorum et aliorum Hierosolimitanorum*, ed. and trans. Rosalind Hill
    (London, 1962), IX.28–9 (pp. 66–9).

21 Raymond d'Aguilers, *Historia Francorum Qui Ceperunt Iherusalem*, ed. and
    trans. John Hugh Hill and Laurita Hill (Philadelphia, 1968), p. 62.

22 William of Tyre, *A History of the Deeds Done Beyond the Sea*, ed. and trans.
    Emily Atwater Babcock and A. C. Krey, 2 vols (New York, 1943), VI.7
    (p. 271), VI.16 (pp. 285–6).

23 Raymond d'Aguilers, *Historia Francorum*, ed. Hill and Hill, pp. 100–1.
    Hill and Hill note that Raymond's account does not appear elsewhere
    and hence is at best 'suspect' (p. 100 n. 17).

24 Tudebode, *Historia*, ed. Hill and Hill, pp. 58, 59.

25 See Renate Blumenfeld-Kosinski and Timea Szell (eds), *Images of
    Sainthood in Medieval Europe* (Ithaca, 1991).

26 Megivern provides a table of bleeding host miracles which shows their
    preponderance during the fourteenth century; see James J. Megivern,
    Concomitance and Communion: A Study in Eucharistic Doctrine and Practice,
    Studia Friburgensia n.s. 33 (Fribourg and New York, 1963), p. 44. On
    bleeding host miracles, see Peter Browe, *Die eucharistischen Wunder des*

Mittelalters (Breslau, 1938). For more selective accounts, see Miri Rubin, *Corpus Christi: The Eucharist in Late Medieval Culture* (Cambridge, 1991), pp. 121–8, and Eamon Duffy, *The Stripping of the Altars: Traditional Religion in England c.1400–c.1580* (New Haven and London, 1992), pp. 102–6. For a perceptive reading of the play in the context of such miracles, see Sarah Beckwith, 'Ritual, church, and theatre: medieval dramas of the sacramental body', in David Aers (ed.), *Culture and History, 1350–1600: Essays on English Communities, Identities, and Writing* (Detroit, 1992), pp. 65–89.

27 Croxton *Play of the Sacrament*, in *Non-Cycle Plays and Fragments*, ed. Norman Davis, EETS s.s. 1 (Oxford, 1970), lines 502, 674. On conversion in the play, see Donnalee Dox, 'Medieval drama as documentation: 'real presence' in the Croxton *Conversion of Ser Jonathas the Jewe by the Myracle of the Blessed Sacrament'*, *Theatre Survey*, 38 (1997), 97–115. On the relationship of the play's antisemitism to contemporary attacks on Lollardy, see Lisa Lampert, 'The once and future Jew: the Croxton *Play of the Sacrament*, little Robert of Bury, and historical memory', *Jewish History*, 15 (2001), 235–55.

28 Croxton *Play of the Sacrament*, in *Non-Cycle Plays*, ed. Davis, line 943.

29 *The Sowdone of Babylone*, in *The Romaunce of the Sowdone of Babylone and of Ferumbras his Sone who conquerede Rome*, ed. Emil Hausknecht, EETS e.s. 38 (London, 1881, repr. Oxford, 1969), lines 1353–62. I follow the punctuation used in Lupack, ed., *Three Middle English Charlemagne Romances*.

30 *Otuel and Roland*, lines 575–7, in *Firumbras and Otuel and Roland*, ed. Mary Isabelle O'Sullivan, EETS o.s. 198 (London, 1935).

31 *The King of Tars*, ed. Judith Perryman (Heidelberg, 1980); conversion scene at lines 877–936.

32 On the priest's role, see John Bossy, 'The Mass as a social institution', *Past and Present*, 100 (1983), 29–61.

33 *Gesta Francorum*, ed. Hill, I. 2 (pp. 2–5).

34 '[C]orpus et sanguis in sacramento altaris sub speciebus panis et vini veraciter continentur; transubstantiatis, pane in corpus, et vino in sanguinem.' *Concilium Laterensae* IV, chapter 1, in *Sacrorum Conciliorum nova, et amplissima collectio*, ed. J. D. Mansi, 31 vols (Venice, 1759–93), vol. 22, cols 981–2. On eucharistic theology up to the Fourth Lateran Council, see Gary Macy, *The Theologies of the Eucharist in the Early Scholastic Period: A Study of the Salvific Function of the Sacrament according to the Theologians c. 1080–c.1220* (Oxford, 1984).

35 '[C]um firmissime credendum sit et nullatenus dubitandum, integrum Christi corpus et sanguinem tam sub specie panis, quam sub specie vini veraciter contineri.' *Concilium Constantiense generale*, in *Sacrorum Conciliorum collectio*, ed. Mansi, vol. 27, col. 727d.

36 On the 'danger' [*periculum*] of spilling expressed by medieval theologians, see Megivern, pp. 240–1; quotation (from Aquinas) on p. 221.

37 Duffy, *Stripping of the Altars*, pp. 95–116.

38 Richard Rolle, 'Meditation B', lines 266–72 in *Richard Rolle: Prose and*

Verse, ed. S. J. Ogilvie-Thomson, EETS 293 (Oxford, 1988), p. 75. On Rolle, see Nicholas Watson, *Richard Rolle and the Invention of Authority*, Cambridge Studies in Medieval Literature 13 (Cambridge, 1991).

39 Richard Kieckhefer, *Unquiet Souls: Fourteenth-Century Saints and Their Religious Milieu* (Chicago, 1984), pp. 89–121; quotation from p. 105. On the blood of Christ in early modern devotion, see J. T. Rhodes, 'The body of Christ in English eucharistic devotion, c. 1500–c. 1620', in Richard Beadle and A. J. Piper (eds), *New Science Out of Old Books: Studies in Manuscripts and Early Printed Books in Honour of A. I. Doyle* (Aldershot, 1995), pp. 388–419.

40 Rossell Hope Robbins, 'Popular prayers in Middle English verse', *Modern Philology*, 36 (1939), 337–56 (p. 344); noted in Duffy, *Stripping of the Altars*, p. 102.

41 *The Prickynge of Love*, ed. Harold Kane, Salzburg Studies in English Literature, Elizabethan and Renaissance Studies 91: 10 (Salzburg, 1983), pp. 9–10, 12. See the perceptive discussion of this text in Sarah Beckwith, *Christ's Body: Identity, Culture and Society in Late Medieval Writings* (London and New York, 1993), pp. 56–62.

42 See V. L. Kennedy, 'The moment of consecration and the elevation of the Host', *Mediaeval Studies*, 6 (1944), 121–50; Rubin, *Corpus Christi*, pp. 55–8.

43 On the sight of Christ's wounds in the host, see Rubin, *Corpus Christi*, pp. 302–6.

44 Miri Rubin, *Gentile Tales: The Narrative Assault on Late Medieval Jews* (New Haven and London, 1999).

45 Text in *Der mittelenglische Versroman über Richard Löwenherz*, ed. Karl Brunner, Wiener Beiträge zur Englischen Philologie 42 (Vienna, 1913). On the eucharistic symbolism, see Suzanne Conklin Akbari, 'The hunger for national identity in *Richard Coer de Lion*', in Robert Stein and Sandra Pierson Prior (eds), *Reading Medieval Culture* (Notre Dame, 2004).

46 E.g. Finlayson, 'Definitions of Middle English romance' (n. 7 above), 164; cf. Hardman, '*Sege of Melayne*' (n. 17 above), p. 72.

47 Finlayson, 'Definitions', p. 165.

48 Thompson, *Robert Thornton* (n. 9 above), p. 48.

49 On the deliberate juxtaposition of these siege poems in the manuscript, see Thompson, *Robert Thornton*, p. 48. For an extended analysis of the *Siege of Jerusalem*, see Bonnie Millar, *The Siege of Jerusalem in its Physical, Literary, and Historical Contexts* (Dublin, 2000). A new edition of the poem is promised by David Lawton and Ralph Hanna III; until then, see *The Siege of Jerusalem*, ed. E. Kölbing and Mabel Day, EETS o.s. 188 (London, 1932).

50 Diane Speed, 'The construction of the nation in Medieval English romance', in Meale (ed.), *Readings in Medieval English Romance* (n. 5 above), pp. 135–57, esp. pp. 146–7.

51 Shepherd, 'Journee', p. 121; Shepherd prints an edition of the *Capystranus*

in his *Middle English Romance* (pp. 388–408). See also Malcolm Hebron, *The Medieval Siege: Theme and Image in Middle English Romance* (Oxford, 1997), pp. 84–90.

52 Hebron, *Medieval Siege*, p. 135.

53 Phillipa Hardman offers a sensitive reading of the *Siege of Melayne* in the context of the Marian poem 'O florum flos' which follows it in the London Thornton manuscript, though her extended argument – 'that the end of the romance involved a miracle of some kind in which Mary intervened in the course of events on behalf of her knights' – is less persuasive. See Hardman, '*Sege*', pp. 82–4 (pp. 82–3). On the sequence of texts in the manuscript, see also her 'Reading the spaces: pictorial intentions in the Thornton manuscripts, Lincoln Cathedral 91 and BL MS Add. 31042', *Medium Aevum*, 63 (1994), 250–74.

54 Noted in Thompson, *Robert Thornton*, p. 48 n. 25.

55 Middleton points out that the potentially jarring presence of *Piers Plowman* along with *Mandeville's Travels* can be attributed to the coherency of the Vernon manuscript and its overall focus on conversion: 'It is a book about the peoples of the Book in their temporal and spiritual establishments.' Anne Middleton, 'The audience and public of *Piers Plowman*', in David Lawton (ed.), *Middle English Alliterative Poetry and its Literary Background* (Cambridge, 1982), pp. 101–23 (p. 106).

56 Childress, 'Between romance and legend', p. 320.

57 On manuscript compilation practices, see Ralph Hanna III, *Pursuing History: Middle English Manuscripts and Their Texts* (Stanford, 1996), pp. 21–34.

2

The twin demons of aristocratic society in *Sir Gowther*

Alcuin Blamires

Sir Gowther is a 700-line narrative probably originating (in its Middle English form) about 1400 in the North Midlands. It is extant in two mildly divergent manuscript texts, which will here be referred to as the 'Advocates' and 'Royal' versions.[1] *Sir Gowther* is conspicuous for that surface crankiness and drastic speed which are often found in medieval English verse romances and which readily provoke a modern reader's suspicion that no very challenging contact with medieval society is being offered.

Gowther is the name of the son born to a hitherto childless duchess after she is first threatened with repudiation by her husband and then apparently impregnated by a devil out in an orchard. This son grows up pursuing a life of reckless helter–skelter sadism. However, when an elderly earl of the region alleges that such tyranny proves he cannot be of human stock, Gowther coerces his mother to admit the devilish identity of his father. He recoils from this revelation into a course of abject penitence. Under the pope's instruction he embraces complete voluntary silence and undertakes a startling regime of self-humiliation, accepting food only from the mouths of dogs. Gowther's spiritual rehabilitation is subsequently consolidated through the agency of an emperor's mute daughter, whom he delivers from the prospect of forced marriage to a Sultan by thrice fighting the Sultan's forces, in successive suits of armour miraculously supplied in response to prayer. Although the daughter falls from her tower when she sees Gowther wounded on her behalf, she arises after three days of 'death' and escapes also from her own mute condition to proclaim news of his divine forgiveness. Gowther marries her and they inherit the empire.

Sir Gowther has seemed in the past too slight and eccentric, too brusque and melodramatic to attract much serious notice apart from classificatory investigation of its folktale affiliations and bureaucratic inquiry into its generic status.[2] What modicum of attention it has otherwise gained has arisen because it draws upon the discourse of demonology on the one hand and the discourse of penitence on the other. The narrative's powerful penitential thrust has been illuminated in particular by the work of Margaret Bradstock and Andrea Hopkins.[3] Bradstock's argument that, 'apprehended at a symbolic level', the text's subject matter 'ceases to be improbable' because it projects a process of spiritual regeneration, is commended by Hopkins as 'the kind of reading [...] essential for a proper understanding of the poem'.[4] Such a symbolic reading covers, for Bradstock, even the devil's paternity. Gowther 'is the son of a devil and therefore inherently evil. This is symbolic of the original sin.'[5] For Hopkins, while Gowther is partly 'Everyman, who has inherited Original Sin', the devil's paternity is also emphatically literal: it causes Gowther to pursue a campaign of mass violence against the church and anyone in orders, thereby 'performing a specific task at the orders of his father, the Devil'.[6]

It is curious that willingness to countenance symbolic meanings in the religious domain has not been complemented by much willingness to consider them in the social domain. In fact, the 'symbolic' value of the fiend's paternity as interpreted by Bradstock and Hopkins has actually been predicated on a readiness to simplify the fiend's role in the narrative, diminishing equivocations which (it will here be argued) make that role socially significant, at least in one of the two surviving manuscript versions. While the present essay is by no means hostile to religious interpretation – and will in fact propose some elaboration of it – a primary concern in my discussion will be to focus sociological implications in *Sir Gowther*. Here is a narrative that emphatically addresses what Stephen Knight considers to be endemic in the romances – a 'range of threats' to the 'tenure of power' by a dominant social group, which romance narrative aims to 'resolve' by 'employing the values' that seem from that group's viewpoint 'the most credible'.[7]

The peculiarity of *Sir Gowther* is that it focuses key anxieties of society's dominant group at such a pitch as to project a kind of worst-case threat to dynastic stability.[8] The questions that loom dramatically in this narrative concern the state of society as well as the state of the soul. An Everyman-orientated reading unwarrantably reduces the 'knightly' dimension to lesser significance. The ideological scope of the narrative is demeaned if that dimension is only held to 'subserve religious concerns' and to 'provide a metaphorical statement of them'.[9] A more positive way of responding to sociological implications in *Sir*

Gowther is offered by Margaret Robson when she reminds us of the common medieval assumption 'that a male child takes its nature from his father and that an ignoble son means an ignoble father'.[10] Robson focuses productively on fears, anxieties and desires in the narrative. Yet her psychoanalytical method situates these primarily as individual needs and anxieties. The romance clamours, I think, for analysis that highlights the text's articulation of deep-seated anxieties in medieval society about breeding and dynasty. *Sir Gowther* speaks trenchantly of the 'twin demons', or spectres, haunting such society: failure of heredity and arrogance.

The culture's obsession with purity and continuity of bloodline and with the social arrogance implicated in that are familiar to us, for example from their presence in the Griselda story. Elevated by marriage to noble rank, Griselda has a daughter. The sex of the child is reckoned disappointing, but the proof of Griselda's fertility is a cause for hope – the prize of a male heir may follow. When she later bears a son, however, her husband voices the sort of plausible sarcasm that might be expected from scandalised 'gentil' society at the prospect of blood of ignoble stock inheriting the marquisate.[11] It is worth recalling that voices were raised about such issues in actuality. A case in point would be Richard II's advancement of Michael de la Pole in 1385 from relatively humble origins to an earldom, provoking incredulous scorn.[12] As for the abiding concern about the precariousness of male succession, one might note the historian's calculation that during the fourteenth and fifteenth centuries in England, 'about one quarter of the peerage families died out in the male line about every twenty-five years and direct male succession over three or more generations was very much the exception'.[13]

To interpose these considerations into a reading of *Gowther* is to engage willy-nilly in controversy about which is the 'best' version of the romance. The penitential readings already referred to take up a position in the editorial 'turf war' which this romance provokes, because penitential readings thrive best on the version in the Advocates manuscript. The recent ascendancy of that version has meant a decline in the repute of the rival Royal version. The variations are not great, but they nevertheless produce an overall difference that is greater than the sum of the particular divergences. Henry Vandelinde is right to assert that there are 'two *Sir Gowther* poems' and that 'each has a specific agenda'.[14] While it is true that the Advocates version develops the romance's latent religious configuration more effectively, it is equally true, I think, that the Royal manuscript dwells more effectively on the story's latent social meaning. What follows concentrates attention on the Royal text, as edited by Rumble in his anthology.[15] It is not a matter of asserting Royal's priority but rather of interpreting its distinctive thrust (though each rendering has had its devotees).[16] The focus will especially be on the early part of the romance, and subsequently on the significance of Gowther's abasement among dogs.

Sir Gowther begins with warnings about the power of the devil. It then introduces a society wedding between a Duke and a bride who seem to have stereotypical credentials for producing noble heirs; she fair of flesh (33) and he, as he ostentatiously demonstrates at a wedding feast tournament, well able to crack the shields of doughty men (47–8). But the union remains childless for seven years. The narrative voice puts this even-handedly: 'He gat no childe, ne none she bere' (53), but the Duke proceeds to place the onus solely on his wife. He issues a simple ultimatum: the marriage will be dissolved unless she bears off-spring 'That myght my londes weld and were!' (59).

The Duke in his untroubled arrogance assumes, first, that fertility is a female responsibility; and second, that effective procreation means strong male issue, to govern and police 'his' lands. The second assumption is routine in romances. The first was also a prejudice widely held in medieval culture despite the availability of a more even-handed medical opinion that sterility might inhere in either sex.[17] *Octavian* is an instructive example of one romance that sustains the more enlightened opinion, since in that instance the seven-year childless marriage of an emperor and wife is perceived (by both of them) in terms of mutual responsibility, a matter of 'their' inability to 'get' a child 'between' them.[18] So in *Sir Gowther*, while the Duke's aggressive masculine egotism is by no means alien to the medieval context, that should not blind us to the fact that it registers nevertheless as egotism. Emperor Octavian, by contrast, stifles and hides his patriarchal misery, which his wife only draws out of him with difficulty.

The Duke's ultimatum prompts the duchess to pray desperately for a child by whatever means ('In what maner she ne rought', 66). The result is her sexual encounter in an orchard with an incubus-fiend bearing her husband's appearance, who informs her that he has impregnated her with a child who will be 'wild' in wielding his weapon (76–8).

The narrative teasingly problematises her perception of this drama, because the identity of the male figure she encounters in the orchard is equivocally unfolded. He is initially perceived as 'a man in a riche aray' (68): he is therefore at first sight an unidentifiable newcomer, but one wealthily dressed (so by implication not a social 'nobody', not a churl on the loose). Since we are then told that the man 'bisowght' her 'of love' (69) there is the momentary impression of a courtly suitor's importuning. Immediately it is added that he appears in the 'liknesse of here lord' (70). Whether the duchess experiences him *as* her husband or as someone else pretending to be her husband remains crucially uncertain. That ambiguity confers an option of legitimacy upon the ensuing sex-act, whereby beneath a chestnut tree 'His will with hire he wrought' (71–2). Yet the imposition of 'will' is redolent of rape, and that is the retrospect we contemplate when the figure brusquely gets up and stands before her announcing that he has fathered a wild progeny on her. At this the duchess, whose reaction during the episode has been unknown but perhaps implicitly compliant, blesses herself – registering her alarm thereby – and runs off indoors.[19]

At some level the incubus fiend must be taken literally. The open-ing lines of *Sir Gowther* in the Royal version insist on the fiend's power to assume the guise of husbands for sex with the men's wives. Corinne Saunders has reminded us of the 'clerical tradition of the incubus as a real and evil threat', whose role it is a mistake to blur by resorting to explanations involving fantasy or the subconscious.[20] Yet a more capacious view is surely possible, allowing the material devil a resonant function in the externalisation of repressed thoughts. Such a view is voiced by Dyan Elliott with regard to the demonic incubus: 'In the high Middle Ages the intimate enemy (namely, erotic thoughts and their physiological consequences), unexamined and repressed intern-ally, was ultimately externalised and began to walk abroad.'[21]

While that may sound a suspiciously modern formulation it is not really discordant with 'clerical' devil-lore. Clerical tradition posits a general symbiotic relation between the mental state of any human who is to be visited, and the physical appearance adopted by the devil visitant. Thus *The Cloud of Unknowing* insists 'þat euermore whan þe deuil takiþ any bodi, he figureþ in som qualite of his body what his seruauntes ben in spirit'.[22] That this general hypothesis might encompass the particular case of the incubus fiend, is suggested by the way in which another treatise of this period notes that, given the eagerness of incubi to assail women, 'þerfor it is perlyous to women *þat desyryn mychil mennys companye* to ben ouyr mychil solitarie withoutyn onest companye' (my emphasis).[23]

If the fiend incarnate reciprocates something in the victim's state of mind, if the incubus may be deemed to 'figure' a woman's desire for male 'companye' – a word carrying latent sexual connotation – then the fiend's role in *Sir Gowther* need not be taken *only* literally. The fiend is called forth by, and in some sense projects, the near-despairing recklessness ('In what maner she ne rought', 66) of the Duchess's need for impregnation by her husband – or by someone who can seem to be him. Driving her need and therefore clearly sharing some responsibility for the 'fiendish' conception is the ruthless patriarchal pressure for ensuring dynastic succession to which she has been subjected.

The duchess's 'fiendish' impregnation is also socially suggestive in another convergent sense. In medieval culture, powerful prejudices surrounded the phenomenon of extra-marital conception. It was bad enough that the purity of the bloodline was contaminated so that 'wrong-heyring' (i.e., an illegitimate heir) ensued. 'Wrong-heyring' is what the romance of *Octavian* calls it when Octavian's mother insinuates that the twins eventually produced by her son's wife must have been fathered by some virile kitchen lad taken as a sexual partner because Octavian himself was seemingly impotent.[24] But such 'contamination' might have further unwanted consequences, because the product of a sexual *mésalliance* might predictably be a wild or *vileyn* offspring, unsusceptible to courtly upbringing.

Put another way – and this is the perspective most often found – where the offspring fails to conform to elite social expectations, medieval society is prepared to allege contamination in the succession. This is familiar in examples such as *Ywain and Gawain*, where Ywain's failure to keep his word to return to his new wife by the promised time provokes the rebuke of her emissary, that he is a false traitor and 'an unkind cumlyng'.[25] This expression is usually thought by editors to gesture towards Ywain's status as a 'newcomer' or 'outsider' in his wife's domain: but more insidious connotations of *cumlyng* are present.[26] In this calculated rebuke, his parentage is being queried by the imputation that he is not a scion of noble stock, but rather (in the transferred sense of *cumlyng*) an 'adopted child', or 'stray', moreover an *unkind* or 'unnatural' one. A classic exemplification of the underlying conviction here, that debased behaviour points to debased pedigree, appears in a monitory story in *The Book of the Knight of the Tower*. A son of the Queen of Naples secretly conceived in adultery inherits the kingdom after her husband's death, but he turns out arrogant, extortionate, a rapist, and violent, with the result that he ruins the country. A hermit discerns the lesson, that this king is 'not trewe heyr' and therefore not of a character able to bring peace to the realm.[27]

It is in such a context that I suggest we consider how *Sir Gowther* raises the question of the potential evil of the son of a husband-substitute whom a noblewoman has taken under pressure of an obligation to reproduce. The objection that it is a category error to start talking of the fiend as a 'husband-substitute' involves the corollary that the extreme penitential drive of the narrative will depend on the literalness of the fiend's paternity in this case. Yet the Royal manuscript version does not proceed to support such a categorical reading, because it does not as a whole rehearse the fiend's paternity of Gowther so emphatically as the Advocates text rehearses it. Indeed it has been noticed before that the devil's fatherhood is an element much more 'thoroughly worked out' in the Advocates version.[28] Perhaps the most crucial difference in this respect is that when Gowther's career of violence is in full spate, the Advocates text comments, 'Erly and late, lowde and styll, / He wolde wyrke is fadur [presumably, the devil's] wyll',[29] whereas Royal has Gowther attacking 'tho that wold not werk his [own] will' (169–70).

In any case, at Gowther's conception both versions immediately set out to blur the situation quite significantly. They compound the curious implications of a look-alike husband in the orchard by having the duchess rush back into her chamber and blurt out to the duke a cover-up story to the effect that by angelic prophecy she and he will now conceive a child 'that shall your londes welde' (84). Consequently that night, we are told (in lines whose juxtaposition in the Royal version is most fascinating) the duchess and duke went to bed and

> He pleid him with that lady hende;
> She was bounde with a fende
> Til Crist wold lose hire bonde. (94–6)

The fact that the Advocates version offers a different construction strongly insinuating a 'but' (the Duke *pleyd* with her, but 'all this time she was carrying the devil's child', as Mills translates Advocates at this point)[30] should not be taken to determine the more ambiguous construction of the Royal lines quoted, which leave ill-defined the connection between the Duke's sexual activity and his wife's being 'bound'.

The lines offer, in fact, a classic example of a kind of ellipsis whose importance in the narrative mode of the English verse romances has been noted by Spearing. There is a shortage of 'syntactical links' in the narration, so 'listeners are left to supply the connections for themselves'.[31] In one perspective the duchess is desperately trying to cleanse or erase the 'bad magic' of fiendish violation by replacing the pseudo-husband's insemination with the real husband's: she is trying to 'make' her husband be the father, to conceive a sanctified and not-wild son.[32] In another perspective the duchess is insuring against the crisis of extra-marital pregnancy caused by rape, by resorting to strategic supplementary coitus. In the most interesting perspective of all, the fact that the fiend had the husband's external appearance (which critics have found baffling), and the fact that the husband as it were now 'seconds' that fiend in the act of conception, invites us to the conclusion that the Duke might just as well be the father, or, that the Duke might as well be a fiend.[33] It is as if the Duke's crude, inhuman, egotistical presumption betrays fiendishness and thence 'engenders' a monster.[34]

Admittedly the narrative proceeds to reassert for a moment the fiend's literal paternity (stating that the very same fiend 'got' Merlin, 97–9). Yet the way in which the fiend/husband identity has been coalesced seems to sustain the option of a reading in which the romance is seen to address profound medieval anxieties about the production of heirs, and particularly of violent and ungovernable heirs, without laying these phenomena exclusively at the door of fiends. 'Exclusively' is the operative word here. The Royal redactor of the Gowther story envisages a demonic impregnation while encouraging the reader to think also about one of the 'demons' of aristocratic society, the relentless imperative of purebred dynastic continuity.

Whereas childlessness is the social nightmare in which the plot of *Sir Gowther* begins, the nightmare into which it proceeds is that of the arrogantly violent 'heir from hell'. Gowther is the horrible product of the story's joint paternity. To the extent that Gowther is not the Duke's biological son, he embodies the danger of debased behaviour resulting from what we have seen referred to in romance as 'wrong-heyring'. On the other hand, to the extent that Gowther in his violent and brutally self-willed youth is, in some secondary sense, the Duke's son, he represents the threat of wayward arrogance, rejection of God, and refusal of courtliness in a son who 'takes after' a domineering, misogynistic and self-oriented father.

The chief characteristics of Gowther's growth into bloodcurdling tyranny are three. First, as an infant he drains the life out of nine wet-nurses in succession and then, when none more are forthcoming, tears his mother's own breast. Here we need to read beyond vampire-like ghoulishness, for this is an emblem of repudiation of nurture. It echoes, as Robson notes, the Duke's own impulse to repudiate his wife (to repudiate the feminine?), but it also signifies – in the eventual violence to the mother's breast – a self-alienation from genetic stock.[35] Here is the heir who will not imbibe maternal pedigree aright, who asserts 'self' violently against that pedigree.[36]

A second characteristic of Gowther as 'the heir from hell' is that, hastily put onto solids, he grows enormously fast. On the one hand his premature size and violent power attest fiendish monstrosity: on the other, they project the danger latent at the extremity of what the culture otherwise holds desirable. Medieval culture conventionally applauds the production of inheritors of notable physique and indomitable power. The limitations of such convention do not go unobserved in romance. In the twelfth century Chrétien de Troyes astutely contrasts Calogrenant's ignorant knee-jerk knightly aggression with the civilised discipline of a 'monster' herdsman in *Yvain*.[37] What Gowther is becoming in the late fourteenth-century English romance is a sinister amalgam of the knee-jerk aggression of the knight with the colossal power of the monster herdsman.

His third characteristic is that once physically mature, he embarks on a reign of terror, partly victimising his mother's own retinue, but more generally victimising members of the church, even whole communities. His most sensationally barbaric act of this kind is to burn a community of nuns in their own convent – an act for which a need for penance is acutely felt later. We should notice also the disruption of specifically *feudal* protocol here. The nuns' fate follows perversely upon a scene where they have processed out to make feudal obeisance to him, kneeling and formally greeting him as liege lord (182). The demonic heir in *Sir Gowther* is an enemy of the faith, as often remarked. But such enmity is also deliberately associated with an expression of sheer wilfulness and caprice that makes him the total antithesis of all feudal responsibility and courtly *mesure*.

That Gowther comes to represent the awful prospect of the corruption of dynasty through an heir out of control is a point articulated more particularly in the Royal narrative. While both texts have the Duke knighting his son in a spirit of resignation ('His fader him myght not chastithe, / But made him knyght that tyde', lines 143–4 in Royal, paralleled at 146–7 in Advocates), only in Royal is this accompanied by an account of the father's gift of his own powerful sword – and hence in theory the transmission of its patrilineal charisma – to Gowther.

> He gaf him his best swerde in honde;
> There was no knyghte in all that londe
> A dent durst him abyde. (145–7)[38]

Although as some readers have argued there may be a hint that the parents see knighting as a last-ditch means of bringing Gowther to an adult sense of responsibility,[39] the paradoxical consequence in the Royal narrative is that in effect the Duke implicates himself as 'father' in the mayhem subsequently caused by the son with this sword. An impression that the son inherits and tyrannically magnifies the Duke's more socially 'acceptable' egotism is made available in this way. That implication of enlarged egotism is confirmed by the same text's comment that Gowther deals mercilessly with any 'that wold not werk his will' (169).

This reading allows Gowther's campaign of destruction against the church to be interpreted in the light of the standard medieval doctrinal connection between faithlessness and *superbia*, pride. In moral analysis, each of these sins was coterminous with the other. For one moralist the first branch of pride was signalled by forgetfulness of God and the second branch by failure to reverence God. Conversely, the first branch of 'mekenesse' was to honour God.[40] For another moralist the branch of pride called 'unobedyens' was typified specifically by acts of hostility against the church, and against parents.[41] In Gowther's case transgression in these aspects of pride would appear to be compounded in terms of the further category of 'unschamfulnes' whereby the perpetrator 'glories' in malice, displaying no conscience, thus recalling the Psalmist's words 'Quid gloriaris in malicia, qui potens est in iniquitate?' ('Why enioyest þou in þi malyce þat art so myghty in wyckydnes?').[42] Gowther shows no sign of remorse or fear of God. In his faithless arrogance he is without 'dreed' or *timor domini*, that is without the first gift of the Holy Spirit, the gift that springs in the ground of humility and thus averts pride.[43]

By understanding these moral inflections aright, I believe we may the better grasp the appropriateness – even the inevitability – of Gowther's drastic self-humiliation in his voluntary debasement among dogs. This ritual self-humiliation occurs when (after the showdown with his mother and an interview with the Pope) he arrives as a penitent at the Emperor of Almayn's palace. The analogue in *Robert of Sicily* is helpful here. King Robert is expressly a Nebuchadnezzar figure; an overweening ruler suddenly deposed by angelic *fiat* for asserting his own indomitability in express opposition to the declaration he has heard in the liturgy that God can put down the mighty.[44] The angel who displaces Robert obliges him to eat on the ground with dogs, his only food-taster now to be a hound: 'Wher is now thi dignité?' (168).

King Robert hits rock bottom for his arrogance, which is also as I have emphasised a denial of faith, and vice-versa. Because critics have sufficiently rehearsed Gowther's denial of faith, I think we need to restore to view the other facet of Gowther's case – the casual arrogance: the more so since this is the facet that sustains the social and dynastic questions that the romance is asking. 'Eating with dogs' invokes, of course, a biblical commonplace about faith and humility. It has nothing to do with the punishment of St Paul as Margaret Bradstock thought,[45] and everything to do with the Woman of Cana. In Matthew's account this woman interrupts Jesus, pleading on behalf of her sick daughter who is 'vexed with a devil'. Since she is a representative of a potentially unreceptive community Jesus probes her with a hostile reaction – 'It is not meet to take the children's bread and cast it to dogs.' Her reply, 'True, yet the dogs eat of the crumbs which fall from their master's table' elicits his admiration: 'great is thy faith' (Matt. 15.21ff.).

The convergence of self-abasement with resolute faith in the woman's statement offers a powerful exemplification of the moralists' insistence that meekness is continuous with the honouring of God. And this explains why Gowther, arriving in his penitential journey at the Emperor of Almayn's castle, carefully makes his way up to 'the hegh bord' and then 'Thereunder he made his sete' (320–1).[46] In this self-abasing position, articulating his new-found humility and faith, Gowther joins the emperor's dogs in eating the scraps from their master's table.

The fact that Gowther specifically has excesses of arrogance to atone for is emphasised subsequently in a line somewhat reminiscent of the chastened status of Sir Gawain at the end of *Sir Gawain and the Green Knight*. When Gowther sets forth in miraculously provided armour for the third time to continue fighting off the heathen who have come for the emperor's daughter, we are told 'Rode he not with brag nor bost' (544).[47] Conversely, Gowther's new found humility is carefully reinforced through a series of moments of interior self-suppression. For example, when people in the emperor's court disdain him as 'Hobbe the Fool' for his dog-ridden behaviour, he mentally commits himself to Christ (359–60). In a similar gesture of self-renunciation he had responded to the arbitrary withdrawal of food-bringing dogs which for three days had sustained him during his prior journey from Rome: he thanked God 'in thowght' (301–6).

It is likely that the narrative emphasises its concern with arrogance in at least one further way, that is, iconographically. The fall of the mute princess from her tower on seeing her champion Gowther wounded in combat with the Saracens, leaves her apparently 'dead' for three days (or for two days in the case of the Advocates version). She returns to life able to speak and to proclaim God's forgiveness of Gowther.[48] Now, falling was the commonplace sign of divine punishment for individual arrogance. Iconographically, from early in the Middle Ages, pride was frequently pictured as a man thrown from a horse.[49] More notably a fall from a tower became precisely the emblem of divine retribution for arrogant faithlessness in the later Middle Ages. In biblical iconography, the favourite illustration for the second book of Kings (Vulgate IV Kings) showed Ahaziah falling from a tower – a fate he earned by turning aside from Jehovah and consulting false gods as recounted at the start of the book.[50] In the vice and virtue designs for *Somme le roi* manuscripts in the thirteenth and fourteenth centuries the same image was adopted.[51] In the *Somme* miniatures he is juxtaposed with a counterpart in the New Testament, the egotistical hypocrite, and contrasted with an antitype in another compartment, the penitent sinner. Of course, any allusion to Ahaziah in *Sir Gowther* would have to be regarded as oblique. The princess herself does not strike us as tainted with arrogance – it is more the case that she is enacting on Gowther's part, as if sacrificially, the paradigm of the 'humbling of the mighty' which now seals his own moral rebirth and re-socialisation.[52]

A final twist to the track we have been following is that the regenerate Gowther does not reclaim his ducal inheritance. On the contrary he hands over that inheritance to the old earl who first brought him to his senses; and he provides also for a marriage between this earl and his mother. However apt it might have been for Gowther to be reinstated as Duke, reasons both pragmatic and delicate seem to hold against it. The pragmatic is that his liaison with the Emperor's daughter, sure enough, will lead towards a grander dynasty. The more delicate reason is that, his human 'father' having died (implicitly traumatised?) during the son's career of ungovernable destruction, Gowther needs to restore, not claim, the paternal position, and at the same time offer his mother a second chance to participate in a normalised dynastic arrangement.[53]

That is somewhat speculative. I hope that what has been more certainly demonstrated is that although the Royal version by no means eliminates the penitential and spiritual potential of the story – the moments when the abject Gowther hears bystanders affirm that he is 'a man' (327) and when he hears the Pope finally declare him to have 'bycome Godes child' (625) articulate a trajectory of profound recovery for one who had been shocked with the information that he 'was goten with a fende' (262) — this is also a narrative that finds fresh ways of addressing some of the dominant class's deepest anxieties about heredity. What were the hidden costs of harping on the provision of *gentil* heirs? If one's heir proved to be the 'heir from hell', what did that imply about his genesis? Who or what is to blame for the presence of self-willed and brutal youths in positions of power — fathers? mothers? the devil? And how does the devil's input work?

In my view the exploration of these issues in the Royal version of *Sir Gowther* is more complex and more interesting than sometimes thought. There has been too much critical wrangling about whether it is a 'knightly' or 'hagiographical' romance. The whole point is that it is both at once. Conceivably it is so in specific historical terms. Given the decisive agency of the Pope in the text, and the horror of a dukedom ravaged for a while by tyranny, it is possibly a narrative that would fit the political circumstances of England at the end of the fourteenth century. Like the Charlemagne romances, it could be said to promote papal authority (damaged at the time by the schism) and to warn against tyrannical lordship (a phenomenon, to be sure, of the last decade of the century).[54]

However, that type of contextual reconstruction is bedevilled by the vagaries of dating. What is more of a constant in the later Middle Ages, and what arguably most needs to be restored to view not only in discussion of *Sir Gowther* but in discussions of many romance narratives, is the work that such romances do on behalf of the ideology of dynasty: their presentation and resolution of the pressures and anxieties and 'demons' besetting a dynastic society.

Notes

1 British Library, MS Royal 17. B. 43 contains *Mandeville's Travels*, then *Gowther*, followed by *Revelation in Patrick's Purgatory* and *Tundale's Vision of Hell, Purgatory and Heaven*. It is evidently a compilation concentrating on the eschatalogical and the exotic. The Royal text of *Gowther* is available in *The Breton Lays in Middle English*, ed. Thomas C. Rumble (Detroit, 1965), pp. 178–204 (supplying some 'omissions' from the Advocates version). The version in National Library of Scotland, MS Advocates' 19. 3. 1, is most conveniently available either in *Six Middle English Romances*, ed. Maldwyn Mills (London, 1973), pp. 148–68 (where it is supplemented with the opening fourteen lines of the Royal version), or in *The Middle English Breton Lays*, ed. Anne Laskaya and Eve Salisbury

(Kalamazoo, MI, 1995); see also *Sir Gowther: Eine englische Romanze aus dem XV Jahrhundert*, ed. Karl Breul (Oppeln, 1886).

2   Shirley Marchalonis, '*Sir Gowther*: the process of a romance', *Chaucer Review*, 6 (1971–72), 14–29; E. M. Bradstock, '*Sir Gowther*: secular hagiography or hagiographical romance or neither?', *AUMLA: Journal of the Australasian Universities Language and Literature Association*, 59 (1983), 26–47.

3   Margaret Bradstock, 'The penitential pattern in *Sir Gowther*', *Parergon*, 20 (1978), 3–10; Andrea Hopkins, *The Sinful Knights: A Study of Middle English Penitential Romance* (Oxford, 1990), pp. 144–78.

4   Bradstock, 'Penitential pattern', p. 9; Hopkins, *Sinful Knights*, pp. 145–6.

5   Bradstock, 'Penitential pattern', p. 3.

6   Hopkins, *Sinful Knights*, p. 152.

7   Stephen Knight, 'The social function of the Middle English romances', in David Aers (ed.), *Medieval Literature: Criticism, Ideology and History* (Brighton, 1986), pp. 99–122 (p. 101).

8   While the designation of a 'dominant social group' is clearly a simplification, there can be no doubt that the issues concerning lineage that are the focus of the present essay were an abiding preoccupation among those who exercised power through substantial family ownership of land in medieval England, from the gentry to the peerage.

9   Bradstock, 'Penitential pattern', p. 6.

10   Margaret Robson, 'Animal magic: moral regeneration in *Sir Gowther*', *Yearbook of English Studies*, 22 (1992), 140–53 (p. 144).

11   *Clerk's Tale* V. 462–8, 631–3, in *The Riverside Chaucer*, ed. Larry Benson *et al.* (Boston, 1987), from which all further Chaucer quotations are taken.

12   Nigel Saul, *Richard II* (New Haven, 1997), pp. 117–18; Chris Given-Wilson, *The English Nobility in the Late Middle Ages* (London, 1987), pp. 48–9 (but see p. 52 for factors other than 'cheapening' of titles in such instances). The theory of the 'heritability of nobility' is insidiously set forth in the influential *De regimine principum* (c. 1277–79) of Aegidius Romanus, as lucidly explained by Larry Scanlon, *Narrative, Authority, and Power: The Medieval Exemplum and the Chaucerian Tradition* (Cambridge, 1994), pp. 111–12.

13   S. H. Rigby, *English Society in the Later Middle Ages: Class, Status and Gender* (Basingstoke, 1995), p. 198.

14   Henry Vandelinde, '*Sir Gowther*: saintly knight and knightly saint', *Neophilologus*, 80 (1996), 139–47 (pp. 139–40). Vandelinde's elaboration of the hypothesis lacks nuance. On the problems posed by multiple versions of the romances, see A. S. G. Edwards, 'Middle English romance: the limits of editing, the limits of criticism', in Tim W. Machan (ed.), *Medieval Literature: Texts and Interpretations* (Binghamton, 1991), pp. 91–104.

15   *The Breton Lays in Middle English*, ed. Rumble, pp. 178–204.

16   The Royal version once ranked the higher in estimation, and was thought to represent an 'original' of greater courtly quality; see Marchalonis, 'Process of a romance', p. 27. More recently the Advocates version has

been acclaimed, Royal being relegated as 'a corrupt and inferior manuscript tradition' on the grounds that it 'weakens' religious themes found
in Advocates that are allegedly 'close to the intentions of *Sir Gowther's*
author', Hopkins, *Sinful Knights*, p. 225. This judgement, and my own,
make it quite paradoxical that it is in the Royal copy, rather than the
Advocates copy, that the scribe was moved to label the story as if it were
a saint's life: 'Explicit Vita Sancti'.

17　Opinions are clarified in Joan Cadden, *Meanings of Sex Difference in the
Middle Ages* (Cambridge, 1993), pp. 228–31 and 249–53. Law would tend
to back up the Duke's threat in *Gowther*, in the sense that 'as a practical
matter, a man might find a way to replace a wife, if the couple were
childless, but not vice-versa' (Cadden, p. 253).

18　'Chylde myght they gete noon, / That tyme betwene them twoo, / That
aftur hym hys londys schulde welde; /…/ A sorowe to hys herte ranne /
That chylde togedur they myght noon han /…/ "And we no chylde
have us between" /…/ "That we togedur may have an heyre",' *Octavian*,
in *Six Middle English Romances*, ed. Mills, lines 32–4, 43–4, 65, and 80.

19　On the element of rape, see Corinne J. Saunders, '"Symtyme the fend";
questions of rape in *Sir Gowther*', in M. J. Toswell and E. M. Tyler (eds),
*Studies in English Language and Literature: 'Doubt Wisely': Papers in Honour
of E. G. Stanley* (London, 1996), pp. 286–303; see also Corinne Saunders,
Rape and Ravishment in the Literature of Medieval England (Cambridge,
2001), pp. 223–8.

20　Saunders, '"Symtyme the fende"', p. 300. Hopkins also discusses incubus-
lore, but her application of it is strained in one particular. She claims that
the lines commenting on the marvel that fiends got women pregnant,
'Tho kynde of men wher thei it tane / (For of homselfe had thei never
nan)' in the Advocates version (ed. Mills, lines 16–17) invoke clerical
arguments that devils 'have to steal' men's nature (i.e. semen) from humans
'because they are themselves incapable of generation'; *Sinful Knights*, p.
165, also pp. 166–7. The lines do not seem capable of this technical construction. Rather, the suggestion is that immaterial fiends can only achieve
human bodily form by 'taking' or assuming humankind through a
woman: it is a parody of the doctrine of God taking human *kynde*
through Mary.

21　Dyan Elliott, *Fallen Bodies: Pollution, Sexuality, and Demonology in the
Middle Ages* (Philadelphia, 1999), p. 29.

22　A point thrice reiterated in *The Cloud of Unknowing*, ed. Phyllis Hodgson,
EETS o.s. 213 (London, 1944), ch. 55, pp. 102–3.

23　*Dives and Pauper*, ed. Priscilla H. Barnum, vol. 1, pt 2, EETS o.s. 280
(Oxford, 1980), p. 119. Even in a case where the incubus is impelled by
a more apocalyptic motive, seeking to travesty and counter the Virgin
Birth by making a maiden conceive Merlin unwittingly in her sleep, care
is taken to sustain a vestigial sinfulness or sensuality in the victim: she has
dropped her guard through failure to bless her room (Lincoln's Inn text

840–2 and Auchinleck text 837–42) preceded by drinking (only in the Lincoln's Inn text, 809–20); see the parallel texts in *Of Arthour and of Merlin*, ed. O. D. Macrae-Gibson, EETS o.s. 268 (London, 1973). This detail is not noted in the illuminating comparison between *Gowther* and Merlin narratives in Saunders, *Rape and Ravishment*, pp. 219–23.

24 'Moche sorowe deryth mee / That Rome schall wrong-heyred bee, / In unkynde honde. /.../ For thou mygt no chylde have, / Thy wyfe hath take a cokys knave': *Octavian*, ed. Mills, lines 106–8, 115–16.

25 *Ywain and Gawain*, ed. Albert B. Friedman and Norman T. Harrington, EETS o.s. 254 (London, 1964), line 1627.

26 *MED* comeling, n., senses 1(a), (b), and (3).

27 William Caxton (trans.), *The Book of the Knight of the Tower*, ed. M. Y. Offord, EETS s.s 2 (London, 1971), p. 83, deriving from ch. 45 of *Le Livre du chevalier de la Tour Landry*, written in the 1370s. Maurice Keen gives a trenchant summary of debates about virtue and breeding in *Chivalry* (New Haven, 1984), pp. 156–61. The type of prejudice that Dante, Chaucer and others sought to counter in this regard appears in a passage cited by Keen from Jean de Bueil: 'I shall never believe that nobles who dishonour their arms were descended from the valiant fathers whose name they bear; one must suppose that their mothers had lechers in their mind when they engendered them. Maybe indeed they were actually in bed with them'; *Le Jouvencel par Jean de Bueil*, ed. Camille Favre and Léon Lecestre, 2 vol (Paris, 1887–89), vol. II, p. 82.

28 Hopkins, *Sinful Knights*, p. 153; see also Bradstock, 'Penitential pattern', p. 4. After the rape scene, allusions to the fiend as father occur in Advocates at 96, 173, 206, 228, 238, 271, and 742, but Royal matches these only at 99, 203, 225, and 264.

29 Advocates, ed. Mills, lines 172–3.

30 'He pleyd hym with that ladé hende, / And ei yode scho bownden with tho fende' (91–2), glossed by Mills on p. 150.

31 A. C. Spearing, 'Early medieval narrative style', in his *Readings in Medieval Poetry* (Cambridge, 1987), pp. 24–55 (pp. 32–3).

32 Critics often note the pathos of the Duchess's account. Saunders suggests that the Lady creates a romance fiction 'where prayer has occasioned a conception more divine than devilish'; *Rape and Ravishment*, p. 225.

33 The only critic who has explored something like this possibility is Jeffrey J. Cohen, among some Lacanian speculations in 'Gowther among the dogs: becoming inhuman c. 1400', in Jeffrey J. Cohen and Bonnie Wheeler (eds), *Becoming Male in the Middle Ages* (New York and London, 1997), pp. 219–44 (p. 229).

34 By a similar logic Donegild is able to argue that the 'horrible [...] feendly creature' allegedly born to Custance shows the mother to be 'an elf'; Chaucer, *Man of Law's Tale*, II. 751–4.

35 This is a more precise point than Cohen's suggestion that Gowther 'resists familialism', 'Gowther among the dogs', p. 225; and see Robson,

'Animal magic', pp. 143, 147. By contrast Jane Gilbert, with psychoanalytical sophistry, maintains that Gowther's ravenous suckling is actually a
rejection of *paternity*, defying 'the paternal authority that would forbid
him absolute access to the maternal body': 'Unnatural mothers and
monstrous children in *The King of Tars* and *Sir Gowther*', in Jocelyn
Wogan-Browne *et al.* (eds), *Medieval Women: Texts and Contexts in Late
Medieval Britain* (Turnhout, 2000), pp. 329–44 (pp. 338–9).

36 The initial resort to a procession of wet-nurses in *Gowther* inscribes the
medieval nobility's tendency to resist in practice the concerted opinion
of moralists that maternal breastfeeding was always to be preferred, since
it gave an infant the chance to imbibe the 'qualities' of the mother: see
Clarissa Atkinson, *The Oldest Vocation: Christian Motherhood in the Middle
Ages* (Ithaca, 1991), pp. 58–60, 120–1, 201–3.

37 See *The Knight with the Lion, or Yvain*, ed. and trans. William W. Kibler
(New York, 1985), lines 269–409.

38 Such transmission is articulated in examples such as Marie de France's
Yonec, in her *Lais*, ed. A. Ewert (Oxford, 1944), lines 421–36; or in *Sir
Degaré*, in *Breton Lays*, ed. Rumble, lines 115–17, 623–32, 949–64. In
both cases the sword explicitly embodies the power of the father. The
Advocates version of *Gowther* eschews any impression of dynastic
transmission because there when he is fifteen years old Gowther makes
his own massive weapon – a falchion that no other man could lift (ed.
Mills, lines 136–9). Hopkins alleges that the writer of the Royal version
'tends to weaken the sword motif, as if unaware of its significance' (*Sinful
Knights*, p. 159) but it will be apparent that I read the variations in Royal
as elements of a coherent alternative production of the story.

39 Bradstock, '*Sir Gowther*: secular hagiography or hagiographical romance',
p. 35; Marchalonis, 'Process of a romance', p. 18.

40 *The Book of Vices and Virtues*, ed. W. Nelson Francis, EETS o.s. 217
(London, 1942), pp. 13, 15–16, 132.

41 *Jacob's Well*, ed. Arthur Brandeis, EETS o.s. 115 (London, 1900), p. 71.
Disobedience is epitomised by an image of a man striking a bishop in one
of the bas-reliefs of the vices and virtues on the walls of Amiens cathedral;
Emile Mâle, *The Gothic Image: Religious Art in France of the Thirteenth
Century*, trans. Dora Nussey (New York, 1968), p. 126 and Fig. 73.

42 *Jacob's Well*, ed. Brandeis, p. 77, quoting Vulgate Psalm 51:1.

43 *Ibid.*, p. 240.

44 In *Middle English Metrical Romances*, ed. W. H. French and C. B. Hale
(New York, 1964), lines 29–60. Hopkins identifies Robert's sin as 'overweening pride, especially in temporal power' which 'causes the sinner to
deny the power of God' (*Sinful Knights*, p. 188).

45 Bradstock finds Gowther's conversion 'reminiscent, in its suddenness and
finality, of the conversion of St Paul'; and suggests that 'his physical afflic-
tions provide a parallel with the punishment of St Paul: "And he was three
days without sight, and neither did eat nor drink" (Acts 9:9).' ('Penitential

pattern', pp. 4–5).

46 The line is matched in Advocates, but the enforcing echoes of it in Royal lines 437 and 499 disappear in Advocates.

47 Compare Gawain, vowing to remind himself of the frailty of the flesh 'When I ride in renoun': *Sir Gawain and the Green Knight*, lines 2434–5, in *Poems of the Pearl Manuscript*, ed. Malcolm Andrew and Ronald Waldron (London, 1978).

48 It is an interesting question whether in its focus on muteness and on the mouth, *Sir Gowther* engages in some way with hypotheses about 'possession' by devils. In Luke 11: 14 'the dumb spoke' after a devil was cast out. The emperor's mute daughter may herself be imagined as possessed prior to her fall. Devils are expelled by Jesus through the mouth from two men whom they are possessing, and made to enter the 'Gadarene swine' through the mouth, in the illustration to Matt. 9: 28–33 in the fourteenth-century *Holkham Bible Picture Book*, London, British Library, MS Additional 47682, fol. 24r. Possibly Gowther's self-imposed muteness betokens a similar recognition of 'possession'.

49 Mâle, *Gothic Image*, trans. Nussey, pp. 100, 104. Joanne Norman notes the variant whereby Superbia falls from her position of power on a throne: *Metamorphoses of an Allegory: The Iconography of the Psychomachia in Medieval Art* (New York, 1988), p. 81.

50 Ahaziah 'scorned the living and true God and instead consulted the god of Ekron': *Fasciculus morum*, ed. S. Wenzel (University Park, PA, 1989), p. 581. Statistics on the widespread dispersal of this image of Ahaziah's (or 'Ochozias's') fall are given in Robert Branner, 'The "Soissons Bible" paintshop in thirteenth-century Paris', *Speculum*, 44 (1969), 13–34 (p. 26), and in his *Manuscript Painting in Paris during the Reign of Saint Louis* (Berkeley, 1977), pp. 184–5, 178–9.

51 For instance, see the miniature by Master Honoré, *Somme le roi*, British Library, MS Additional 54180 (French, *c.* 1290), fol. 97v, reproduced in Andrew Martindale, *The Rise of the Artist in the Middle Ages and Early Renaissance* (London, 1972), p. 25.

52 It is a literal rendering of that 'putting down of the mighty' at which King Robert scoffs in *Robert of Sicily*, in *Middle English Metrical Romances*, ed. French and Hale, lines 29–57. Bradstock sees an allusion not to the iconography of humility but to a miracle in the life of St Paul, who brought back to life a youth who fell from a tower while listening to his preaching ('Secular hagiography or hagiographical romance', p. 46).

53 It is at this point in the narrative that I would find most use for Gilbert's overall hypothesis that Gowther needs above all to defer, not so much to a 'father' as to what Lacan calls 'the Name-of-the-Father' ('Unnatural mothers and monstrous children', p. 331).

54 See Robert Warm, 'Identity, narrative and participation: defining a context for the Middle English Charlemagne romances', in Rosalind Field (ed.), *Tradition and Transformation in Medieval Romance* (Cambridge, 1999), pp. 87–100.

3

A, A and B: coding same-sex union in *Amis and Amiloun*

Sheila Delany

Form

I take my title from the rhyme scheme of a tantalising but little studied Middle English romance, *Amis and Amiloun*.[1] The poem is composed in twelve-line stanzas, rhymed AAB AAB CCB DDB, with a metrical scheme of four, four and three stresses corresponding to the rhyme. This is a variant of the well-known 'tail-rhyme' stanza found in some Middle English lyrics and in over twenty Middle English romances. Six of these tail-rhyme romances appear for the first time in the famous Auchinleck manuscript (written about 1330), which contains a total of eighteen romances and provides the earliest witness of the Middle English *Amis*.[2] There is no solid reason to believe that the poem antedates the manuscript, and the historicisation provided here argues for a composition date approximately contemporaneous with that of production of the manuscript.[3]

Though the rhyme scheme of our romance is thus by no means unique, in this setting it is distinctively linked with content and meaning. The triplet rhyme scheme in *Amis* makes a theme statement: same, same, and different, two of one thing and one of another. A similar usage appears in philosophical discourse, where different category is denoted by the letters A and B.[4] The story does indeed engage important philosophical issues in a fairly schematic manner – especially intentionality and sin – though space limits prevent my demonstrating this here. On the narrative level, the issues are framed in terms of same-sex and other-sex relations: friendship, courtship, marriage. I propose, then, that AAB represents the three protagonists: two men and the woman whom one of them marries.

Not coincidentally, the names of these three characters begin with those initials: Amys, Amylion, and Belesaunt. These initials anchor the story in a sex-linked A and B scheme in virtually all its versions. The oldest extant text is a short Latin verse narrative in the form of an epistle by Ralph Tortaire (Rodolfus Tortarius, Raoul de la Torte), a scholar-poet and monk at the Abbey of Fleury.[5] This text has Amelius, Amicus and Beliardis as the main characters; it extends the AB scheme to the jealous courtier, Ardradus, and to the girl's mother, Queen Berta. The next surviving version, a twelfth-century anonymous Latin prose text, has Amelius, Amicus, and Belixenda as the main figures, with the villainous count Ardericus.[6] The late twelfth-century *chanson de geste*, in monorhymed laisses, has Ami, Amile and Belissant; the evil courtier is (H)ardré.[7] The Anglo-Norman version, in couplets, has Amys and Amillyoun, and the latter's faithful young kinsman is called Amorant (though his real name is Uwein), as in the Auchinleck text of the English version (but not in Douce). The spying seneschal is anonymous, and the girl has both a real name and a nickname, neither of which begins with B.[8] This exception in a sense 'proves the rule', showing that any author, redactor or scribe could have changed the names, but nearly all chose to retain the alphabetical scheme.

In my view, the AAB rhyme scheme of the Middle English poem operates on both a semantic and a semiotic axis. Semantically it designates the names of the three main characters; semiotically it represents the relationship among those characters: two men paired (AA) but one of them also linked with the woman (AB).[9] Given the meticulous attention to formal structure that characterises much medieval poetry, such care for a meaning-laden rhyme scheme need not surprise us. Teodolinda Barolini offers a meditation on the meaning of Dante's *terza rima*, a verse form invented for the *Commedia* only a few years before the production of the Auchinleck manuscript. She relates the rhyme scheme to Dante's 'poetics of the new'; it

> mimics the voyage of life by providing both unceasing forward motion and recurrent backward glances. If we consider *aba/bcb/cdc*, we see that in each tercet … the rhyme that was 'new' in the previous tercet becomes 'old'… This process … imitates the genealogical flow of human history, in which the creation of each new identity requires the grafting of alterity onto a previous identity … [a] combining of past and future, old and new, motion progressive and regressive.[10]

To generalise: in some medieval poetry, rhyme is a formal aspect of rhetoric and meaning, with a presence at once visual and aural; thus it can serve as a point of entry to the social dimensions of a poem. Having begun with form, I proceed to genre and history, and their importance for our text.

Genre

Although both eponymous heroes of the romance marry, it is clear that they form the 'real' couple. Theirs is the completely voluntary, intensely committed life partnership which neither of the heterosexual marital unions can match and which forms the centre of narrative, moral, and psychological interest. In this sense the two heroes constitute what John Boswell designated a 'same-sex union', and to the extent that our version of the romance is loosely framed as hagiography it resembles nothing so much as the double male legends Boswell cites as early instances of the literary representation of same-sex union.[11] Indeed, it may well be that the generic ambiguity of this work – hagiographical romance or secular legend? – exists precisely to remind the audience of archetypal Christian precedents for same-sex union as fictional motif and social fact.

At this point, a brief plot summary of the Middle English poem is required to facilitate the reader's tracking my argument. Two adolescent nobles, not related but identical in appearance, swear a brotherhood covenant and become officials at a ducal court. One of them, Amiloun, leaves court to marry; he has identical gold cups made for himself and Amis. Meanwhile, at court, the duke's daughter, Belisant, aggressively seduces Amis, and an evil steward offers Amis his friendship; rejected, the steward accuses the young man of fornicating with Belisant. Amis claims innocence; then, forced to duel with the steward, knows he cannot win because he has lied. Amiloun – legitimately able to claim innocence of the sexual offence – therefore poses as Amis, wins the duel, but is punished with leprosy for the imposture. Amiloun's wife, revolted by his disease, chases him from home. Accompanied by a faithful young kinsman, Amiloun comes to the castle of the now happily married Amis and Belisant, and is taken in. An angelic vision reveals that the blood of Amis's children will cure his friend. Amis kills his children and Amiloun is cured; the children revive miraculously; Amiloun takes vengeance on his uncharitable wife and lives happily ever after with Amis. They found an abbey, die on the same day, and are buried in the same grave.

Variants of this story appear in several genres: romance, *chanson de geste,* verse epistle, prose sketch, miracle play; some scholars have detected folkloristic motifs. In his 1937 EETS edition, Leach proposed that 'The Amis and Amiloun stories fall into two groups: the romantic and the hagiographic', and that the English version is 'fundamentally non-Christian and non-hagiographic … [with] no conception of Amis and Amiloun as saints'. The theme is 'the testing of friendship, not the exposition of Christian character or Christian virtue'.[12] Hagiographical elements are 'late' (that is, not present in early versions of the tale) and 'extraneous' (to the story of a tested friendship). Implicit here is the conviction of impermeable genre borders, a conviction at odds not only with the text but with literary history generally, as V. Propp observed in 1928: 'Just as elements are assimilated within a tale, whole *genres* are also assimilated and intermingled.'[13]

The 'romance vs. hagiography' debate looms large in scholarship on the English, French, and Anglo-Norman narratives: hagiographical romance? secularised hagiography? romance with Christian overtones but not really hagiographical? This debate strikes me as a red herring, for the history of hagiographical literature shows that saints' legends are a deeply syncretic genre from the beginning, always already full of romance, folktale and mythic motifs. We may think of princesses imprisoned in a tower (SS Christine and Barbara), of dragon-killers (SS George and Margaret), of a long sea journey with the heroes fed by an eagle (SS Vitus and Modestus), of disguise (numerous cross-dressing women saints). Early Christian hagiography borrowed from even earlier Greek or Latin romance or other classical genres, as well as from late-classical Jewish martyrology; reciprocally, some later hagiography unashamedly modelled itself on secular romance.[14] Likewise, romance itself is a mongrel, some of its motifs and characters taken from hagiography, others from epic or folklore. A redactor of the *South English Legendary* makes it clear that romance was the popular literary-cultural matrix in which and against which the hagiographer often wrote:

> Men wilneth uche to hure telle. of bataille of kynge
> And of knightes that hardy were. that muchel is lesynge
> Wo so wilneth muche to hure. tales of suche thinge
> Hardi batailles he may hure. here that nis no lesinge
> Of apostles & martirs. that hardy knightes were
> That studevast were in bataille. & ne fleide noght for fere.[15]

Slippage of genre categories should therefore be understood as a natural condition of the saint's life; we might even consider the fictional (as opposed to genuinely biographical) legend a subcategory of what Northrop Frye called 'the master-genre', romance.[16] There can be no doubt of the existence of romance motifs in *Amis and Amiloun*; indeed, the poem could be seen as an anti-*Tristan*. In both stories, a noble girl and her mother conspire, on behalf of the hero, to subvert the father's decision about her marriage. In both, a sword separates a bedded, but not wedded, couple. In both, an ordeal is won by a technical 'truth' accomplished by disguise; in both, this deception averts the burning alive of the noble girl. (In *Tristan*, of course, the impostor-hero is not punished; in the English poem he is.) Lastly, both romances concern a triangle of two men and the woman married to one of them, although *Amis* completely revises the dynamic among the three. Yet along with these and other romance themes and motifs, hagiography is also present in our tale.

It is thus at the foundational level of genre that our text begins its subversion of rigid categories and 'norms'. It is not the first to do so, for even the earliest version, that of Ralph of Fleury – categorised by Leach in the romantic, non-hagiographic group – borrows hagiographical motifs: crucifixion is threatened as punishment, miracles of healing and resurrection occur, and the heroes share a grave. And little wonder, for Ralph himself was a hagiographer, having composed lives of Saints Maur and Benedict. Fleury itself was proud custodian of the relics of Benedict, founder of the wealthy and influential Benedictine order. It is fair to infer then, that hagiographical consciousness ran deep here, and could tinge almost any literary production of the place. Moreover, we cannot know in what form Ralph encountered the story. It could have been a lost *chanson de geste*, as Francis Bar suggests.[17] But a *chanson de geste* itself might be a militarised version of a paired-saints' life (think of Roland and Oliver); or reciprocally, a paired-saints' life could be an ecclesiasticised version of an epic, or of a folktale; a folktale could be a simplified version of a *chanson de geste* or of a paired-saints' life, and so on.

Despite generic ambiguity, though, the narrative itself generates no category crisis; there is no gender slippage as there might be in a tale of cross-dressing.[18] The paired protagonists are fully masculine physically and socially. They are not effeminate; they marry women and one of them reproduces; they are militarily brave and bold; they inherit property, exert lordship and impose moral and legal judgement; their friendship is at no point portrayed explicitly as a sexual one. Nevertheless, the social reality of homoerotic relations, especially in clerical and courtly milieux, has been amply documented.[19] Is there any textual reason to think of the homosocial bond of Amis and Amiloun as also homoerotic?

The confrontation between Amis and the steward suggests this interpretation. This scene just precedes, and dramatically parallels, Belisant's successful seduction attempt, so a parallel erotic motive is already hinted at structurally. This parallel is underscored by verbal echoes, especially in the demand for a mutual plighting of troth made by both the aggressive steward and the aggressive girl. The dynamic of the steward's exchange with Amis heightens the erotic atmosphere. When the steward asks Amis to be his special friend, his request is framed as competition with the absent Amiloun: 'Y schal þe be a better frende/ þan euer ȝete was he' (lines 359–60). The steward urges Amis to 'swere ous boþe broþerhed/ & pliȝt we our trewþes to' (362–3) in a lifelong affective bond, aiming to replace Amiloun in Amis's affections. Amis's rejection cites the exclusivity of his bond with Amiloun: he will 'Chaunge him for no newe' (384) – just as Belisant, a few stanzas later, asks Amis to 'chaunge me for no newe' (584). This competition and exclusivity suggest a more than social bond, for surely if the issue were only friendship, a person has room in his life for more than one friend. Friendship is not necessarily exclusive, but an ongoing erotic relationship usually is. Indeed, Amis appears to make this point himself, saying,

> 'Gete me frendes whare y may,
> Y no schal neuer bi nyȝt no day
> Chaunge him for no newe.' (382–4)

Here, Amis acknowledges that while there may be other friends for him in general, this particular proposal is beyond simple friendship. As well, the 'night or day' phrase may be more than convenient rhyme: it may mark out one difference between friendship, a daytime relationship, and a homoerotic bond which includes bedding down together. After this firm rejection, the steward goes nearly insane with wrath (386). He threatens lifelong enmity, adding, in effect, 'You'll be sorry!' ('þou schalt abigge þis nay', line 390). Again, the emotional intensity suggests more at stake than a mere tactical alliance; the steward responds like the proverbial scorned woman. I do not want to imply that he is effeminate, only that the emotional pitch is so high that eroticism seems to be at issue.

Later, the steward spies on Belisant's seduction of Amis, lurking in the room next door specifically in order to witness the couple's lovemaking through a little hole in the wall – a detail unique to the English version. Much is made of sight here: 'He seiʒe hem boþe ... he seyʒe hem boþe wiþ siʒt' (773–5). What is odd about this voyeuristic scene is that the steward already knows that the pair are involved because the indiscreet and aggressive Belisant ogles Amis at dinner (694–705). Rather than warning the duke, or scolding the girl, the steward simmers, awaiting the opportunity to betray the young couple (705–8). Perhaps he requires ocular evidence of their affair before denouncing them; perhaps it is part of his degenerate character that he likes to watch, for he runs after them them in order to do so: 'For to aspie hem boþe þat tide, / After swiþe he ran' (731–2). And, having seen, he is once again insanely wrathful (778–9).

It can be argued, and rightly, that the steward's job is to protect his overlord's interests and property, including the reputation of the duke's daughter. But the emotional intensity once more suggests another level of motivation: jealousy that the girl has landed Amis, resentment that he himself has been rejected from this very scenario and is now reduced to the undignified position of spying – addressing a different little hole than what he might have hoped.

Are there other 'little holes' in the story – openings where a queer reading might make sense? Here are two more. Amoraunt, now a strong fifteen-year old, takes great care of his lord Amylion and 'at his rigge he diʒt him ʒare' (1832): on his (Amoraunt's) back he (Amoraunt) placed or carried him (Amiloun) readily. This is clearly the narrative meaning required, for the boy does carry his uncle. Still, as a submerged but grammatically correct sexual pun, the phrase could read: at his (Amiloun's) back he (Amoraunt) did/serviced him (Amiloun).[20] Later, when the two arrive before Amis's gate, Amis's officers note the extraordinary beauty of Amoraunt, the 'naked swain' (1972). This nakedness shows the boy's utter poverty, but given his attractiveness it also adds a hint of erotic titillation to the knight's offer to introduce Amoraunt to Amis's court and ensure his success there.

My point, then, is that at certain moments the text permits an erotic reading of the male–male relationships in the story. It is, moreover, precisely the hagiographic background that encourages such a reading, specifically the thousand-year old tradition of lives of paired male saints.

Paired saints of both sexes were not uncommon in hagiographical literature, quite apart from the often coupled apostles Philip and Bartholomew, Simon and Jude, Peter and Paul. According to Boswell, the first documented male pair were the third-century Armenians

Polyeuct and Nearchos; next, the popular Serge and Bacchus, Roman soldiers. Boswell's list of other male pairs includes Marcellus and Apuleius, Cyprian and Justinus, Cosmas and Damian, Dionysius and Eleutherius;[21] Butler[22] adds Abdon and Sennen, Cyril and Methodius, Crispin and Crispinian, Processus and Martinian, Marcus and Marcellian, while the *Golden Legend* provides another (and different) fourteen male–male pairs.

Some of these *vitae* have motifs similar to those in the Amis and Amiloun tale, again illustrating the artificiality of a too-strict demarcation of genre lines. Common topoi are fidelity to a vow, miraculous healing, angelic voices, wandering, disguise and poverty, and ability to revive the dead. Though these appear in many legends paired or not, burial in the same grave (as in *Amis*) is normally limited to paired saints and is usual for them. Nearly all the paired saints in the *Golden Legend* and in Butler's *Patron Saints* are buried together, whether as friends, siblings or spouses. Occasionally they are buried together even when the two saints were neither friends nor martyred together (Gordianus and Epimachus, for example).

Like Amis and Amiloun, saints Serge and Bacchus are said by one writer to resemble each other 'in size, appearance, greatness, and youth of body and soul'.[23] Like the convoluted plot of *Amis and Amiloun*, the ordeal of Serge and Bacchus begins with denunciation by a courtier envious of the protagonists' closeness to the ruler. In the legend, as in many others, the emperor Maximian reacts with the rage typical of the persecuting tyrant. This conventional rage survives in the Middle English text in the person of the wrathful, impulsively violent duke, Belisant's father, who tries to kill the offending Amis rather than investigate the steward's charge of fornication. In the Niarchos–Polyeuct legend, Polyeuct, 'joined to Nearchos by boundless love, was prepared, he said, to subordinate everything to his absolute love for Nearchos – injury, death, or anything else, to such an extent that he would not even spare his children for the sake of Nearchos, since he counted them, too, as less important than his love for the latter'.[24] This sentiment – paternal love superseded by the bond of friendship – is precisely what provides the grisly dénouement of our tale.

What these parallels suggest is that the elements of same-sex paired saints' legend found in our romance may be a way of representing same-sex union in the high Middle Ages. Boswell argues – convincingly, in my view – that the early lives themselves perform exactly this coding; indeed, his argument is even more radical in claiming that the early legends did not encode (in the sense of disguise) but rather represented social reality fairly straightforwardly. This may have been true even for the earliest author, the monastic hagiographer-poet Ralph Tortaire, and I think it is indubitably so for the Middle English redactor, especially given his social context. What might be, then, the pragmatics of this story in its English treatment?

History

Two dimensions of medieval political history emerge from my reading: one international and of relatively long duration, the other distinctively English and contemporaneous with the Auchinleck manuscript. No historicisation, on either level, has yet been attempted with this richly signifying work.

On the international level, the ecclesiastical reform movement initiated by Pope Gregory VII did not die when Gregory did in 1085, but intensified as the Catholic Church strove to increase its political power, social influence and wealth, especially *vis-à-vis* the secular state. To those ends it campaigned to purify the lives of its ministers. Homosexuality per se was not a major focus of the reform movement: simony and clerical marriage were the main targets. Nonetheless, Boswell suggests that from the mid-eleventh century, two orientations toward homosexuality and homosociality began to develop. One was the ascetic, anti-sodomy lobby (e.g., Peter Damian or Ivo of Chartres), which met with little positive response from the hierarchy; the other celebrated the positive value of homoerotic relations in poetry, letters, and treatises on spiritual friendship (e.g., Anselm of Laon, Aelred of Rievaulx, and many known and anonymous clerical poets).[25] A story of impassioned same-sex friendship such as that narrated by Ralph Tortaire, schoolmaster and writer at the distinguished monastery of Fleury, can only have fortified the latter tendency. Perhaps this is one reason why the heavily ecclesiasticised French version of *Amis and Amiloun*, the so-called *chanson de geste,* must develop the leper-hero's marriage as extensively as it does, along with the military dimension: precisely to prevent the audience seeing it in light of pro-homosociality and its threatening erotic undercurrent. On the other hand, the English version, in effacing clerics, minimising marriage, and sanctifying the male couple, magnifies the homosocial and potentially homoerotic dimension. Clearly neither the original author nor the English redactor would have much sympathy with the draconian ruling of the late thirteenth-century law treatise *Fleta*, which recommended live burial for those guilty of intercourse with Jews, animals or persons of the same sex.[26]

In fact, the so-called 'genre' question should probably be seen as a covert political question inasmuch as the greater or lesser ecclesiastical content in a given version of our tale creates an alignment on major issues confronting the Church during just this two-century period between its earliest Latin version and its first Middle English version. As an illustration we may cite the episode in the heavily ecclesiasticised *chanson de geste* in which the leper's aristocratic wife, the evil Lubias, tries to bribe a bishop with thirty pieces of silver to grant her a divorce; she is rebuffed. Here, the French Church asserts its virtue against seigneurial nobility and the feudal state, and against women's treacherous, Judas-like wiles. The Church is portrayed as pro-marriage, anti-simony, and superior to lay power, hence as enacting the rulings of various ecclesiastical councils, especially the Third Lateran of 1179.[27]

At the time of its first surviving inscription by Ralph Tortaire, the story may already have had a historical basis, perhaps the famous friendship of two homonymic Aquitainian lords: William, fifth duke of Aquitaine and William, fourth count of Angoulême.[28] The historical thrust of this ur-version must remain speculative, but not that of the Middle English text. In early fourteenth-century England, the question of same-sex union had a quite practical application, for no less a personage than the young king Edward II was partner in a same-sex union. This well-documented relationship was not only known throughout the country but became a major political issue of the day.[29] We do well to recall that the compendious Auchinleck manuscript contains – besides its romances and religious texts – a metrical chronicle of England, a list of Norman barons who supposedly fought at Hastings, a verse life of Richard I, and a stanzaic poem on the various ills England experienced during the reign of Edward II. If we read a political subtext in *Amis and Amiloun*, another crossing of genres emerges, this one with political commentary.

Parallels between our romance and the reality of Edward II and Piers Gaveston are striking. I do not propose an allegory, translatable at every point from fiction into history: for one thing, the original long predates Edward's reign; for another, detailed allegory is not required in order to establish points of contact. I do not maintain that Amis or Amiloun 'is' Edward or Piers, only that distinctive features of their story have been added to a tale which might well already have been modeled on the real relationship of two noblemen. Points of contact there certainly are, and far too many to be merely coincidental. I suggest that in this story an English writer found material suitable for indirect representation of issues of his day, and that he shaped this material to make its suitability even more apparent.

Like the two fictional heroes, the real pair were notably handsome noble youths, Edward particularly strong and athletic.[30] They met in 1297, when Piers was brought into Edward's retinue, having been sent out for service as was the custom amongst European nobility and as is the case in our romance. By order of Edward I the two youths were educated together, probably a reward to Piers's father for his years of service.[31] Chroniclers write that the young men's relationship was intense, loving and exclusive; we know that Edward's attachment outlasted Piers's death by several years. Probably the relation was contractual, for Edward referred to Piers as his 'brother' in letters and documents, just as Amis and Amiloun do verbally, and the *Vita* says that the king adopted Piers as a brother. This was said to have been one reason why Edward I banished Gaveston in 1307.[32] The *Vita* likens their friendship to that of David and Jonathan or Achilles and Patroclus, but even stronger; it is, like David's, a 'love … which is said to have surpassed the love of women'.[33] What other points of contact are there?

Item: Only in the English poem are the boys taken to the ducal court by their parents to be educated there, and much is made of their being away from home so young. Piers was brought to the English court by his father in person, to be educated there.

Item: Only the English author specifies that it is between the age of twelve (when they begin courtly service) and fifteen (when they are knighted: line 163) that Amis and Amiloun pledge their personal covenant of 'trouth'. Edward and Gaveston met at about thirteen. The romance pair are knighted together; Edward and Piers were knighted within a few days of one another.

Item: The violent temper of a father and ruler is manifested in reality and in fiction: When Edward requested a large land grant for Piers in 1306, his notoriously violent father viciously assaulted him, much as the Duke assaults Amis on learning of his relationship with Belisant. In both cases, the motive may be less moral outrage at an offspring's irregular sexual relationship than anger at the alienation of territory into the hands of a person of less exalted rank. (We recall that Amis pleads his 'poverty' as a reason not to marry Belisant. Piers, though of noble background, was still a squire in England, not yet created the prince he would become when Edward, once crowned, was free to endow him generously as Earl of Cornwall and with many other lands and gifts.)

Item: The two fictional heroes are undone by the jealous intervention of an envious baron, the Duke's steward. The English barons' hatred of Piers Gaveston began as early as Edward's coronation in 1307, at which the young Gascon squire played a very prominent role. It nearly erupted into civil war over the next five years and eventuated in his murder; Hamilton observes that 'baronial animosity toward him is the central feature of English domestic policies during the years 1307–13.'[34] Gaveston was hated and resented because he was a foreigner; because he was arrogant and flamboyant; because he monopolised the king's attention; because he was not by birth at the same level of nobility as the English peers whom he supplanted; and above all because it was felt that Edward advanced him beyond his merit, to the disadvantage of older and more experienced English barons.

Item: When Amiloun has to return to his own land to claim his inheritance, Amis escorts him a day's journey on his way; this is the youths' first separation. The detail of personal escort appears only in the English version. When Piers Gaveston was exiled in April, 1307, Edward personally escorted him to Dover. Again in 1308, when Piers was exiled to Ireland, Edward, now king, escorted him to the port of Bristol, in both instances with lavish send-offs and extravagant gifts.

Item: Like the two romance heroes, both Piers and Edward married, fought well, and governed (Gaveston in Ireland and in his own territories).

Item: The fact that Amiloun's wife swears by 'Seyn Denis of Fraunce' (1567) and is governed by traditional feudal principles marks her as French. Edward's wife was Princess Isabella of France. The oath is unique to the English version.

Item: Amiloun wins a tournament against the older, jealous steward through deceit (he poses as Amis and takes an equivocal oath of innocence). Piers Gaveston and his athletic young cohort won a tournament against a group of older, jealous barons at Wallingford in December, 1307; he was accused of deceitfully bringing onto the field many more men than were allowed.

Item: Amiloun's wife drives him from bedchamber, dining table, castle and homeland to wander with his lone faithful retainer. Isabella's invasion of England in September, 1326 drove the king from Westminster and then from London, forcing him to wander for two months in the west country and Wales until he was betrayed, captured, deposed and, the following year, killed.

Item: Amiloun's wife arranges a bigamous and adulterous marriage with another knight.[35] Isabella's adulterous, long-term liaison with Roger Mortimer, the rebel earl of March, was notorious by the end of 1325.

Item: When Amiloun and the faithful Amorant are living in exile, the English narrator accounts for their poverty by telling of a great dearth of grain resulting in rising prices and famine (1736 ff.). This is unique to the English version. In 1316, an unusual dearth of grain struck England, followed by rising prices and famine: 'Such a scarcity has not been seen in our time in England, nor heard of for a hundred years.' It lasted about two and a half years, ending in 1318.[36]

Item: At Amis's castle, Amiloun is accused of having stolen the precious golden cup that he shows just before the anagnorisis. Curiously, he is not denounced as a thief but as a *traitor* (2045, 2077) – a specifically political offence – and said to be worthy a traitor's punishment: drawing (that is, being dragged by a horse around the city). This punishment was a not uncommon public spectacle in London and other cities. Piers Gaveston was accused in the baronial Ordinances of 1311 of having appropriated royal treasure and sent it abroad, to the impoverishment of the kingdom. This charge was repeated in 1312, after Gaveston's murder as a traitor, in connection with a hoard of jewels and other precious items, the so-called Newcastle inventory of royal treasures. The barons desired Edward II to denounce Gaveston as a traitor because of this alleged 'theft', but Edward refused to do so. Chaplais concludes that the charges, 'unsupported as they are by any record evidence, cannot be taken seriously'.[37]

Item: Though we lack the ending of the Auchinleck version, other manuscripts have the two heroes buried in the same grave, like so many of the paired male saints whose legends offer a literary analogue. Piers Gaveston was beheaded, like many a saint, and after two years with the Oxford Dominicans his corpse was moved – translated, we might say – to Langley, site of his and Edward's favorite haunt, and buried there.

Writing of his own work on Dante's poetics, John Freccero remarked, 'To begin with an abstract form is to proceed in a manner that is the reverse of what one might expect of a cultural historian'. To this the best rejoinder – as Freccero knew – is Roland Barthes's epigram: 'A little formalism turns one away from History, but ... a lot brings one back to it.'[38] Much remains to be said about the intriguing tale of Amis and Amiloun – about its philosophical stance, its religious orientation, its rhetoric. I hope that this essay, focusing as it does on form, genre, and historical context, may suggest further avenues of research and fields of play for current critical methods.

Notes

I would like to thank my research assistant, Margot Kaminski, who assembled much of the source material used in this paper and prepared it for publication. Also the Social Sciences and Humanities Research Council of Canada, whose grant enabled me to hire her and to present a short version of the paper at the Kalamazoo Medieval Congress in 2000.

1   The romance is extant in four manuscripts, of which the earliest, the Auchinleck, is at the National Library of Scotland. This is the manuscript on which the EETS edition by MacEdward Leach is based (London, 1937; EETS o.s. 203), but since it has been damaged at the beginning and end of the poem, Leach supplements from Egerton 2862, a late fourteenth-century manuscript also known as Sutherland after an early owner, the duke of Sutherland. Leach's edition will be my citation text. The edition by Françoise Le Saux (*Amys and Amylion,* Exeter, 1993) uses Douce 326, a late fifteenth-century manuscript at the Bodleian Library. This is the fullest version, and the edition is extremely convenient for teaching. The latest text is Harleian 2386, also at the British Library; it contains only about a third of the poem. Apparently none of the four used one of the others as exemplar.

Le Saux's bibliography lists only five short critical studies of the ME poem before 1993, all of them published between 1966 and 1983; one is primarily a comparison with the Anglo-Norman version. The poem has been mentioned briefly in various books, and there are a number of articles, mainly in French, about the Anglo-Norman and French versions.

2   For a facsimile edition, see *The Auchinleck Manuscript,* eds Derek Pearsall and C. Cunningham (London, 1977). Conditions of production and consumption of the manuscript were first studied by Laura Hibbard Loomis, 'The Auchinleck manuscript and a possible London bookshop of 1330–1340', *PMLA,* 57 (1942), 595–627; reprinted in Laura Hibbard Loomis, *Adventures in the Middle Ages* (New York, 1962). Loomis's workshop hypothesis has been challenged by Timothy A. Shonk, 'A study of the Auchinleck manuscript: bookmen and bookmaking in the early fourteenth century', *Speculum* 60 (1985), 71–91; he argues for a less centralised system: still secular and commercial but with a dealer-seller-editor and perhaps translator farming out work to freelance scribes. The manuscript may have been used by Geoffrey Chaucer in composing his 'Tale of Sir Thopas', as Loomis argued in 'Chaucer and the Auchinleck manuscript', in P. W. Long (ed.), *Essays and Studies in Honor of Carleton Brown* (New York, 1940), pp. 111–28.

3   The most that can be said about this is that since the later manuscripts of the poem contain material that the Auchinleck version lacks, they may derive from another (very similar) source. However, this hypothetical source may not be much earlier than what we have; it may be, as Pearsall and Cunningham suggest in the Scolar facsimile, 'the bookshop translation

or the bookshop copy that lies behind the Auchinleck copy' (p. x). There are, of course, other ways of accounting for the different material that would save the idea of Auchinleck as the original Middle English version.

4   Aristotle used letters to designate propositions, qualities, and categories in various treatises. For instance, *Topica:* 'Thus if A defines a better than B defines b, and B is a definition of b, so too is A of a' (Book 7.3. 154a) or *Ethica Nichomachea* : 'Let A be a builder, B a shoemaker, C a house, D a shoe … Let A be a house, B ten minae, C a bed. A is half of B, if the house is worth five minae …; the bed, C, is a tenth of B …' (Book 5. 5. 1133a and 1133b) in *The Works of Aristotle,* ed. W. D. Ross (Oxford, 1908–52), vols 1 and 9. I am indebted to D. W. Luscombe's kind assistance for these Aristotle references; also see *Analytica Priora, Analytica Posteriora,* and *De Sophisticis* in volume 1. Given the overwhelming authority of Aristotle, it is not surprising that the habit was well established among medieval scholars by the time Ralph Tortaire wrote the first known version of the Amis and Amiloun story (in the eleventh or twelfth century – see the following note), even though much of Aristotle's work was not translated until the thirteenth century. However, various treatises of Aristotle had been translated by Boethius in the sixth century. In original works and in commentaries on Aristotle, the convention was widespread. The eleventh-century Garlandus Compotista uses it in his *Dialectica,* ed. L. M. De Rijk (Assen, 1959), pp. 147, 148, 149, 156, 169, as did Abelard, a younger contemporary of Rodolfus, in his logical works, e.g., *Ypoteticarum,* in the *Dialectica,* ed. L. M. De Rijk (Assen, 1970), and Aquinas in commenting on Aristotle's *Posterior Analytics, passim*; trans. F. R. Larcher (Albany, 1970). In lecture 28, Aquinas uses sex as an example of predication: 'Thus we may take some middle which is predicated particularly of A and of B, say "male", which is predicated particularly of animal and of man. Now if C is taken in every A, say "Every animal is male", and in no B, say "No man is male", each proposition will be false … etc.': *Posterior Analytics,* trans. Larcher, p. 93. The thirteenth-century English logician William of Sherwood has 'Let the whole of Socrates be called "*a*", … but his foot "*b*". Thus *a* is an animal, and *b* is an animal', *Treatise on Syncategorematic Words,* ed. Norman Kretzmann (Minneapolis, 1968), p. 60. The thirteenth-century Portuguese logician Peter of Spain uses letters for both propositions ('assertibles') and categories, e.g., 'The one running is *a* … Man is a' in 'Treatise on obligations', in *Tractatus Syncategorematum,* ed. Joseph P. Mullally (Milwaukee, 1964), p. 127. The thirteenth-century English courtier-cleric John Blund uses category-letters in his *Tractatus de Anima,* ed. D. A. Callus and R. W. Hunt (London, 1970), pp. 36–8. The usage is common in the work of Duns Scotus on the existence and unicity of God; cf. his *Philosophical Writings,* ed. Allan Wolter (London, 1962), pp. 39, 51 *et alibi*. Also see the essays and texts collected in P. Osmond Lewry (ed.), *The Rise of British Logic* (Toronto, 1983), where A and B can designate a proposition,

a place, an entity, a moment or a person. In Oxford mathematical treatises, 'letters A, B, C, etc., were used to represent ... velocities, or degrees of quality, or propositions, or distances, or instants': Edith Dudley Sylla, 'The Oxford calculators', in Norman Kretzmann *et al.* (eds), *The Cambridge History of Later Medieval Philosophy* (Cambridge, 1982), p. 562.

My argument does not, of course, depend on rhyme schemes being designated with letters in the Middle Ages, only on end rhymes being perceived as same or different, men and women being perceived as same or different, and similarity and difference being designated by letters.

5 See *Rodolfi Tortarii Carmina,* ed. Marbury B. Ogle and Dorothy M. Schullian (Rome, 1933). A translation appears in Leach's Appendix A, and Le Saux includes a summary in her Appendix 1. Life-dates and composition dates are not known precisely, but Ralph could have been born about 1065 and would have lived to a ripe old age if he is indeed responsible for the epitaphs to Abelard attributed to him, for Abelard died in 1142. Prefatory poems about Ralph attached to the manuscript praise his lifelong ('a puero') study, impeccable life, and fine reputation. The other epistles reveal a taste for exotica and enjoyment, strong ties of affectionate friendship, and a confident, self-aware poetic sensibility.

6 This is summarised in Le Saux's Appendix 2.

7 *Ami et Amile, Chanson de Geste,* ed. Peter F. Dembowski (Paris, 1969).

8 *Amys e Amillyoun*, ed. Hideka Fukui, Anglo-Norman Text Society Plain Texts series 7 (London, 1990).

9 On the simultaneous incorporation of semantic and semiotic axes into Middle English poetry, see my *Naked Text: Chaucer's Legend of Good Women* (Berkeley, 1994), pp. 154–64.

10 Teodolinda Barolini, *The Undivine Comedy: Detheologizing Dante* (Princeton, 1992), pp. 24–5; see also John Freccero, 'The significance of *terza rima*' in Rachel Jacoff (ed.), *Dante: The Poetics of Conversion* (Cambridge, MA, 1986).

11 John Boswell, *Same-Sex Unions in Premodern Europe* (New York, 1994), ch. 3. A. H. Krappe suggested that 'twin saints' are a Christian substitute for pagan twin-god cults such as that of Castor and Pollux; they are 'twin legends in hagiographic garb': 'The legend of Amicus and Amelius', *Modern Language Review*, 18 (1929), 152–61.

12 *Amis and Amiloun*, ed. Leach, pp. ix, xxvii, xxvi.

13 Vladimir Propp, *Morphology of the Folktale* (Austin, Texas, 1975), p. 100; italics in original.

14 A case in point for early hagiography borrowing from earlier classical literature is the story of St Faith (Foi) as a christianised /inverted version of the story of Dido and Aeneas; see my *Impolitic Bodies: Poetry, Saints, and Society in Fifteenth Century England* (Oxford, 1998), pp. 40–1. Also Thomas McAlindon, 'The medieval assimilation of Greek romance', *REAL: The Yearbook of Research in English and American Literature*, 3 (1985), 23–56. The fifteenth-century Augustinian John Capgrave modelled his

Life of St Katharine on Chaucer's *Troilus*: cf. M. A. Stouck, 'Chaucer and Capgrave's *Life of St. Katherine*', *American Benedictine Review*, 33 (1982), 276–91 and Derek Pearsall, 'John Capgrave's *Life of St Katharine* and popular romance style', *Medievalia et Humanistica*, 6 (1975), 121–37. See also Jocelyn Wogan-Browne, '"Bet ... to ... rede ... on holy seyntes lyves ...": romance and hagiography again', in Carol M. Meale (ed.), *Readings in Middle English Romance* (Cambridge, 1994), pp. 83–97.

15 *South English Legendary: Corpus Christi MS 145*, ed. Charlotte d'Evelyn and Anna J. Mill, 2 vols, EETS 235, 236 (London, 1956), lines 59–64.

16 Hagiography certainly fits Northrop Frye's description of romance: 'The complete form of the romance is clearly the successful quest, and such a completed form has three main stages: the stage of the perilous journey and the preliminary minor adventures; the crucial struggle, usually some kind of battle in which either the hero or his foe, or both, must die; and the exaltation of the hero. We may call these three stages ... the *agon* or conflict, the *pathos* or death-struggle, and the *anagnorisis* or discovery, the recognition of the hero, who has clearly proved himself to be a hero even if he does not survive the conflict.' Northrop Frye, *Anatomy of Criticism* (Princeton, 1957), p. 187.

17 Francis Bar, 'Raoul le Tourtier et la chanson de geste d'*Ami et Amile*', in *La Chanson de geste et le mythe Carolingien. Mélanges René Louis*, 2 vols (Vézelay, 1982), vol. 1, pp. 973–86.

18 See Simon Gaunt, 'Straight minds / 'Queer' wishes in Old French hagiography: *La Vie de Sainte Euphrosine*', in Louise Fradenburg and Carla Freccero (eds), *Premodern Sexualities* (New York, 1996); also see Allen J. Frantzen's discussion of this legend and critique of Gaunt's essay, in *Before the Closet: Same-Sex Love from Beowulf to Angels in America* (Chicago, 1998).

19 For example in Thomas Stehling (trans.), *Medieval Latin Poems of Male Love and Friendship* (New York and London, 1984); Michael Goodich, *Homosexuality in the Later Medieval Period* (Oxford, 1979); John Boswell, *Christianity, Social Tolerance, and Homosexuality: Gay People in Western Europe from the Beginning of the Christian Era to the Fourteenth Century* (Chicago, 1980). Many social historians and queer-theory scholars emphasise the nineteenth-century invention of the category 'homosexual', but Bernadette Brooten documents the medical identity-categorisation for homosexuality (using various terms) from various cultures in much earlier periods: *Love Between Women: Early Christian Responses to Female Homoeroticism* (Chicago, 1996).

20 *MED* includes among its meanings for 'dight' to get ready for use, and to have sexual intercourse with.

21 Boswell, *Same-Sex Unions*, p. 154, n. 205.

22 *Butler's Lives of Patron Saints*, ed. Michael Walsh (San Francisco, 1987); *Jacobus de Voragine: The Golden Legend*, trans. William G. Ryan, 2 vols (Princeton, 1993).

23 Boswell, *Same-Sex Unions*, p. 155; the writer is Severus of Antioch, early-sixth-century. Boswell adds that 'these are all obvious generalities of

Greek erotic writing, and it is easy to imagine that Severus simply added them as a rhetorical flourish' (p. 155, n. 210). Another approach to the resemblance motif is that it may originate in ancient cults of twin gods, which David Greenberg suggests may have practised cult homosexuality: *The Construction of Homosexuality* (Chicago and London, 1988), pp. 243–4. The motif of the double or twin is also known in folktale: cf., among others, Gédéon Huet, 'Ami et Amile. Les origines de la légende', *Le Moyen Age*, 31 (1919), 162–86, esp. pp. 167–8.

24 Boswell, *Same-Sex Unions*, pp. 142–3.

25 Boswell, *Christianity, Social Tolerance, and Homosexuality*, pp. 210–22 and ch. 9 documenting this 'gay subculture' (p. 243). See also Mark D. Jordan, *The Invention of Sodomy in Christian Theology* (Chicago, 1997).

26 Boswell, *Christianity, Social Tolerance, and Homosexuality*, p. 292.

27 This episode is discussed by Geneviève Pichon, 'La lèpre dans *Ami et Amile*,' in *Ami et Amile. Une Chanson de geste de l'amitié*, ed. Jean Dufournet (Paris, 1987). Also of interest is Lubias' subsequent provocation of an anti-clerical bourgeois revolt. For rulings of ecumenical councils of the Church, see *Conciliorum Oecumenicorum Decreta*, ed. Joseph Alberigo *et al.* (Freiburg, 1962).

28 Bar, 'Raoul le Tourtier', pp. 984–5, n. 66. Bar notes that the latter William received Blaye as fief from the former. Bar is following a suggestion made by J. Koch in 1875. Ralph writes that although his tale is considered merely fictional ('fabula ficta'), it mixes truths and falsity (Epistula 2, lines 119–22, in *Carmina*, ed. Ogle and Schullian). He might mean historical truth, moral truth or both.

29 My main sources for Edward and Piers are Harold F. Hutchison, *Edward II: The Pliant King* (London, 1971); J. S. Hamilton, *Piers Gaveston, Earl of Cornwall, 1307–1312: Politics and Patronage in the Reign of Edward II* (Detroit and London, 1988); Pierre Chaplais, *Piers Gaveston, Edward II's Adoptive Brother* (Oxford, 1994); and the anonymous *Vita Edwardi Secundi*, ed. and trans. N. Denholm-Young (London, 1957). This text breaks off in 1326 and the editor makes a good case for its authorship by one John Walwyn, a government official with lay and ecclesiastical education, who died in that year. Though the manuscript in which the *Vita* appears was held for a time at the Benedictine Abbey at Malmesbury, there is no indication that it 'was composed there, or that the author was ever a monk at Malmesbury or anywhere else' (p. xv).

30 Piers was not a nobody but son of an important baronial family from Gascony, an English-controlled territory; his father served Edward I for twenty years in Wales, Scotland and elsewhere; his brothers served Edward II. Contemporary chronicles attest to the handsomeness and fine physical build of both young men.

31 James Conway Davies, *The Baronial Opposition to Edward II* (London, 1918), p. 82.

32 *Vita Edwardi Secundi*, ed. Denholm-Young, p. 28 ('quem rex adoptauerat

in fratrem'); Davies, *Baronial Opposition*, p. 84.

33 *Vita Edwardi Secundi*, ed. Denholm-Young, p. 30.

34 Hamilton, *Piers Gaveston*, p.15. The reasons had little if anything to do with sexual matters; rather the emphasis was on Edward's slighting other barons in order to advance the young foreigner, and on Piers's tactless behavior and financial recklessness.

35 This does not occur in the French. In the Anglo-Norman, it does, but the wife believes that Amyllion is dead, while the English says nothing about such a mistake. In any case, there is disagreement as to whether her ignorance of Amiloun's cure would legally free his wife from the bond of marriage. In 1180, Pope Alexander III ruled that a spouse's leprosy did not justify divorce; the well spouse should either care for the ill one or, if separated, live chaste: Peter Richards, *The Medieval Leper and his Northern Heirs* (Cambridge, 1977), p. 62.

   Hutchison observes that 'one chronicler suggests that' in 1324 Edward's baronial supporters were 'actually attempting to obtain a papal annulment of the marriage' (*Edward II*, p. 129); for her part, Isabella claimed that her marriage had been broken by the presence of a third party (Hugh Despenser) occupying the king's attention; cf. *Vita Edwardi Secundi*, ed. Denholm-Young, p. 143.

36 *Vita Edwardi Secundi*, ed. Denholm-Young, p. 69. The last item in the Auchinleck manuscript, a long social complaint in verse, makes much of the great dearth of grain and the famine, as God's punishment of English lay and ecclesiastical wrongdoing. See the Scolar Press facsimile edition.

37 Chaplais, *Piers Gaveston*, p. 101.

38 Freccero, 'Terza rima' (above, n. 10), p. 260; Roland Barthes, 'Myth today', in *Mythologies*, trans. Annette Lavers (New York, 1978; originally published Paris, 1957), p. 112.

4

Sir Degrevant: **what lovers want**

Arlyn Diamond

According to *Sir Degrevant*, an early fifteenth-century romance with a lively plot and remarkable density of description, what women want is a handsome, valiant, wealthy and noble lover, triumph over fierce paternal opposition, a splendid wardrobe, and a fabulous room of their own.[1] What men want is a noble reputation, a huge deer park in which to spend their days hunting, extensive and prosperous estates, triumph over would-be oppressors, and a beautiful opinionated heiress. And, the happy ending suggests, they both ought to get what they want. In *Degrevant* marriage reconciles two enemies, incorporating into an established household and lineage new blood on the basis of merit, not just inherited rank, and validating women's right to choose a husband. Moreover, as so often in Middle English popular romances, (*Havelok* or *William of Palerne* or *The King of Tars*, for instance) the marriage between hero and heroine delineates the intersection of the personal and the social, the masculine and the feminine, intersections which will form the focus of this essay.

Degrevant is written in the sixteen-line tail-rhyme stanza often characteristic of popular romances, and, although it has no identifiable main source or close analogues, it also incorporates a number of conventional thematic and verbal formulas. The meeting of lovers in a garden, the rival suitors clashing in a splendid tournament, the feasts, the unsympathetic fathers and helpful maids, are all elements which had proven their literary appeal to a wide range of audiences for more than a century. At the same time, as W. A. Davenport points out, 'this romance is closer than many to the actual concerns of the landowning class of the time – property, fences, hunting rights, being just to one's tenants, seeking proper legal redress for wrongs, and eventually, after much harm done, compromise and reconciliation'.[2]

While agreeing with Davenport's desire to place the narrative in a knowable historical context, I think he defines the audience and its 'actual concerns' too narrowly. Without disputing the justice of his formulation, I would argue that the very term landowning class, however accurate, tends to occlude women's social and cultural activities. My reading centres on the term 'household' as a way of understanding the social imagination of the romance, and its representation of gendered lives and desires. In the fourteenth and fifteenth centuries the term indicates both a place – the heart of a landed estate – and a social and economic institution – a powerful landholding family with its servants and retainers.[3] It is the site of the reproduction of families through marriage, and of the household itself through the inheritance of goods and status, ideally from father to eldest son. It exists to satisfy the desires of the ones who head it, but in its splendid displays of possessions and extravagant hospitality it advertises their power, attracting adherents and intimidating would-be rivals.[4] In her engrossing and thorough study of the noble household (a term which can stretch to include both the aristocracy and the wealthy gentry who shared their values), Kate Mertes claims that 'it cannot be dismissed as a mere domestic organisation, nor yet as a simple political tool of the noble classes. It functioned as an important structure in helping men and women of the later middle ages to conceive, comprehend and carry out their existence.'[5] Thus, for poet and audience, it is easy to understand the conflict between the two men as a struggle for power between rival households. Moreover, because the household is a familial institution, it offers a possible site for the representation of female initiative and desires, particularly as they concern marriage.

In the getting and maintaining of wealth and power, a particularly demanding task in the political and economic upheavals of the fifteenth century, the making of marriages was a way of brokering alliances and providing for the orderly transfer of wealth.[6] Among those with property, medieval marriages were as much part of familial social strategy as they were personal relationships. Although canon law required that both parties consent to a marriage, dependent children, especially daughters, were not expected to choose partners against their family's wishes.[7] When this romance, as I hope to show, endorses the love-match between the daughter of an arrogant earl and the less well-born knight whose lands he has attacked, it links female autonomy with the widespread social fantasy that through marriage and luck one could aspire to enter the ranks of the nobility. The marriage insures the continuation of the earl's line, and the man he has despised will inherit his father-in-law's estate, becoming his peer in wealth and status if not birth. The idea of marrying up was not a radical one in English society, which was, in Dyer's terms, 'remarkably resilient and flexible', although the great barons in practice married among themselves.[8] However, such flexibility was never without its tensions, as the rise of the ambitious encountered the inherent conservatism of a class where rank and wealth were based on birth. *Degrevant* reveals the potential for conflict in a shifting social landscape. Underlying the reconciliation with which the romance ends is a deployment of the trappings of chivalry to endorse aggression and violence as the normative way to achieve a social harmony identified with the privileges and property rights of great householders, both male and female.

In many ways the plot is a pastiche of familiar elements, situated in a recognisable contemporary landscape.[9] While Degrevant is on crusade a neighbouring earl, without apparent motive, attacks his deer park and kills his foresters. Degrevant's attempts to appeal first to the earl's sense of justice and then to his chivalric honour are equally futile, forcing him to fight back. When Degrevant challenges his enemy on his own ground, the earl's daughter, Melidor, watches from the castle walls. He is at once enamoured and pursues her into the castle, in the end winning her love. There are clandestine meetings in Melidor's chamber, a higher-ranking suitor who is defeated at a grand tournament, a spying steward, a helpful maid and numerous battles. In the end Melidor and her mother convince the earl that he has no choice but to accept Degrevant. They live long and prosper, and after his wife's death Degrevant returns to the Holy Land, to die on crusade.

Although the distinction is far too neat, it is possible to divide our attention between the plot, with its focus on the actions and motivations of the main characters, and the poem's extended description of the possessions which define them and the world in which they are placed. Both plot and description can be read as forms of social discourse, circumscribing the uneasy mix of violence and desire which defines the ethos of the romance. One of the few critical essays ever written on this romance argues that it is about the establishment of social order through the reconciliation of masculine aggression (Degrevant and the Earl) and the feminine commitment to order and harmony (Melidor, her mother) through marriage.[10] This seems at first a plausible reading, but its reliance upon traditional moral schema and gender divisions prevents the author, A. S. G. Edwards, from noticing the ways in which the poem does not really reaffirm the binary opposition of male and female, private and public. His assumption that the poem is neatly divided into 'two worlds ... this inner world of love and civilisation and an outer world of conflict and violence', is not borne out by a close examination of the loci of action in the romance, as I hope to show below, or even by history.[11] Recent work by scholars has revealed the extent to which women participated in what we would now define as social and economic activities – managing estates, pursuing legal actions, making and contesting wills, acting as cultural and religious patrons, seeking the favour of the powerful and the good will of peers.[12] Melidor and her mother and maid are as invested as men in the establishment of a household able to provide them with all that the romance represents as desirable – glamorous trappings, servants, and the power to enforce their desires.

Harmony may be a good thing, but it is not a virtue particularly associated with the strong-willed Melidor. Moreover the plot demonstrates that the impulse to order and peacefulness is impotent, unless enforced by superior strength. The first demonstration of this social reality comes when Degrevant, who 'thought werke be lawe / And wyth non oþer schore' (151–2), sends a letter to the Earl, asking for restitution, or an explanation. The Earl's reply to the messenger makes adherence to the law a matter of personal choice, or 'will', a word which recurs frequently in this text: 'I wull, for thy lordes tene, / Honte hys foresstus and grene, / And breke his parkes by-dene' (189–91). The Earl's wife voices her objections to her husband's aggression (373–80) but he is deterred by Degrevant's deeds, not her words. Degrevant in turn is unpersuaded by the Countess's plea to leave them alone, now that he has won (425–8). What Degrevant wants is to 'quite hem his mede' (443), make the Earl pay in some way unspecified except for the 'many dowghty [who] schall dey / Or hyt ende soo' (463–4). The restoration of damages Degrevant earlier sought, he tells his future mother-in-law, is no longer sufficient to end their private war. The narrative is triggered by an act of violence, and continues to pit knight against earl, daughter against father, until the Earl is utterly defeated. Degrevant's seemingly inexhaustible appetite for revenge poses a dilemma which has no social resolution, in a world without even the nominal presence of kings or prelates or judges or sheriffs or other lords, until the wedding at the end. The political and legal landscape is subsumed by the two rival households, with their adherents, dependants and allies circling in orbit around them. Only the appearance of Melidor, 'jentell and small / And louesom to seyght' (419–20) appears to offer a way out of this cycle of injury and retaliation.

The love affair does not evoke a truly alternative set of values, although the lovers' meetings do offer a refuge from the fighting. Even as they feast and snuggle in Melidor's chamber, the hostilities continue outside. The bodies of the Earl's supporters continue to pile up, until the Earl is forced by his daughter and wife to agree to his daughter's choice of a husband. Degrevant never doubts his ability to win Melidor, any more than he doubts his abilities to injure his enemies, and the two activities are always intermeshed. When he first sees her Degrevant promises himself 'that he shall loue þat swet wyȝt, / Acheue how hit wold' (479–80). Even though he meets her first in an orchard, the traditional refuge of lovers, he has come there fully armed. When she insults him as a traitor, he dares her to call out her men, boasting that he will kill them all. Not surprisingly, she flees, but he is undeterred by the failure of his martial approach to courtship, and throughout the course of the affair his protestations of love alternate with threats to potential rivals. As he tells the maid who acts as go-between, no emperor or king is powerful enough 'hyr to bed bryng' (902) against his will. It is almost as if his fierce pride requires an unobtainable object of desire.

The maid plays a crucial role in bringing the lovers together – warning Degrevant of potential dangers and telling him how to get in to the castle. After Melidor has fled from her demanding suitor, it is the maid who forces her hand, saying she herself would be glad to accept him. Without admitting that negotiations are being opened, Melidor grudgingly tells her servant-companion to welcome him herself, 'in all þe devyl way' (792). Her jealous suspicions of what might have happened in the private supper her maid arranges are allayed when she is told that Degrevant has rewarded his squire, who acts as his confidant, with knighthood, marriage to Melidor's maid, and exactly 100 pounds of land, a remarkably extravagant grant. There is even a written charter which the maid offers as proof to her doubting mistress, who goes to the trouble of reading it carefully (975–8). In arranging their marriage Degrevant is doing more than rewarding faithful servants, or exhibiting the disinterested generosity appropriate to worthy heroes. The specificity of the transaction makes it clear it is more than one of the happy ancillary pairings so frequent in romance. Both in form (the bond confirming the grant, the formally plighted marriage intentions) and intent, the gift is an example of the romance's almost obsessive attention to legal and fiscal matters. Squire and maid will form the nucleus of the new household their marriage will create, and both rise with the fortunes of their lord and lady. The squire's loyalty and the maid's initiative suggest the multiple strategies ambitious servants can employ to advance their own interests in a system based on the exchange of obligations and gifts.[13] If the relationships of peers are seen as inevitably competitive, the relationship with sub-ordinates is shown as mutually beneficial.

As a historian, Felicity Heal uses the this romance as a literary (and therefore exaggerated) example of the disorder created in the fifteenth century by rivalries between households, citing as exemplary the scene after the tournament in which Degrevant has mastered all his oppon-ents. The knight, despite his victory, has not been proclaimed the victor by the Earl, or invited to the celebratory feast at the Earl's castle. Aggressively and dramatically Degrevant rides up to the dais where the Earl is feasting: 'To Mayd Myldor he ches, / And chalangys þat fre' (1219–20). By refusing to offer him the hospitality which Degrevant, knowing his obligations, has offered to his own retinue, the earl is refusing to acknowledge his right to 'gentilesse'. Degrevant has trium-phed over a higher ranking suitor for Melidor's hand, winning the admiration of men and the love of countesses and queens for his skill, and in bursting in to his enemy's hall he is making the Earl's dishonour at denying him the prize 'public in the most dramatic manner possible for a householder'.[14] The tournament brings their conflict into public viewing, providing the external audience which their feud lacks, in a forum which is meant to demonstrate and reinforce knightly values.[15] And, from the beginning, the tournament, like the poem itself, makes public its conflation of the hero's love for his mistress with his contest for supremacy with other men.

Melidor is no mere bone of contention between men, however. She is as strong-willed as Degrevant, and unlike her mother appears uninterested in peace for its own sake. Like her lover and father she lives in the declarative mode, insisting dramatically that she will marry Degrevant despite her father's threats, and the presence of a much higher-ranking suitor: 'Shall I hym neuer for-sake, / What deþe þat I take' (1750–1). Their first encounter matches his militant boldness with her sharp tongue. Even though we are told later that she too loves at first sight, her initial response is to berate him, and then the maid who intercedes on his behalf. Melidor is no representative of a femin-ised alternative to violence – indeed, Casson calls her a 'heroine of rather shrewish temper'.[16] There is none of the interior debate associated with 'courtly love', rather an unexpected melange of self-protective prudence and the bold actions of romance. At one moment she demands to see the charter which confirms her maid's claim that Degrevant has betrothed her to his squire and settled 100 pounds of land on them (973–8). At another she marches in to the middle of the tournament with a horse for her lover, announcing: 'On þis stede wol I ryde / By my lemmanus syde' (1318–19). Her determination to make her own choice is not justified by immoderate romantic passion, since she never lets love overwhelm her sense of her own prerogatives. For her, lover and potential marital partner are inseparable. When Degrevant begs for 'mercy' she tells him sternly that he will regret making such a request. Not even a king could 'touchest … swych þing' without a formal marriage, and for that he needs her father's assent, or 'wylle' (1530–50 *passim*). That will, initially the source of conflict between the two households, is finally overwhelmed by Degrevant's slaughter of his men, his wife's advice to make peace with the man he has wronged, and his daughter's inflexible resolve. Her final threat 'And giff ȝe holde vs a gret, / Shall I neuer ete mete' (1785–6) seems to break his spirit:

> ȝe eorl for angur gan swet,
>   And syȝthe ful sar.
> 'Damesele, ar þou be spylte,
> I for-giff þe þe gylte;
> Hit is all as þou wylte,
> I can say na mar.' (1787–92)

Degrevant might not seem a suitable vehicle for expressing the ambitions of those who considered themselves 'gentle' without belonging to the nobility, for we are told at the beginning that he is Arthur's nephew (perhaps a confusion with Agravain). Nonetheless the poet essentially forgets about his supposedly royal connections. In the beginning of the poem they seem to operate as a formulaic indicator of prestige and personal merit, as opposed to inherited status, since what is emphasised later is his social distance from Melidor's family. As her maid tells him:

> Hyr proferrys par amoure
> Boþ dukes and emperoure,
> Hyt were hyr disonowre
>   For to taken þe. (857–60)

Just before she receives him in her chamber, the poet reminds us that she is a 'lady of heye kynn' (1363).

Kate Mertes says that 'every document discovered, every text reinterpreted confirms the view that all nobles and gentles, male and female, expected their marriages to serve their families economically and politically'.[17] Although *Degrevant,* with its insistence on the daughter's independence, might seem by this account a subversive text, in fact the marriage does serve Melidor's family, as she and her mother are astute enough to perceive. The earl's intransigence, representing the mindset of a closed class, is seen as both ineffective and short-sighted, since in all ways, from his prowess in battle to his generosity to minstrels to his hospitality to his own household, Degrevant is in fact a worthy custodian of his new family's line. Their extravagant wedding, attended by Emperors, cardinals, the douze peers of France, the King of Portugal, *et al.*, advances the message of the plot: men of wealth and gentility deserve access to the highest class, but only their own fiercest exertions will enable them to rise in a world where great magnates have the power to ride roughshod over such aspirations.

Love does in the romance what royal authority was often called upon to do in history – reconcile the warring parties. Marriage brings about a peaceful countryside and happy lovers, although in actual practice marriages were supposed to be arranged by parents and guardians, who saw marriage 'as a way of augmenting and consolidating their lands and rising in political power and influence … [and ensuring] heirs to whom the inheritance would pass and who would safeguard it for future generations'.[18] According to May McKisack, 'failure of heirs constituted by far the most serious threat to baronial stability … [and] fathers of wealthy heiresses could take their pick among likely suitors'.[19] Clearly however fathers and daughters do not always agree on what defines 'likely' and in this romance women prove that their judgement is superior. When the women in *Degrevant* urge the Earl to let his daughter marry as she wishes, they are speaking not just for individual happiness and peace but for a union which will strengthen the power of the landholding elite by recruiting someone worthy to support its claims.[20]

And, in so speaking, they underline their essential role in household formation. Melidor can not be read as a mere token of alliance between men. The Paston letters, an extensive collection, among the earliest in English and arguably the most interesting, provide ample evidence that women can be crucial to a family's success. The Pastons were an ambitious and energetic family moving up the ranks in fifteenth-century Norfolk, and the letters show women making marriages, hectoring children to push themselves forward at court, organising family resources, negotiating with potential allies and rivals and sometimes literally holding the fort.[21] 'Ryt wurchipful hwsbond', begins one letter from Margaret Paston to her husband, John, 'I recomawnd me to you, and prey yow to gete som crosse bowis, and wyndacys to bynd them wyth.'[22] When gaining and maintaining status and property was as consuming and potentially dangerous as it was in the later Middle Ages, a family which could count on the efforts of all its members in its collective drive to succeed was much more likely to prevail over its rivals.[23] As John Carmi Parsons points out, 'marriage, motherhood, and kinship ... were indispensable to the family ... women thus retained claims to power and influence within the feudal family'.[24] In the late Middle Ages a noble home is not the Victorian 'haven in a heartless world' but a kind of command post in the constant struggle for familial aggrandisement.

Like Edwards and Davenport in their readings of the poem, I have constantly referred to violence as a problem to be 'solved' by the happy ending. However, this reading is both too simple and anachronistic, since those in the upper ranks saw violence as a legitimate tool for defending their honour, and the law and social practice enabled them to do so in a way we would find intolerable.[25] Degrevant's actions are never directly critiqued. As Philippa Maddern says, 'the violent and destructive activities of fifteenth-century knights were thus surrounded by so great a cloud of laudatory adjectives – worthy, worshipful, manly, doughty, invincible, fierce – that no disapproval could touch them'.[26] What makes Degrevant's role as landholder different from his role as crusader is that the earl is not a pagan, a distant enemy, a usurper – he is a neighbour. Nonetheless, even among neighbours, violence is 'one option available to county families in their constant pursuit of land, status and power'.[27] Even intimate relations are not exempt. Mertes refers to marriage and the family as 'calculated battlegrounds', a formulation painfully represented in the story of poor Margery Paston, who chose to marry the family bailiff and was beaten and repudiated by her family at her mother's instigation.[28] We need to understand the way violence appears culturally normal, inseparable from the highest chivalric ideals which make Degrevant so appealing a hero, for Melidor, the audience at the tournament, and lay members of late medieval society.[29] Since the earl cannot be dislodged, Degrevant must turn to the feud as a way of settling disputes, combining defence of his property and dependants with forced negotiations, in the guise of chivalric heroism.

Against this reading of incessant social strife in the action of the narrative, I want to juxtapose a complementary reading of stability, tradition and public power embedded in its descriptive elements. Here I would like to focus on the class and gender implications of its particular materiality, its noteworthy attention to the trappings of wealth and status as both economic and symbolic capital. In a poem of fewer than 2,000 lines, over 200 by my count are devoted to extended representations of possessions. The concerns of a social order based on adherence to law and protection of property are associated with Degrevant. He is a peculiar mix of romance hero and prudent land-owner. On the one hand he is a crusader and a member of the Round Table, compared to Gawain and Perceval in prestige, Arthur's nephew. He triumphs in battle and tournament, a figure aligned with courtly (and even aristocratic) romance. What Melidor sees is a figure who 'with gold and aȝour ful schen / ... / Was ioy to be-hold' (470–2). At first Degrevant appears to belong to a literary tradition which exists in many places and no particular place at all. As the tale progresses we see a somewhat different figure, a prudent landowner, whose wealth comes from carefully guarded possessions – his parks and woods, his rivers, his game, his towns, his tenants and their farms, all precisely enumerated:

> Ther was sesyd in hys hand
> A þousand poundus worth off land
> Off rentes well settand,
> And muchell dell more;
> An houndered plows in demaynus,
> Fayer parkes in-wyth haynus,
> Grett herdus in þe playnus,
> Wyth muchell tame store;
> Castelos wyth heygh wallus,
> Chambors wyth noble hallus,
> Fayer stedes in the stallus,
> Lyard and soore. (65–76)

This hero is rooted in a particular social landscape and set of material practices. We are given the details of his stewardship when the poet describes how he rebuilds what the Earl has destroyed, re-enclosing parks, loaning seed, oxen, wagons and horses to his dependants (145–50). His first instinct seems to be to conserve and to 'werke be lawe' (151). In the poem's lovingly itemised enumeration of the possessions which define a noble life, it is the deer park, however, rather than cattle and serfs, which is most suffused with meaning, representing what I have called the nexus of symbolic and actual capital. We are told, in more detail than we are told about his activities as a knight of the Round Table, that hunting is Degrevant's greatest pleasure, and the park is the terrain in which the he and the Earl contest for supremacy. As Christopher Dyer notes,

> game symbolised the aristocratic style of life. It was nurtured in private parks or protected in forests and chases. The fences that separated the game from the non-aristocrats, like moats, castle walls and monastic precincts, gave physical expression to social barriers. Hunting parties provided the aristocracy with their principal diversion, and they accompanied the chase with rituals and ceremonies. If the cost of game is counted in terms of the expense of fencing parks, the loss of rent from land of potential agricultural use, and the labour expended in its capture, every piece of venison would have been very valuable indeed.[30]

In English history, from the forest laws of the Plantagenets on, the right to hunt was inextricably linked to the power to prevent others from hunting. The Earl's literal overriding of Degrevant's rights to an aristocratic way of life is a denial of law, and of a chivalric ideal:

> He hade a grete spyt of þe knyght
> That was so hardy and wyght,
> And thought howe he best myght
> That dowghty to grade. (101–4)

The Earl's unmotivated disdain for his neighbour, his aggressive contempt, seems to identify social rigidity, the aristocratic desire to maintain social exclusivity, with social destructiveness. 'To grade' means to put down from high rank, demote, depose, humble, according to the *Middle English Dictionary*.[31] The deer park, rather than the castle, is the field on which competing claims are fought out. One might argue that what separates the Earl from Degrevant is not class, but rank. He is not a landless knight who needs a wealthy marriage, since we are told both that he is rich in his own right, and that he wants no dowry with Melidor, preferring 'hyr body all bare' (571–6), by which he obviously means stripped of the trappings of wealth.

Degrevant's noble character makes him an ideal match for the Earl's daughter, despite his lack of title. His exemplary qualities as knight and landowner seem then to identify social investment – the literal and figurative care of land and tenants – with his worthiness to rise in status. In the figure of Degrevant we can see a rewriting of nobility in ways which value individual worth, a term with both economic and social implications, as well as birth. In many romances the apparently lower-ranking suitor – *Havelok, William of Palerne* – turns out to be of equal or higher rank. However, Degrevant's lower rank is no impediment either to the poet or to those who celebrate the wedding at the end. When Melidor chooses Degrevant, she validates the aspirations of a landholding elite which defined itself as 'gentle', and hoped to be able to advance through marriage. He is a chivalric hero, who is aggressive in his own defence, but does not share the Earl's destructive appropriation of the wealth of those under him, his contempt for their rights. Degrevant, of course, gets to marry up, because he is represented as 'just as good as' if not better than the Earl, not in alternate, but in the same ways. Both Dyer and Mertes argue that, for the late Middle Ages, despite an overwhelming concern with rank and birth, in cultural and ideological terms, gentle, noble, and aristocratic are roughly equivalent labels.[32] In *Degrevant*, as in the *Wife of Bath's Tale*, true gentilesse is pitted against the snobbery of a titled class, which has to open up to those worthy of it, but is not transformed in its fundamental values.

Melidor, as a dependent female, does not of course have investment capital of her own, but as her father's daughter she is a conduit to his estates, and she is loaded with symbolic capital. She is not the 'body all bare' Degrevant claims to be the object of his desire (574), but a body that bears all the signs of her family's rank and status. At first sight merely 'jentell and small' (419) she becomes at next sight 'comlech y-clade', and accompanied by 'to ryche banrettes' (473–4), knights of the same rank as Degrevant. When he actually meets with her in the orchard, her body is armored with clothing which delights Degrevant without being sexually enticing, since it never hints at the nakedness beneath. For two stanzas the poet emphasises the wealth and fashion of her attire:

> Sche come in a vyolet
> With whyȝth perl ouerfret,
> And saphyrus þerinne i-sett
> On eueryche a syde;
> All of pall-work fyn
> With nouche and nevyn,
> Anurled with ermyn,
> And ouert for pryde.
> To tell hur botenus was toor,
> Anamelede with aȝour;
> With topyes hur trechour

Ouertrasyd þat tyde.
Sche was receuyd a spanne
Of any lyuand manne;
Off rede golde þe rybanne
    Glemyd hur gyde. (641–56)

Structurally, this passage is very similar to the one which describes Degrevant's coat-of-arms (1045–56), or the scene cited above (465–72) in which Melidor first watches him from the walls. In these descriptions clothes identify the wearer to an observant world, and the symmetry of the descriptions suggests that neither for men nor women is there an identity – an embodied self – distinct from the social self.[33]

More famous than her clothes, although equally significant of her family's wealth and power, is her chamber, which is described at enormous length. (William Morris apparently painted scenes from the romance on the walls of the 'House Beautiful' in Kent.)[34] For five full stanzas the poem describes the architecture and decoration of this 'chamber of love'. L. F. Casson calls this description ambitious, but a failure: it is meant to be a Bower of Bliss, but the details seem jumbled and unlikely to 'stupefy the … senses'.[35] Davenport, on the other hand, finds it 'the stuff of fantasy and dream, the emotional high point of the poem … Here the indoor world of the castle has its fullest realisation; Degrevant has penetrated to the heart of the castle; he has successfully moved from outside the walls, into the orchard, the hall, and now the private chamber, which proves to be an Aladdin's cave of wealth, art and history as well as a chapel of Venus.'[36] A close reading of the actual text makes it hard to agree with such judgements, without accepting the literary and gender assumptions upon which they are based. As I have already argued, women's sphere in the great households might have been distinct, but it did not represent an alternative set of values. Looking at the details without the preconception that they must represent, as Edwards says, 'the inner world of love and civilisation … the world of the feminine,' can make us understand the description differently. What follows gives some sense of the exuberance of the poet's description of what the chamber contains:

Þer was a ryal rooffe
In þe chaumbur of loffe;
Hyt was buskyd a-boue
    With besauntus ful bryȝth;
…

Endentyd and dyȝth;
Þer men myȝth se, ho þat wolde,
Arcangelus of rede golde,
Fyfty mad of o molde,
    Lowynge ful lyȝth;
With þe Pocalyps of Jon,
Þe Powlus Pystolus euerychon,
Þe Parabolus of Salamon. (1441–55)

This is hardly the intimate space associated with the bedchambers of romance, where Lancelot and Guenevere, Floris and Blanchefleur, Troilus and Criseyde, find erotic joy. Although Melidor's bed has silken sheets and is decorated with the story of Ydoine and Amadace, 'þe kyngus owun banere' on the tester is a potent reminder of what she represents (1501–2). In real life even the pope had birds and flowers in his bedchamber at Avignon, not saints or theologians or political symbols. There is a long tradition of detailed description of building decoration in medieval literature and various models have been suggested for this remarkable scheme. Davenport looks at both the well-known wall paintings at Longthorpe Tower, French and English romances, and allegorical court poetry, without finding any particular source. However, the wall paintings or statues in French romances or Chaucer's dream visions act to reinforce the text's themes – the story of Dido and Aeneas, statues of Venus, scenes from the *Romance of the Rose* – in a way which does not seem to happen here. The details are too abstract and confused to allow for an iconographic analysis, but it is clear that they have nothing to do with stories of lovers, nor do they have any particular female associations – no Mary, no female saints, just unrelieved patriarchy.

I would like to suggest two other models, both of which seem to me to offer a better reading of what is actually in the poem, rather than what we expect of women's chambers. The first is the bedchamber of the Countess Adela de Blois, daughter of William the Conqueror, as described by Baudri de Bourgueil, in a panegyric addressed to her. According to Baudri, who admits that he might be exaggerating for the sake of praise, she has a mappemounde, tapestries with scenes from the bible and pagan mythology, and one showing her father's conquest of England, bedposts with figures of philosophy and the seven liberal arts – in short, the possessions of her father's daughter. Historians have primarily been interested in Baudri's poem because the extensively described tapestry of William's English invasion might be the earliest reference to the Bayeux tapestry, but for us it is of interest because the room's furnishings are meant to demonstrate Adela's learning, her religious virtues and connection to her father.[37] Although the details are different from those in the English text, the effect is the same — a space which is a public announcement of the inhabitant's status as female heir.

The other model I want to suggest is the great architectural and artistic works associated with Westminster, which in the second half of the fourteenth century benefited from royal and ecclesiastical interest in building and decoration.[38] Edith Rickert mentions as evidence of the splendid art of the period the hammerbeam roof and carved and painted angels of Westminster Hall which offers a possible inspiration for the elaborate ceiling of Melidor's room, with its fifty archangels.[39] Another possible inspiration was the king's 'Painted Chamber', which was both bedroom and state apartment. The Chapel of St Stephen, like Melidor's chamber, had elaborate paintings and stained glass windows. The most striking analogue to the details listed in the romance, however, can be found in the chapter house at Westminster, which contained a series of depictions of the Apocalypse. My study of Kathleen Scott's index of British manuscript images reveals no comparable combination of subjects elsewhere, nor does A. Caiger-Smith's catalogue of surviving English wall paintings.[40] According to Rickert, these pictures, which constitute the best-known paintings of the Apocalypse in England, are unique in being accompanied by text.[41] In Melidor's chamber the Epistles of Paul and the parables of Solomon may exist as text rather than image — the wording is ambiguous. The Chapter House would have been well known since parliament met there in the fourteenth century.[42] Its paintings, arranged in five arcades, are crammed with details, just like the chamber. Each scene is divided into smaller units, packed with figures, including symbols of the evangelists, and heads of angels in the corners, although it would take a miniaturist and a larger building to include the nine worthies and the story of Absalon and the four doctors and the philosophers which the poet enumerates.

These two models suggest that in fact the division between public and private which the chamber is taken to represent, like the division between male and female audiences, is a misleading opposition. There are certainly romances, such as *Troilus and Criseyde* or *Gawain and the Green Knight*, where the lovers meet in a secluded and sexually charged space. However, Melidor meets her suitor in a room in which the private — the conversation of the lovers — and the public — the cultural heritage represented by the art and artefacts — are interwoven. This interpenetration of spheres is not an anomaly, in a world filled with servants, where queens received petitioners in their bedchambers, where ladies gathered with their attendants to read, sew, converse and take care of household and religious business and where receiving visitors was part of the duty of the nobility.[43] Because the economic and social work of the household takes place in chambers as well as halls, the medieval bedchamber can never be assumed to be private or intimate – the so-called 'inner world of the feminine' – in the ways that we understand the modern bedroom to be. In the provocatively titled, 'In Bed with Joan of Kent', W. M. Ormrod discusses the 'spatial politics' of noble women's bedchambers, arguing that they must inevitably carry connotations beyond the personal.[44]

So far in my essay I have focused on the material and symbolic context in which the action of the romance is immersed. I want to conclude by looking briefly at the two manuscripts in which the romance is found, each representing very distinctive tastes. These two very different collections show that the romance appealed to different audiences, crossing the boundaries of gender and position. The claim that this work is a legitimate representation of female desire is justified by its appearance in the famous Findern Manuscript (Cambridge University Ff.1.6), a fifteenth-century collection of courtly poetry associated with the North-East Midlands family of the Finderns, a gentry family with aristocratic connections.[45] This is just the sort of household that might have been attracted to a story about social triumph through marriage. Over a long period of time the family and their friends assembled poetry by Chaucer, Lydgate, Gower and others written in a courtly style and concerned with sentiment, especially love. The manuscript shows a remarkable consistency of taste, and a number of amateur hands, suggesting a very personal connection between owners and contents. Because of the presence of women's names at various points in the manuscript, some scholars have gone so far as to argue that some of the poems, including *Degrevant*, the only romance in the collection, were copied by female scribes. Although not everyone would agree that Elisabet Koton and Elisabet frauncys, whose names appear at the end of the romance, were its actual copyists, it is fair to say that women were among its eager readers and enjoyed its endorsement of its heroine's determination to get her own way in love.[46] Of course, it would also be fair to title a study of this romance 'What Men Want' since the only other place it appears is in an even better-known collection, the Thornton manuscript (Lincoln Cathedral 91), an important anthology of romances compiled by Robert Thornton, also a member of a gentry family, around 1440.[47] His more eclectic collection of romances and saints' lives includes among other works the only copy of the decidedly unsentimental *Alliterative Morte Arthure*, *The Erl of Tolous*, *Sir Perceval*, *Octavian* and *Isumbras*, works which can be seen as articulating more conventionally moral and patriarchal values than *Degrevant*. Its presence in two such different but equally individual sets of texts has interesting implications for a study of romance's ability as a genre to appeal simultaneously to multiple audiences. Men and women, sharing the same culture and the same households, might equally enjoy the story. Men identifying with the heroic Degrevant and women with the intrepid Melidor would both be participating imaginatively in the world of display and power of the great landholding magnates. Melidor's extravagant possessions remind us that women's identity can not be separated from their class position, as the romance amply demonstrates. What she desires is what makes her desirable – Degrevant is a suitable consort for the space which surrounds her, just as she guarantees his right to his deer. Together they will form the nucleus of the ideal household – one earned by chivalric violence and female will.

Notes

1   The best edition is *The Romance of Sir Degrevant: A Parallel-Text Edition from MSS. Lincoln Cathedral A. 5. 2 and Cambridge University Ff. I. 6*, ed. L. F. Casson, EETS o.s. 221 (London, 1949). All citations will be from the Cambridge text, which is the most complete.

2   W. A. Davenport, 'Sir Degrevant and composite romance', in Judith Weiss, Jennifer Fellows, Morgan Dickson (eds), *Medieval Insular Romance* (Cambridge, 2000), pp. 111–31 (p. 114).

3   Kate Mertes, *The English Noble Household: 1250–1600* (Oxford, 1988). See also her article, 'Aristocracy', in Rosemary Horrox (ed.), *Fifteenth Century Attitudes* (Cambridge, 1994), pp. 42–60.

4   'The late Middle Ages has, with much justification, been described as "the age of the household" and peculiarly of the noble household', according to Felicity Heal, nor is she alone in that judgement. See her 'Reciprocity and exchange in the late medieval household', in Barbara Hanawalt and David Wallace (eds), *Bodies and Disciplines* (Minneapolis, 1996), pp. 179–98 (p. 179). David Starkey says, 'In the later Middle Ages household and family were (to an extent inconceivable today) the central institution of society': 'The age of the household: politics, society and the arts c. 1350–c. 1550', in Stephen Medcalf (ed.), *The Later Middle Ages* (New York, 1981), pp. 225–90 (p. 225).

5   Mertes, *The English Noble Household*, p. 184.

6   See, for example, Christopher Dyer, *Standards of Living in the Later Middle*

Ages (Cambridge, 1989), pp. 50, 90, 108. Dyer routinely includes marriage as an economic activity, as do Mertes, Starkey and Heal.

7 Two articles in Constance M. Rousseau and Joel T. Rosenthal (eds), *Women, Marriage, and Family in Medieval Christendom*, Studies in Medieval Culture 37 (Kalamazoo, 1998) deal with the tension between individual choice and family control in the making of English marriages: Jacqueline Murray, 'Individualism and consensual marriage: some evidence from medieval England' (pp. 121–51), and Shannon McSheffrey, '"I will never have none ayenst my faders will": consent and the making of marriage in the late medieval diocese of London' (pp. 153–74).

8 Dyer, *Standards of Living*, p. 47.

9 Davenport, '*Degrevant* and composite romance', shows in the course of his discussion how many traditions and texts this romance draws upon. See also *Sir Degrevant*, ed. Casson, pp. lxii–lxxii, and Laura Hibbard, *Mediaeval Romance in England* (1924, rept. New York 1963), pp. 306–11, for a discussion of sources and analogues.

10 A. S. G. Edwards, 'Gender, order and reconciliation in *Sir Degrevant*', in Carol M. Meale (ed.), *Readings in Medieval English Romance* (Cambridge, 1994), pp. 53–64.

11 Edwards, 'Gender, order and reconciliation', p. 56.

12 Jennifer Ward, *English Noblewomen in the Later Middle Ages* (London, 1992) and (ed.), *Women of the English Nobility and Gentry* (Manchester, 1995), a collection of documents. These contain the most extensive study of English women of the upper classes. Karen Jambeck, 'Patterns of women's literary patronage: England, 1200–ca. 1475', in June Hall McCash (ed.), *The Cultural Patronage of Medieval Women* (Athens, GA, 1996), pp. 228–65.

13 See Heal, 'Reciprocity and exchange', p. 180 and Mertes, 'Aristocracy', p. 48.

14 Heal, 'Reciprocity and exchange', p. 192.

15 Maurice Keen calls tournaments 'a powerful force towards generalising both the standards and the rituals of European chivalry'. *Chivalry* (New Haven, 1984), p. 83; he devotes an entire chapter to the tournament.

16 *Sir Degrevant*, ed. Casson, p. lxxv.

17 Mertes, 'Aristocracy', p. 45.

18 Ward, *English Noblewomen*, p. 15.

19 May McKisack, *The Fourteenth Century* (Oxford, 1959), pp. 259–60.

20 Jennifer Ward discusses the ways in which noble families sought to maintain their lineage, through inheritance and marriage, in 'Noblewomen, family and identity in later medieval Europe', in Anne J. Duggan (ed.), *Nobles and Nobility in Medieval Europe* (Woodbridge, 2000), pp. 245–62.

21 *Paston Letters*, ed. and selected by Norman Davis (Oxford, 1958).

22 *Ibid.*, p. 9.

23 Mertes, 'Aristocracy', pp. 45–7.

24 John Carmi Parsons, 'Introduction: family, sex, and power', in John Carmi Parsons (ed.), *Medieval Queenship* (New York, 1993), pp. 1–22 (p. 3).

25 Richard Kaeuper, *Chivalry and Violence in Medieval Europe* (Oxford, 1999), p. 28.

26 Philippa Maddern, *Violence and Social Order* (Oxford, 1992), p. 78.

27 *Ibid.*, p. 18.

28 Mertes, 'Aristocracy', p. 45; *Paston Letters*, ed. Davis, pp. 74–6.

29 Maddern, *Violence and Social Order*, p. 12.

30 Dyer, *Standards of Living*, p. 61.

31 *MED*, grade, v. 2.

32 Dyer, *Standards of Living*, p. 47; Mertes, 'Aristocracy', p. 44.

33 Nicola McDonald points out how 'bright women who shine, like costly treasures, incite the adventure-lust of ambitious men': '*The Seege of Troye*: "[f]for wham was wakened al this wo"?', in Ad Putter and Jane Gilbert (eds), *The Spirit of Medieval English Popular Romance* (London, 2000), pp. 181–99 (p. 195). In *Degrevant* both men and women are desired for their ornamented beauty. See also Susan Crane, *The Performance of the Self: Ritual, Clothing, and Identity during the Hundred Years War* (Philadelphia, 2002).

34 Hibbard, *Medieval Romance*, p. 308.

35 *Sir Degrevant*, ed. Casson, p. lxxiv.

36 Davenport, '*Degrevant* and composite romance', pp. 124–5.

37 Shirley Ann Brown and Michael Herren, 'The *Adelae Comitissae* of Baudri of Bourgueil and the Bayeux Tapestry', in Richard Gameson (ed.), *The Study of the Bayeux Tapestry* (Woodbridge, 1997), pp. 139–55 (p. 153). I am indebted to Jocelyn Wogan-Browne for pointing out this parallel.

38 Edith Rickert, *Painting in Britain: The Middle Ages* (Harmondsworth, 1954), pp. 147–51.

39 *Ibid.*, p. 147.

40 Kathleen Scott, *Later Gothic Manuscripts*, 2 vols (London, 1996), vol. 2; A. Caiger-Smith, *English Medieval Mural Paintings* (Oxford, 1963).

41 Rickert, *Painting in Britain*, pp. 162–3.

42 Caroline Babington, Tracy Manning and Sophie Stewart, *Our Painted Past* (London, 1999), p. 30. McKisack lists the wide range of those invited to attend parliament in the later Middle Ages: 'lords spiritual and temporal, certain councillors and officials, proctors for the clergy, and representatives of shires, cities, and boroughs': *The Fourteenth Century*, p. 182.

43 Ward, *English Noblewomen*, pp. 71–3; Parsons, 'Introduction', p. 10.

44 W. M. Ormrod, 'In bed with Joan of Kent', in Jocelyn Wogan-Browne *et al.* (eds), *Medieval Women: Texts and Contexts* (Turnhout, 2000), pp. 277–92. See also, in the same volume, Colin Richmond, 'Elizabeth Clere: Friend of the Pastons' (pp. 251–73), which is a detailed study of the ways in which 'business' is taken care of during women's talk.

45 Rossell Hope Robbins, 'The Findern anthology', *PMLA*, 69 (1954), 610–42, and Sarah McNamer, 'Female authors, provincial setting: the reversing of courtly love in the Findern manuscript', *Viator*, 22 (1991), 279–310. Davenport also notes the association of the Findern manuscript

and female interests, '*Degrevant* and composite romance', pp. 112–13.

46 John J. Thompson, 'Collecting Middle English romances and some related book-production activities in the later Middle Ages', in Maldwyn Mills, Jennifer Fellows and Carol M. Meale (eds), *Romance in Medieval England* (Woodbridge, 1991), pp. 17–38 (p. 34).

47 *Ibid.*, p. 19.

5

Putting the pulp into fiction: the lump-child and its parents in *The King of Tars*

Jane Gilbert

The central figure of the Middle English popular romance known as *The King of Tars* (hereafter *KT*) – a formless lump of flesh born instead of a child – defines a certain view of popular literature. The birth is an outrageously sensationalist event; the ideological message conveyed by its subsequent transformation into a human being through baptism is simplistic, vulgar and racist. By its unfinished aspect, moreover, the formless lump parallels the work's rudimentary and unsophisticated poetic quality. And yet, the lump is a powerful image, which repels and fascinates by its very crudity. In a manner characteristic of popular art, it exceeds the limitations of the work which presents it, while attempts to reduce it to a merely aesthetic or rational object fail to capture its quiddity.

It is around this central void of the interpretation-defying thing, however, that the ideological and literary systems of individual versions of the story are organised; and these systems demand analysis. This essay concentrates on the treatment of the lump in order to show how its treatment throws into relief the different configurations of paternity and maternity, of gender roles and of religious politics put forward in a range of re-tellings. Three kinds of critical analysis are put forward, progressively narrowing the focus of study. Building on Lillian Herlands Hornstein's impressive scholarship, I begin by study-ing analogues of *KT* drawn from medieval chronicles; these analogues allow an appreciation of features shared by the different narratives. The second section turns to the Auchinleck text of *KT*. Here my argument will be constructed around two sorts of theory equally concerned with problems of order: medieval physiology and Lacanian psychoanalysis. Integrating historical conceptualisation with modern conceptualisa-tion deepens both, for it allows the historical specificities of the texts under discussion and of the discussion itself to emerge more sharply. Finally, important ideological issues are clarified through detailed textual comparison of the Auchinleck text with the Vernon, another of the three surviving redactions of the poem.[1]

The plot of *KT* relates how the Sultan of Damascus falls in love by hearsay with the daughter of the Christian King of Tars.[2] Initially the Princess rejects him, but after the Christian army is routed she relents to spare her people further suffering, and pleads with her father to allow the match. Once at his court, she discovers that the Sultan will not marry her until she adopts his religion; this she outwardly does, although in her heart she keeps faith with Christ. When in due course she bears a child, it is a formless lump of flesh, without life or limb:

> & when þe child was ybore
> Wel sori wimen were þerfore,
> > For lim no hadde it non.
> Bot as a rond of flesche yschore
> In chaumber it lay hem bifore
> > Wiþouten blod & bon.
> For sorwe þe leuedi wald dye
> For it hadde noiþer nose no eye,
> > Bot lay ded as þe ston.
> Þe soudan com to chaumber þat tide,
> & wiþ his wiif he gan to chide
> > Þat wo was hir bigon.[3]

Attributing this misfortune to his wife's insincere conversion, the Sultan takes the lump to his temple and prays to his 'goddes' (625) to give it human form, but to no avail. He destroys the idols and returns the lump to the Princess, who proposes that the whole episode be treated as a duel of faiths: both husband and wife will embrace whichever god can transform the lump. The Princess summons a Christian priest from her husband's dungeons to christen the lump, whereupon it instantly becomes a beautiful boy. Overwhelmed, the Sultan has himself christened, occasioning a further miracle:

> His hide, þat blac & loþely was,
> Al white bicom, þurth Godes gras,
> > & clere wiþouten blame. (928–30)

The Sultan calls on his Christian father-in-law to help him convert his people and a battle against heathen lords ensues. The Auchinleck manuscript text breaks off in what look like the concluding moments of this battle, with the triumph of Christianity and the conversion or massacre of the Saracen prisoners; the ending of manuscripts Vernon and Simeon will be discussed below.

Most of the medieval analogues discussed by Lillian Herlands Hornstein, the principal authority on this subject, derive from chronicles recounting the conversion to Christianity of the heathen Cassanus, king of the Tartars. This conversion is brought about by the birth to Cassanus and a Christian woman of a monstrous child miraculously transformed into a beautiful boy through baptism. Its result is, according to the version, either a Tartar victory over the Sultan of Damascus and a possible Christian reconquest of Jerusalem, or the mass conversion of the Tartars.[4] Some of these analogues have the child born half-animal and half-human, others half-hairy and half-smooth or completely hairy: 'hispidus et pilosus, velut ursus'[5] (hairy and shaggy, like a bear). The analogy is echoed in one of the versions in which the child is a formless lump:

> Accidit ut regina die sancti [Francisci] primum ederet partum, pudibundum regno magis quam jucundum, ursi non viri praeferens pignus, utpote frustum informe carnis, non filium.[6]

> [It happened that on St Francis's day the queen gave birth to her first child, more to the kingdom's shame than to its rejoicing, bringing forth the child of a bear not a man, rather a formless piece of flesh than a son.]

Bear-cubs in bestiary and Physiologus tradition are said to be born small lumps of eyeless white flesh which their mothers gradually shape by licking and animate by breathing life into them.[7] In the majority of these analogues, therefore, the child can be understood to be semi-bestial. This semi-bestiality is open to different interpretations. In a number of cases the father fails to recognise his own son and accuses the mother of adultery.[8] The outcome implies, however, that the child's illegitimate form symbolises the interfaith marriage from which it arises. Moreover, the child's animal side suggests a sub-human aspect to its father. This is accentuated in *KT*, where both narrator and characters repeatedly compare the Sultan and his men to animals. To cite only one of many examples: when his messengers claim that the

King has described him as a 'heþen hounde' (93) the Sultan rages like a 'wilde bore' (98) and a 'lyoun' (105), thus ironically exceeding the designation to which he objects. If this understanding is valid, the monstrosity of the lump-child is directly inherited from its heathen father in a process comparable to what today would be called genetic inheritance. The same thinking probably lies behind those of Hornstein's analogues which make the child black on its left and white on its right side. These resonate with the racial theme of *KT*, in which the Princess is 'white as feþer of swan' (12) and the Sultan before his transformation 'blac & loþely' (928). However, neither of those two analogues discussed by Hornstein which have a parti-coloured child refers to colour difference between the parents; the argument seems instead to be religious, for the public event explained by the private miracle in these versions is the Tartar king's request to the Pope for religious teachers and the consequent mission of two friars, rather than the military crusade to liberate the Holy Land favoured by most other versions.[9] In the chronicle analogues, the child's physical imperfection is the symbol and embodiment of its father's spiritual irregularity, the fleshly revelation of his inferior religious status. Before their christening, father and son are deemed sub-human to the degree that each represents only the crude form of a human being, lacking that spiritual dimension which properly distinguishes humans from the other animals. Baptism refines the animal-heathen substance to create a superior being – hairless, white, fully human.

Where the analogues present the lump primarily as its father's child, the Auchinleck text of *KT* draws on Aristotelian conception theory, in which the mother contributes only the basic matter, the material, fleshly substance, from which the child will be made. *Mater* (mother), as we are often reminded, was thought in the Middle Ages to be derived etymologically from *materia* (matter).[10] The father, through his seed, supplies the 'life or spirit or form', that vital principle which transforms the matter into a human child and animates it.[11] As the Princess knows, it is this second element that the lump lacks:

> Ʒif it were cristned ariʒt
> It schuld haue fourme to se bi siʒt
> Wiþ lim & liif to wake. (760–2)

Fourme here has its technical sense. Shapeless, lifeless chunk of flesh, the lump-child is a fictional approximation to Aristotelian matter, the result of a conception in which the paternal role has failed. While the

Sultan's biological parenthood is admitted, the lump's inhumanity is not, as in the analogues, its father's contribution, the direct transmission of his paganism; here there is simply no paternal input at all. The particular monstrosity of the lump in *KT* results from the fact that it is exclusively its mother's child. The wider ideological implications of this paternal failure are clear in the scene in which the Sultan begs his gods to give the lump human shape:

> & when he hadde al ypreyd,
> & alle þat euer he couþe he seyd,
> Þe flesche lay stille as ston. (637–9)

Stille as ston, a repeated phrase, links the lump's insensibility to that of the idols which will fail either to heed the Sultan's prayer or to feel the blows by which he renders them as formless and limbless as his child (659).[12] Lump and idols are equally deficient in being confined to the material world, which is also the maternal world. The crude stuff of incomplete humanity is denoted moreover by the term *þe flesche*, used consistently to describe the lump before its transformation. Historians argue for a conceptual distinction in the Middle Ages between body and flesh, the former a symbolically ordered entity allied with the soul but the latter vulnerable and excessive.[13] Body was gendered masculine, flesh feminine.[14] These terms are helpful in considering *KT*, where the lump begins as maternal, feminine flesh and ends as paternal, masculine body; the transition occurring at the moment when the child passes by baptism from the domain of the mother, herself a Christian but, paradoxically, associated figuratively with unredeemed heathendom, to enter the Christian order.

Aristotle's view of the father as giver of the form that shapes matter is paralleled by Lacan's description of the paternal function as the imposition of order on the chaos of nature (by this means the father symbolises the differential structure of the Law). Whereas Aristotle's focus is on the insufficiencies of the mother, however, Lacan's is on those of the father; moreover, Aristotle grounds his discussions of paternity and maternity in biology (thus providing them with the ideological camouflage afforded by an association with 'nature'), while Lacan emphasises the political dimensions of both. Lacan's writings of the early and mid 1950s, in particular, provide an analytical tool for understanding the complex construction of and the anxieties about paternity which ring through these medieval texts.[15] Like many medieval works, they pose the question which, according to Lacan, is the great question of

Freudian psychoanalysis: 'what does it mean to be a father?'[16] For Lacan, the distinctive paternal task is above all a matter of rendering humans distinct from animals, especially by regulating sexuality:

> The primordial Law is ... that which in regulating marriage ties superimposes the kingdom of culture on that of a nature abandoned to the law of mating. The prohibition of incest is merely its subjective pivot, revealed by the modern tendency to reduce to the mother and the sister the objects forbidden to the subject's choice, although full licence outside of these is not yet entirely open.
>
> This law, then, is revealed clearly enough as identical with an order of language. For without kinship nominations, no power is capable of instituting the order of preferences and taboos that bind and weave the yarn of lineage through succeeding generations.[17]

The paternal function thus appears symbolically in two activities which distinguish human marriage practices from the unconstrained copulation of animals: the creation and enforcement, on the one hand of kin groups defined by the inscription of a lineage descending through the father, and on the other, of marriage rules forbidding certain relations between members of the various groups. Lacan proposes a characteristically punning mnemonic to delineate the intimate connection he sees between the two essential activities which define paternal authority: 'le nom du père' (the father's name) is also by homophony 'le non du père' (the father's no).

In *KT*, the Sultan's failure to father his child relates to precisely these two activities. Lacan's proposal to extend the regulation of marriage ties beyond the incest taboo (dear to structuralist anthropology) allows it to include the mixed-religion marriage that *KT* designates as unlawful:

> Wel loþe war a Cristen man
> To wedde an heþen woman
>   Þat leued on fals lawe;
> Als loþ was þat soudan
> To wed a Cristen woman,
>   As y finde in mi sawe. (409–14)

By resolving that his bride must convert before he will consummate their marriage, the heathen Sultan attempts to impose a sexual prohibition whose legitimacy is upheld by the text. However, he is deceived by her outward show of conversion and unwittingly breaks his own rule, thus aligning himself with what Lacan terms 'nature abandoned to the law of mating'. The Sultan's inability to impose the symbolic separation of the human from the natural domain is confirmed by the numerous comparisons of him and other Saracens to wild beasts (e.g. 93, 98, 105) and by the repeated derogatory references to his wild or near-insane behaviour (e.g. 196, 404). It seems that the desire to produce oneself and others as true human beings by adhering to the tenets of a symbolic law is common to all human creatures; but, according to the poem, only dupes believe that a 'heþen lawe' (504) can fulfil this symbolic function. The Christian God is the sole creator of human beings. Baptism installs this God as Father and enables the child to be born out of the maternal substance, which in itself is insufficiently differentiated from the animal domain.

Yet the child's baptism is not the end, for although it raises the child to human status, it does not permit the Sultan to impose a line of patrilineal descent. As the Princess tells him after the lump's transformation, this is not a question of biology; symbolic paternity can function only within Christianity:

> Þe soudan seyd, 'Leman min,
> Ywis ich am glad afin
>   Of þis child þat y se.'
> 'Ʒa, sir, bi seyn Martin,
> Ʒif þe haluendel wer þin
>   Wel glad miʒt þou be.'
> 'O dame,' he seyd, 'hou is þat?
> Is it nouʒt min þat y biʒat?'
> 'No sir,' þan seyd sche,
> 'Bot þou were cristned so it is
> Þou no hast no part þeron, ywis,
>   Noiþer of þe child ne of me.' (805–16)

The paternity lacking pertains not to the Sultan's acknowledged physical fatherhood but to his right to be named as the child's father. For a father to be so recognised in any society a whole range of cultural and institutional forces must be mobilised and criteria met. The single criterion highlighted in *KT*, however, is Christianity. Patrilineage, which Lacan claims to be a defining characteristic of encultured humanity, is not established with the baptism of the son but must wait until the father takes the plunge. As he does so, his skin colour turns from black to white, an expressive and racist image for his entry into the paternal order, here identified with the Christian regime and the colouring of northern Europeans. The Sultan's insertion into patriliny is confirmed as he gains not only a son but also a father: the King of Tars, his father-in-law (the relationship is more obviously symbolic for being divorced from the biological), with whom he promptly embarks on a crusade against his own people, and whose name and honour he may perhaps have inherited in the lost ending of the Auchinleck version.[18] Such a conclusion would match what we have seen in the text; the title borne by both men and by the poem itself, and which indicates a patrilineage stretching into past and future, would be a fictional approximation to what Lacan in slightly later work terms the Name-of-the-Father.

This latter concept builds on that of the (lower-case, unhyphenated) name of the father, discussed above, but adds a transcendental dimension typical of the development of Lacan's thinking from the later 1950s onwards: 'The attribution of procreation to the father can only be the effect of a pure signifier, of a recognition, not of a real father, but of what religion has taught us to refer to as the Name-of-the-Father.'[19] The Nom-du-Père points to a transcendental source for paternal authority, which source Lacan calls the symbolic Father. According to Lacan, no actual father can attain to the transcendent status of the symbolic Father; any individual will necessarily fall short of the ideal. Nevertheless, the human institution of paternity relies on the supposed existence of someone, somewhere, who can properly assume the role, and thus the symbolic Father provides an 'alibi éternel' on which all actual fathers depend.[20] The Auchinleck redaction of *KT* identifies the Christian God as the symbolic Father, making him the sole and all-powerful guarantor of paternity. Procreation cannot be attributed to the man who does not acknowledge this God as fatherhood's eternal alibi, and an individual father can only accede to the capacities and rights of paternity insofar as he is a channel for the Name-of-the-Christian-Father – which the Sultan before his conversion clearly is not. After the christening at which he takes the name of his priestly godfather, his former inadequacy is transformed into a capability which enhances the very name of father, as he imposes his authority in both the domestic and the political spheres.

According to Lacan, however, the claim by any named individual to exercise the paternal function fully could only be made within the order called the imaginary.[21] Lacan's repeated assertion that the position of the symbolic Father cannot be filled without losing the very symbolic status which is its essence highlights the political agenda served by *KT*'s identification of the Christian God with the transcendent Father. However, Lacan does allow that earthly fathers, denied the inaccessible, may perform limited paternal functions, albeit with varying degrees of inadequacy. But *KT* eschews problematic degrees of competence and unattainable symbolic essence in favour of an uncompromising choice between accessible states of respectively, exclusion from and glorious fulfilment of the paternal role. In *KT*'s stark schema the lump-child represents not some naive popular belief that certain historical peoples could literally not procreate, but the ideological contention that non-Christians are incapable of exercising the paternal function. And without symbolic paternity human beings cannot reproduce, in the sense that they cannot pass on the cultural qualities that distinguish people from animals. Therefore *KT*, like the analogues, makes the father responsible for the child's monstrosity. Whereas in those versions his heathen presence imprinted itself as physical irregularity, in the Middle English romance his religion is interpreted as a symbolic absence which leaves his child fatherless, unable to take the crucial step from maternal flesh to paternal body.

A possible objection to this argument is that paternal failure is not restricted to the heathen Sultan. The Christian King of Tars also fails to impose sexual prohibition and patrilineal filiation, since he cannot prevent the marriage between his daughter and the Sultan. His military defeat and the slaughter of his army confirm his impotence in the face of the Sultan's inhuman onslaught. White Christians are identified as bearers of the entire paternal function only after the redemption of the potentially lost soul has made fully manifest the power of the Christian God, and this delay emphasises the dependence of their potency on his. Initially, however, the Christian father shows the same inadequacy as will the heathen.

This inadequacy has a doctrinal function, for into the breach steps the Princess. The text's exemplar of humility and Christian fortitude, the Princess plays a crucial mediating role as the material and moral means by which Christ gains entry into the earthly world of the narrative. Overwhelmed with 'sorwe & wo' (265) at the spectacle of so many deaths, she affirms her innocence of the blood spilt for her by taking charge of the situation in the only way open to her, and persuades her parents to allow her to marry the Sultan. This is the first of three pivotal acts, individually necessary but only together securing the final release from heathendom in a consummation which will unite father, son and mother under the sign of Christian paternity. The second redeems the son, and here too the Princess is a key figure. She it is who has borne the lump-child, she who now directs the Christian priest:

> For þurth þine help in þis stounde
> We schul make Cristen men of houndes.
> God graunt it ʒif it be his wille. (742–4)[22]

The third act is the Sultan's conversion, achieved after the Princess withholds paternal status from him until baptism, in the speech quoted earlier. The Princess's role in ushering in the Christian-paternal order recalls that of the Virgin Mary, and this connection enhances our understanding of the *flesche* associated with her. From the thirteenth century onwards, medieval theology and piety concentrated increasingly on Christ's carnal nature rather than on his divinity. Christ's humanity itself became sacred, and depended centrally on his physical existence. According to Bynum, the focus of piety was not only Christ's body, but his 'fertile and vulnerable' flesh and blood.[23] This flesh and blood, already associated metonymically and metaphorically with femininity, were considered to derive from his only human parent, herself the product of the Immaculate Conception. A double revaluation thus took place. The flesh acquired a value different from that which it was often accorded in earlier Christianity; no longer interpretable only as the home of sin and decay, it was also the stuff of Christ's Incarnation. The Virgin Mary too gained new importance both as a human and as a mother. Her maternity, if not her womanhood, revered as the source of Christ's sacred humanity, she was lauded as a necessary though not sufficient condition of the salvation Christ offers. Her role was considered analogous to that of a priest, for it was she who first brought Christ's flesh and blood to the congregation; in *KT*, the Princess brings in the priest who will officiate over the conversion of the heathen.[24] This conversion not only extends the Christian faith, but brings paternal potency into the text, empowering both King and Sultan. Where the father is lacking, it is the mother who introduces the paternal regime.

A central agent of the Christian-paternal order, the Princess is still allotted a limited role in that order as provider of raw human material, waiting on intervention by God and a Christian husband. So much is orthodox. However, she is not wholly absorbed into the cultural model of the Virgin Mary. The lump she produces presents a graphic image of what her maternity would be if it could exist outside the symbolic order; its compelling and repellent qualities are those she would own if not under paternal control. Unacceptable at both the personal and the cultural levels, it is figuratively associated with a heathenism conceived as absence from the divine Father. Maternal *flesche* is in this narrative not only the necessary support of the symbolic body but also dramatically other to it. Despite the Princess's centrality, her Christian faith and her energetic and submissive service, an elemental quality she owns as a mother remains alien to the Christian-paternal regime. Its radical indeterminacy, translated into culturally intelligible terms, opens her figure to dual and equivocal interpretation.

I have been treating *KT* on the basis of one manuscript, the Auchinleck. The Vernon and Simeon texts, which strongly resemble each other, are still less discussed.[25] Crucially, the lump to which the Princess gives birth is treated differently in the Auchinleck and Vernon versions. Therefore the texts' political and aesthetic systems, constructed as they are around that central (missing) point, are also different. The final section of this essay examines how paternity and maternity are configured in the Vernon redaction. Quite another poem emerges from this later manuscript, in some respects in polar opposition to Auchinleck and certainly prompting re-interpretation of the tale.

Instead of referring to the lump as 'þe flesche', Vernon calls it 'child', 'hit' or, on one occasion, 'þat wrecche' (V, 710). Thus the later redaction lacks the strict terminological distinction drawn by the earlier between the lump before its insertion into human relations through the patriarchal order and the child after baptism gives it a place within that order. This is not mere imprecision, however, but part of the distinct thematic structure which Vernon weaves. The alteration contributes to a change in the portrayal of the Sultan. In Auchinleck he stands out as the only character to refer to the lump as a child, 'þis litel faunt' who is 'lorn' (A, 599). These wistful references only reveal his lack of understanding of the symbolic situation, in contrast to the Princess whose unsentimental and precise terminology underlines her accurate perception of the causes of and remedies for the lump's inhumanity. In Auchinleck the Sultan's sorrow can afford the audience some outlet for any painful feelings the compelling image of the lump-child may arouse, but identification with him is disavowed in favour of that with the crisper and more energetic Princess. She sees through her grief to seize the opportunity for ideological confrontation, and in her emotional muscularity she exemplifies the subordination of sentiment to doctrine which befits a Christian heroine. In Vernon, however, the Sultan's grief transmits itself directly to the audience. There is a genuinely touching quality in the scene which follows the Sultan's destruction of his idols:

> Whon þei weore bete ful good won,
> Þe child lay stille as eny ston
>   Vppon his auteere.
> Þe child he tok vp sone anon
> In to his chaumbre he gan gon
>   & seide: 'Dame, haue hit here;
> Ichaue i-don al þat i con,
> To don hit formen after mon
>   Wiþ beodes and wiþ preyere;
> To alle my goddes ich haue bi-souht,
> Non of hem con helpe hit nouht,
>   Þe deuel set hem on fuyre!' (V, 619–30)

This quality is lacking in Auchinleck:

> & when he hadde beten hem gode won,
> Ȝete lay þe flesche stille so ston
>   An heye on his auter.
> He tok it in his hond anon,
> & into chaumber he gan gon,
>   & seyd, 'Lo, haue it here.
> Ich haue don al þat y can
> To make it fourmed after a man
>   Wiþ kneleing & preier.
> & for alle þat ichaue hem bisouȝt
> Mine godes no may help me nouȝt.
>   Þe deuel hem sette afere!' (A, 661–72)

Subtle changes effect a major overall shift. In Vernon the child is a helpless would-be subject of divine help (V, 629), whereas in Auchinleck it has no such status (A, 671). The pathos of Vernon lines 619–21 replaces the irony of the Auchinleck scene, where the lump's mocking refusal to respond makes it less the victim than the ally of the idols, like them an uncannily resisting representative of the material world. In each version the futility of the father's activity is emphasised, but the repeated use of the word *child* in Vernon vindicates the Sultan's emotions of grief, powerlessness and inadequacy. One major effect of this is to highlight and authorise those emotions which Auchinleck subordinates to didacticism by restricting them to the Sultan as symptoms of his limited insight. Vernon presents the Sultan's feelings in such a way that they appear representative and even exemplary, worthy of being shared by the audience.[26]

In Vernon's reworking, the Sultan accedes to the status of father before his christening, but earthly paternity is much more distant from the divine prototype on which it depends. Perceiving the lump as a child makes him a father, the one designation validating the other in a way unacceptable to Auchinleck. His sorrow recalls that of the King of Tars himself when, at the beginning of the poem, he too loses a child, the Princess whom he cannot protect against her ravisher. In Auchinleck the losses suffered by the Christian and heathen fathers are contrasted. The extreme grief of the Christian parents, rendered vividly and at length, attracts our sympathy (A, 325–6, 349–72), while the Sultan's emotions are given short and somewhat bathetic shrift to minimise the impress of fatherhood:

> Oft he kneled & oft he ros,
> & crid so long til he was hos;
>   & al he tint his while. (A, 634–6)

Audiences of Vernon are encouraged to sympathise with both fathers and not, as in Auchinleck, to identify with one alone. It lessens the Christian parents' expression of grief, and adds lines describing their resignation to God's will:

> Þei seȝe, hit mihte non oþer go;
> Þe kyng and þe qwene also,
>   Þei custe heore douhter þare,
> Bi-tauȝten hire god for euer mo;
> Hem self aȝeyn þei tornede þo,
>   Of blisse þei weore al bare. (V, 337–42)

What is lacking in the Sultan's response is not the depth of feeling which Auchinleck allows only to the true (because Christian) parent, but the comfort afforded by a trust in providence. The fathers' emotions are comparable; the contrast now concerns the consolation available to each. Moreover, because both his love for the child he has begotten and his sense of failing that child are instrumental in the Sultan's moral preparation for conversion, the role of biological fatherhood as a stage in the progress towards that conversion is underscored. The link between physical and symbolic fatherhood, emphatically denied in Auchinleck, is restored in Vernon. On the one hand, this means that the heathen realm is no longer opposed to the Christian as, respectively, exclusion from and fulfilment of paternity. Vernon lacks Auchinleck's presentation of a biological father cut off from the Nom-du-Père. On the other hand, in Vernon mortal fatherhood seems to be further removed from its all-powerful divine prototype than is the case in Auchinleck. A degree of failure and frustration appears to be the lot of the human father, whatever his religion. Instead of investing Christian fathers with full paternal powers as Auchinleck ultimately does, Vernon takes the birth of a child as initiating its father into a consciousness of power-lessness and inadequacy which the poem presents, as does Lacan, as the universal condition of paternity on earth; though appreciation of that condition's spiritual meaning, and therefore a measure of reconcilia-tion, remains a privilege open only to Christians. Thus Vernon situates itself differently from Auchinleck in relation to what Lacan calls the symbolic and the imaginary orders. The later redaction retains the imaginary identification of the Christian God as Father found in the earlier version, but allots to Christian (as to heathen) fathers a more symbolic – because frustrated and defective – status. Thus the division between symbolic and imaginary orders is relocated, shifting from a Christian-heathen axis to an earthly-heavenly one.

Turning now to how maternity is altered by Vernon's treatment of the lump: a further consequence of the poet's decision not to refer to it as *þe flesche* is that the maternal associations the term carries in Auchinleck disappear. Paganism remains animal as well as mineral in Vernon, for this version also contains many references to the heathen as beasts.[27] The idea that pagan inhumanity can be represented by brute maternity, however, is barely if at all implied in Vernon, reinforcing the impression that the lump is its father's child rather than its mother's. Its imperfection is referred predominantly and directly to him, as his vain struggle to perform the paternal function takes centre stage. The text concentrates squarely on the father's responsibility for his child's condition and on his failure in respect of the symbolic order, without diverting attention to the Princess's role in relation to a double-faceted maternity, at once obstacle and means of access to the sym-bolic. According to the Vernon redaction, the heathen state is defi-cient in paternity without therefore being more maternal. Whether through choice or because its redactor lacked the necessary education and eye for theory, Vernon forgoes Auchinleck's rationalisation of the lump in terms of Aristotelian physiology.

In place of Auchinleck's ambiguously valued maternity, Vernon invokes a femininity celebrated for its privileged relation to the symbolic order. Thus Vernon's Princess appeals to St Katherine the learned teacher rather than to Auchinleck's St Martin when convincing her husband that only his conversion will make him the child's father (A, 808; V, 766). The concluding stanza draws the moral:

> Þus þe ladi wiþ hire lore
> Brouȝte hire frendes out of sore
>   Þorw Jesu Cristes grace. (V, 1,111–13)

Both versions portray the married woman as helpmeet and insist on an analogy and a compatibility between a successful secular career and spiritual progress, but Vernon consistently presents the female role as teacherly and virginal, whereas Auchinleck sees it more as maternal.[28] In the Vernon *KT*, woman helps to lead others towards the truth; her creativity relates not to biology but to culture and spirituality, and it is by acting in those domains that she makes men. Insofar as the Virgin Mary is a model in this redaction, her function of agent in and mediator of man's salvation is considered more under its aspect of transmitting divine (paternal) light to a benighted earth than of introducing a human (maternal) element into the divinity. Female subordination is represented by the circumscribed place of the handmaiden within the symbolic order and not, as in Auchinleck, by an ineradicable association with the abject stuff which both supports and resists that order.

Not that this contradicts the emphasis on marriage as the proper female sphere; each text makes it clear that the Princess would have been morally and generically wrong to have demanded the path of virgin martyrdom at her people's expense, while the greater Christian community within the text is shown ultimately to profit from her marriage just as in hagiography it does from a virgin martyr's death or from a married saint's refusal of worldliness. Although the poem begins with the opposition, familiar from virgin martyrs' lives, between Christ and the pagan suitor, in this case the two turn out to be miraculously compatible, a resolution prefigured in the Princess's erotically charged dream of an aggressive black hound transformed into a white knight who promises her Christ's protection. Her reaction to this dream is intense, physical and, in Auchinleck, ambivalent:

> & when þe maiden was awaked,
> For drede of þat wel sore sche quaked
>   For loue of her sweuening.
> On hir bed sche sat al naked,
> To Ihesu hir preier sche maked,
>   Al miȝtful heuen king:
> As wis as he hir dere bouȝt
> Of þat sweuening, in slepe sche þouȝt,
>   Schuld turn to gode ending. (A, 457–65)

In Auchinleck's version, the Princess responds to both the fearsome and the erotic qualities of the dream that prefigures her own trials in a heathen land and her bridegroom's metamorphosis in the font. Her desire fits thematically with the poem's emphasis on marriage as a pious woman's vocation, yet it also exceeds that.[29] Aroused by a mixture of cruelty and tenderness and by a cultural disorientation signified by the heathen clothes in which she has been dressed for the Sultan's delectation, the maiden's sensuality seems to relate directly to a heathen and hence outlandish context. Female sexuality is simultaneously acknowledged and disavowed by this association with the exotic other, but it is not wholly denied to the character presented by the text as an exemplary Christian daughter, woman and wife. In this version, domestic submission is supported by a sexual enjoyment which, although not an integral part of the Christian-paternal order, is recognised to function in this case as a positive force for that order. Justified by the Virgin Mary whose mediating role she emulates, Auchinleck's Princess is licensed to exercise her sexuality within her transgressively mixed marriage. The delights of the flesh are redeemed by their association with the eternally immaculate and virginal.[30]

Vernon's account of the Princess's response to her dream is almost identical to that of Auchinleck except in the opening lines:

> Whon þe mayde was awaked,
> Hire flesch, i-wis, was al aquaked
>   For drede of hire sweuenynge. (V, 427–9)

By the removal of Auchinleck's 'loue' (A, 459) the erotic response is eliminated, the fearful being correspondingly expanded into two lines. Both female sexuality and feminine ambiguity are erased, moves borne out by the rest of the text. The Princess's fear and physical revulsion are consistent with the text's use of virgin role-models, as described above, and her reaction is perhaps to be read as the proper feminine response to sexuality in any instance. Repulsed rather than responsive *flesch* signifies a vulnerability and distress which the text endorses and encourages even while it commiserates. Whereas the dream's message of a future merging of Christ and her heathen lord affords the Auchinleck lady pleasure and promises future sensual rewards, in Vernon it only makes clear where her unpleasant duty lies. Vernon's Princess must continue with her wedding without the desire accorded to her counterpart in the earlier manuscript. She is unlike St Katherine not only because it is her duty to accept her heathen suitor, but also because she manifests no strong wish for any bridegroom, be it Christ himself. There is no indication in the text that her feelings towards the Sultan change after his conversion. Marriage and its consummation appear to her a painful and frightening ordeal; this is the martyrdom to which she must submit.

Vernon directs towards its heroine a double refusal: she can neither have what she wants nor want what she has. There is to be no enjoyment for her in secular life, but the virago role of the virgin saint is not a licit alternative. These twin prohibitions are reinforced elsewhere in the text. On the religious side, despite the references to Katherine and to the lady's lore, a notable omission from Vernon is the Princess's sermon to the Sultan (A, 841–76) in which she briefly summarises some fundamental points of Christian doctrine. Although the Vernon text advocates an image of femininity which implies that women's exercise of learning is valid when it brings others to Christ, it suppresses the principal scene in which a female character puts that theory into practice.[31] On the secular side, the Vernon redaction shows dislike for and disapproval of the courtly milieu in which its heroine is forced to live. The tournament with which the Sultan celebrates his wedding is in Vernon gory and unrestrained, in contrast to Auchinleck, where the poet calls it 'a semly si3t' (A, 535) and distinguishes it stylistically from the accounts of battle which begin and end the narrative.[32] What in Auchinleck is favourably rendered as entertaining or socially useful chivalry becomes in Vernon brutal violence, implying that the enjoyment of such pastimes befits neither Christian characters nor Christian audiences. A similar distaste for courtly entertainments is manifest in the treatment of minstrel activity at the wedding, which Auchinleck celebrates in a whole stanza (A, 553–64) omitted from Vernon, where the festivities seem relatively austere.[33] Both manuscripts feature the exotically alien, including heathen violence and feminine sexuality as well as courtly and festive activities, elements common in romance and contributing significantly to audience enjoyment. But the Auchinleck version allows us to approve of our pleasure as supporting the poem's greater ideological ends. It portrays the heathen court as a repository of values not to be despised, and the Sultan, denied the validated parental anguish of his Vernon counterpart but judged on these different criteria, as a man of some merit; though initially outside the Christian and paternal pale, he is not unworthy of ultimate redemption, while after his baptism his chivalric virtues bring a superior potency to Christian paternity. In short, secular activities are not only compatible with pious pursuits but can cultivate virtues which enhance them.

The Vernon redaction, alert to the moral danger in every worldly action, seeks to diminish both our opportunities for enjoyment and the pleasure we take in that enjoyment; in this version, courtliness is much more distant from godliness and secular life can only be endured, not enjoyed.[34] Overall, Vernon gives the impression of simultaneously exploiting the romance form for its popularity and condemning it for its ideology. Auchinleck, by contrast, appears much more comfortable with the status of pulp fiction.

Notes

An earlier version of this article, including a comparison with *Sir Gowther*, was published in Jocelyn Wogan-Browne *et al.* (eds), *Medieval Women: Texts and Contexts in Late Medieval Britain: Essays for Felicity Riddy* (Turnhout, 2000); reproduced by permission of the publisher. I wish to thank my father, Malcolm Gilbert, for imposing form on the chaos this revision originally presented.

1 The Auchinleck manuscript is thought to have been produced around 1330, the Vernon at the end of the fourteenth century. Both can be consulted in facsimile: *The Auchinleck Manuscript: National Library of Scotland Advocates' MS 19.2.1*, with an introduction by Derek Pearsall and I. C. Cunningham (London, 1977), and *The Vernon Manuscript: A Facsimile of Bodleian Library, Oxford, MS. Eng. Poet. a.1*, with an introduction by A. I. Doyle (Cambridge, 1987). Doyle also describes the manuscript containing the third extant text of *KT*, the Simeon manuscript, London, British Library, Additional MS 22283. Slightly later in date than Vernon, Simeon is closely linked to it, and the texts of *KT* found in each are very similar. On the relation between the two manuscripts, see especially A. I. Doyle, 'The shaping of the Vernon and Simeon manuscript', in Derek Pearsall (ed.), *Studies in the Vernon Manuscript* (Cambridge, 1990), pp. 1–13 and Robert E. Lewis, 'The relationship of the Vernon and Simeon texts

of the *Pricke of Conscience*', in Michael Benskin and M. L. Samuels (eds), *So Meny People Longages and Tonges: Philological Essays in Scots and Mediaeval English Presented to Angus McIntosh* (Edinburgh, 1981), pp. 251–64.

2 On the whereabouts of Tars, see Lillian Herlands Hornstein, 'The historical background of *The King of Tars*', *Speculum*, 16 (1941), 404–14 (pp. 405–6).

3 Quotations are from *The King of Tars*, ed. Judith Perryman (Heidelberg, 1980), lines 576–88. Further references to the Auchinleck version will be to Perryman's edition and will be given in the text.

4 Full details are to be found in Lillian Herlands Hornstein, 'New analogues to the *King of Tars*', *Modern Language Review*, 36 (1941), 433–42. Most of the chronicles Hornstein cites relate these events to the date 1299, but it also appears in relation to dates ranging from 1280 to 1338.

5 Hornstein, 'New analogues', p. 434.

6 *Ibid.*, pp. 441–2 (p. 442). In another article where she quotes these lines, Hornstein seems from her syntax to understand 'child' as the object of *ederet*, subject of *praeferens* and then object of *ederet* again. The point that this is a somewhat tortuous (although possible) reading was made in private correspondence by Shelagh Sneddon, who proposes the alternative translation I have transmitted above. Compare Lillian Herlands Hornstein, 'A folklore theme in the *King of Tars*', *Philological Quarterly*, 20 (1941), 82–7 (p. 84). The version quoted, which occurs in the Anglo-Latin *Chronicon de Lanercost*, distinguishes itself by its historical context: it relates the birth of Eric II, King of Norway. No justification is given for the monstrous child. Its transformation into the future King Eric is ascribed to St Francis, to whom Eric's father has a special devotion. Franciscan associations are common to a number of the analogues collected by Hornstein. The Lanercost version is also noteworthy for having a double transformation, like *KT*. In adulthood Eric marries an initially reluctant Scottish princess whose influence civilises her adopted country by improving its mores, teaching it French ('Gallicum') and English and improving its institutions.

7 Florence McCulloch, *Mediaeval Latin and French Bestiaries* (Chapel Hill, 1960), pp. 94–5. Hornstein, 'Folklore theme', p. 84, speculates that the variation between these analogues may be accounted for by scribal confusion between the terms *hirsus* (rough, shaggy) and *ursus* (bear), which brought the idea of hairiness into association with that of formless birth, although she also points out that the bear simile might imply formlessness to one redactor but hairiness to another.

8 On stories including accusations against women of adultery or of monstrous or animal birth, see Margaret Schlauch, *Chaucer's Constance and Accused Queens* (New York, 1927). Schlauch summarises the story of Hirlanda of Brittany, accused of giving birth to a shapeless and inanimate child (pp. 126–7).

9 Hornstein, 'New analogues', pp. 438–41. Hornstein traces elsewhere some ideas other than the strictly racial which may have contributed to this

account, and identifies some other black-and-white children in medieval literature.

10 Isidore of Seville, *Etymolgiae*, IX. v. 6: 'Mater dicitur, quod exinde efficiatur aliquid; mater enim quasi materia, nam causa pater est' (*Patrologia Latina* vol. 82, col. 354). See also Judith Butler, 'Bodies that matter', in *Bodies That Matter: On the Discursive Limits of 'Sex'* (New York, 1993), pp. 27–55.

11 Caroline Walker Bynum, 'The body of Christ in the later Middle Ages: a reply to Leo Steinberg', in *Fragmentation and Redemption: Essays on Gender and the Human Body in Medieval Religion* (New York, 1992), pp. 79–117 (p. 100). A brief and clear description of the male and female roles in Aristotelian, Hippocratic and Galenic theories of conception is given in Clarissa W. Atkinson, *The Oldest Vocation: Christian Motherhood in the Middle Ages* (Ithaca, 1991), pp. 46–51. Joan Cadden, *Meanings of Sex Difference in the Middle Ages: Medicine, Science and Culture* (Cambridge, 1993), has a much more detailed account of the theories in their classical (pp. 19–39) and medieval (pp. 117–30) forms, as well as a description of their transmission to the medieval West (pp. 39–53). Of the authorities Cadden cites, the closest to *KT* is Albertus Magnus (pp. 121, 126–30).

12 'Stille as ston' recurs at line 662, after the Sultan has destroyed his idols. When the lump is first introduced, it is described as 'ded as þe ston' (585).

13 Alain Boureau, 'The sacrality of one's own body in the Middle Ages', *Yale French Studies*, 86 (1994), 5–17.

14 Bynum, 'Body of Christ', opposes the 'paradigmatic male body' as 'the form or quiddity of what we are as humans' (p. 109) to the 'womanly, nurturing flesh' (p. 114). Pages 98–101 provide a succinct account of the associations between the feminine and the flesh.

15 The case for distinguishing between the phases of Lacan's thought is eloquently made in the preface to David Macey's *Lacan in Contexts* (London, 1988), pp. ix–xi. Apart from the texts cited below, I have also drawn in my account of the lump on Lacan's seventh seminar, translated as *The Ethics of Psychoanalysis, 1959–60: The Seminar of Jacques Lacan*, Book VII, ed. Jacques-Alain Miller, trans. with notes by Dennis Porter (London, 1992).

16 '[T]oute l'interrogation freudienne se résume à ceci – *Qu'est-ce que c'est qu'être un père?*', Jacques Lacan, *Le Séminaire, Livre IV: La relation d'objet, 1956–57*, ed. Jacques-Alain Miller (Paris, 1994), p. 204; italics in original. No English translation of this seminar is yet published.

17 'The function and field of speech and language in psychoanalysis', in Jacques Lacan, *Écrits: A Selection*, trans. Alan Sheridan (New York, 1977), pp. 30–113 (p. 66). This paper, also known as the Rome discourse, was originally delivered on 18 November 1953.

18 Perryman (*KT*, p. 9) calculates that a maximum of 169 lines of the Auchinleck *KT* have been lost, but notes that Pearsall estimates forty to sixty. Auchinleck heads the tale 'þe king of tars', whereas the incipit and explicit found in Vernon and Simeon respectively refer to both the King of Tars and the Sultan of Damascus.

19 Lacan, 'On a question preliminary to any possible treatment of psychosis', in *Écrits: A Selection*, trans. Sheridan, pp. 179–225 (p. 199). First published 1959.

20 *Séminaire IV*, ed. Miller, p. 210.

21 *Ibid.*, pp. 210, 276. Whereas the symbolic order is an abstract, mathematical structure, the imaginary is the domain of images, identifications and phenomena. For a helpful account of the three orders (real, imaginary and symbolic), see Malcolm Bowie, *Lacan* (London, 1991), pp. 88–121.

22 For line 742, Perryman gives the Vernon and Simeon reading 'þin help and myn'; I have restored the Auchinleck reading. Quotations from the Vernon manuscript refer to F. Krause, 'Kleine Publicationen aus der Auchinleck-hs.', *Englische Studien*, 11 (1888), 1–62; further references will be given in the text.

23 Bynum, 'Body of Christ', p. 116, and further: 'As mystics and theologians in the thirteenth, fourteenth and fifteenth centuries increasingly emphasised the human body of Christ, that body could be seen both as the paradigmatic male body of Aristotelian physiological theory and as the womanly, nurturing flesh that Christ's holy mother received immaculately from her female forebear', p. 114.

24 On the Virgin Mary as priest, see Bynum, 'Body of Christ', pp. 100–1. The Princess is more directly like a priest in Vernon, where she views conversion as her own as well as the priest's task – see note 22, above.

25 Karl Reichl analyses in detail the dialect of *KT* in Auchinleck and in Vernon/Simeon and considers the poem's transmission from the earlier to the later manuscripts: '*The King of Tars*: language and textual transmission', in Pearsall (ed.), *Studies in the Vernon Manuscript*, pp. 171–86. In her introduction to *KT*, pp. 58–69, Perryman considers the themes of the tale in both Auchinleck and Vernon/Simeon versions, concluding that the latter shows 'a weaker grasp of the ideas' (p. 69). I have used many of Perryman's detailed observations but generally interpret their effect differently.

26 The Princess also refers to the lump as 'child' (V, 706), which would be unthinkable in Auchinleck.

27 By likening the Sultan to an animal and an insane human, V implies that both are equally improper to the true human.

28 For example, Mary is described as 'moder fre' (A, 65) or 'mayden freo' (V, 64).

29 Karen A. Winstead demonstrates the use *KT* makes of hagiographic conventions in its representation of marriage: 'Saints, wives, and other "hooly thynges": pious laywomen in Middle English romance', *Chaucer Yearbook*, 2 (1995), 137–54.

30 Jocelyn Wogan-Browne, *Saints' Lives and Women's Literary Culture, c. 1150–1300: Virginity and its Authorizations* (Oxford, 2001), shows how virgin identifications were available and often useful to medieval women living in a wide variety of situations.

31 Vernon's removal of the Princess's preaching might imply a redactor

more sensitised to heresy than is the case in Auchinleck, which could be an effect of the later date. N. F. Blake notes the orthodox nature of the Vernon texts as a whole and suggests that 'the onset of the Lollard heresy may have prompted someone to prepare a collection that was free of heresy for those who might not so easily be able to judge those things for themselves, such as women religious'; 'Vernon manuscript: contents and organisation', in Pearsall (ed.), *Studies*, pp. 45–59. It has often been suggested that Vernon's original audience was female; certainly pious femininity is a major theme of the collection. A. S. G. Edwards argues that 'medieval compilers were clearly conscious of [*KT*'s] place among Biblical narratives emphasising the power of pious women as agents of Divine power'; 'The contexts of the Vernon romances', in Pearsall (ed.), *Studies*, pp. 159–70 (p. 168). Edwards notes, however, that although in Auchinleck and Simeon *KT* is grouped with other texts focusing on the lives of holy women, Vernon lacks this arrangement. On the other hand, Winstead warns against the presumption of a female audience or patrons on such grounds. Observing that the three *Canterbury Tales* which concentrate on what she calls '"martyred" laywomen' are told by and elicit commentary only from male characters, she proposes that Chaucer's presentation of these tales 'raises … questions about the motives and prejudices of the people who tell secularised saints' lives'; 'Saints, wives', p. 150.

32 Perryman, *KT*, p. 66. Edwards notes the predominance of devotional over chivalric themes in *KT* as in *Robert of Sicily* and *Joseph of Arimathea*, the other two romances contained in Vernon ('Contexts', pp. 159–61).

33 Also cut is a stanza near the beginning (A, 289–300) in which the Sultan is seen behaving with princely generosity towards the messengers who tell him of the Princess's capitulation. In my view, Vernon's omissions relate more to disapproval of the esteem in which courtliness is held than to a condemnation of the Sultan, although this sometimes takes the form of reminding us that he is a heathen, as where the knights he sends to fetch the Princess in Auchinleck (316) become 'Sarazins' in Vernon (298).

34 Perryman argues for a different approach to the story in the two versions: 'The MSS VS redactor seems to have viewed the tale not as an entertaining diversion [as did the Auchinleck redactor] but as history', *KT*, p. 64. There has been substantial critical discussion of *KT*'s mixture of lay and religious elements. For a useful summary of discussions relating to genre, see Reichl, '*The King of Tars*', pp. 171–2. Dieter Mehl points out that *KT* appears in Auchinleck among the exemplary rather than romance texts; *The Middle English Romances of the Thirteenth and Fourteenth Centuries* (London, 1968), p. 122. S. S. Hussey gives a nuanced analysis of the balance of interest in the contemplative and the mixed lives shown by the texts found in part IV of Vernon (*KT* appears in part III); 'Implications of choice and arrangement of texts in part 4', in Pearsall (ed.), *Studies*, 61–74.

6

Eating people and the alimentary logic of *Richard Cœur de Lion*

Nicola McDonald

I

Test de Turt. Foille de pastee bon sarrays, & iplaunted þrin con-ynges & volatils, dates ywaschen & isouced in hony, chese neowe icoruen þryn; clouwes, quibebes, sucre abouen. Soþþen on legge of fassyng of festigade gret plentee, þe colour of þe farsure red, ȝolou & grene. Þat hed schal beon blake adressed oþe manere of hier of wymmon on an blake dische, & a monnes visage abouen. *Diuersa Cibaria* (c. 1300).[1]

[Turk's Head. Take a well-rolled sheet of pastry; fill it with rabbit, fowl and honey-soaked dates; add fresh cheese and put cloves, cubebs and sugar on top. Then lay on a face with plenty of ground pistachio; the filling will be coloured red, yellow and green. Dress the head in black, in the manner of a woman's hair, and place it on a black dish. A man's face should be visible on the top.]

'Eating people is wrong.'[2] Western culture has always treated the eating of human flesh as taboo. Reluctant or not, cannibals evoke fear, loathing or, at best, horrified pity; by disturbing the neat, almost sacred, divide between edible and inedible, they challenge the very integrity of what it is to be human. And that taboo is, apparently, timeless: just as today deeply ingrained codes of gustatory behaviour prevent us serving dead relatives or despised neighbours for dinner, so too in the Middle Ages it was neither proper nor permissible to feast on the flesh of another human being. That said, cannibalism is not simply 'wrong'; cannibals – more appropriately anthropophagi, since the former term signals little more than Columbus' wilful slander of the Carib natives[3] – inhabit a world of nightmare, but it is a nightmare in which cultural prohibitions are played out against fantasies of race, sex and imperialism. *We* don't eat people, *they* do: medieval *mappaemundi*, like John Mandeville, conveniently locate the man-eater on the margins of the known world; responsibility for the gruesome tales of anthropophagy that, inevitably, surface nearer home is levelled at those already beyond the pale, Jews and other outcasts.[4] Yet for all of its determination to purge itself of blame, and squeamishness aside, Western culture (medieval and modern) is no stranger to the notion that eating people is also a palatable pastime.

No fourteenth-century English cook is known to have prepared for consumption the flesh of a real Turk, yet the Turk's Head, a sweet-and-sour meat pie shaped and decorated to resemble the outlandish features of a stereotyped Saracen, was a familiar late medieval dish. Instructions for how to prepare *test de turt*, all carefully delineating the colours and features of the upturned face, survive in no fewer than three manuscripts, two English and one, the earliest, in Anglo-Norman. Most medieval cookery books are assumed to serve the noble household – the cost and diversity of the ingredients (in particular meats and spices) and the quantities invoked require a large, well-funded kitchen – but *Diuersa Cibaria*, the collection which includes the Turk's Head, found a broader, albeit still exclusive, audience: the earliest English manuscript belonged to Friar William Herebert of Hereford and the recipes' *explicit* is written in his hand. Neither Herebert nor any of the other fourteenth-century English householders who served up the Turk's Head were, I am confident, practising anthropophagi. The dish is designed not to remind them of 'Turks I have eaten' but to bring a touch of exotic levity to the table. Like the *cokantrice* (a fantastical beast composed of the forefront of a chicken and the hind quarters of a suckling pig) or the popular plate of mock raw meat ('how somme mete schalle seme raw'), the Turk's Head is evidence of the medieval penchant for illusion, or counterfeit, food: dishes that surprise or entertain by the way in which they counter, either in composition or appearance, culinary and/or gustatory expectations.[5] The Turk's Head shares with other early fourteenth-century *entremets* (the generic term for a small dish served between the primary courses or *mets*) a fundamental edibleness. These are not the flamboyant spectacles of fifteenth-century court feasts that, constructed from cardboard, spun sugar and other inedibles, are intended not for consumption but solely for shock and astonishment.[6] It is the very edibleness of the Turk's Head – the lip-smacking relish with which the diner bites into the aromatic flesh, the grinding of teeth and satisfied swallow, the appetite for more – that makes it more than just a neat piece of propaganda (like the battle between Saracens and Christians staged at Charles V's Twelfth Night dinner in 1378).[7] It is a licence, metaphorically at least, to eat people.

According to structuralist anthropologists, food must be not only 'good to eat' but 'good to think'.[8] Cuisine, the transformation of raw into cooked, is a language that encodes both the essential ordering (the structure) of a society and its hidden contradictions. Key to any understanding of the Turk's Head as a cultural sign is, surely, a recognition of its inherent contradiction, or destabilisation, of the neatly ordered binaries that, so the structuralists tell us, produce and regulate meaning: edible/inedible, literal/metaphoric. It is only when we confront the inadequacy of binary opposition – when we unpick the comfortable, easy categories that make us confident that medieval (and modern) diners don't eat people – that we can begin to understand what is at stake in the early fourteenth-century recipe for *test de turt*. On the one hand, eating the Turk's Head mirrors crusader fantasy: Christians consume Saracens in their conquest, real or desired, of the Holy Land. On the other hand, by literalising the rhetoric of conquest, it makes the unimaginable transgression (eating Saracens) completely imaginable. Like sex and commerce, medieval politics, in particular the politics of national expansion, is fraught with the anthropophagic urge: lords 'etheþ' their underlings and 'deuouren' the poor; knights 'swolwe' one another and so too do kingdoms; enemies are 'glotons'; and victors 'feste' on hard-won land.[9] Structured as opposites, edible and inedible, literal and metaphoric are rather points on a continuum. The Christian fantasy of Muslim genocide – the total decimation of land and people imagined in a Middle English romance as an act of ingestion ('þou … destroyyst hys [the Sultan's] countrays, / Slees hys men, and eetes among')[10] – is, if we are being honest, pretty much coincident with the diner's ingestion of a pie not only imagined as, but made out to look like, a Turk. Both invoke eating people as a trope to make real (imaginatively and materially) a fantasy of total power. Once that power has been acknowledged, then the next step – only a small shift along the continuum – becomes possible: the material Turk (human flesh and blood) is imagined – and prepared/*cuisiné* – as a dish and his ingestion stands in for, and confirms, the fantasy of power.

I remarked above that Western culture has, if not embraced, then at least normalised some forms of eating people. The medieval Turk's Head is one example of how anthropophagy functions alongside, or, more precisely, within, conventional methods of nourishment, but it is not unique. Indeed, it is the very ordinariness of the anthropophagic gesture and its longevity that interests me. The most rarefied instance of culturally validated anthropophagy is, of course, the theophagy at the heart of Christian ritual: Catholic doctrine, confirmed in 1215 at the Fourth Lateran Council, teaches that the eucharist is truly the flesh and blood of Christ (*corpus verum*).[11] I will look more closely at theophagy in section III of this essay, but for the moment, the less exalted evidence is more relevant. The medieval Turk's Head has no identifiable progeny (the meat-pie version disappears after the Middle Ages), yet the trope is remarkably resilient. Jellies depicting the Turk's distinctive turban – called alternately Turk's Heads or Turk's Caps – are popular in England in the eighteenth century (and the moulds remain in catalogues of household ceramics into the twentieth); they are said to commemorate the Christian victory over the Ottoman Turks at the Siege of Vienna in 1683. The Turk's Head surfaces in American kitchens at the start of the nineteenth century, this time as a cake whose form resembles the turban-like, central European *kugelhupf* (itself associated with the gustatory aftermath of 1683); bakeware giants, like Hillside Metal Ware, still manufacture a ring-shaped, aluminium 'Turk Head' mould.[12] And the trope is by no means limited to Anglo-American cuisine; sweet domed pastries, topped with chocolate and called variously Schwartzkopf, Möhrenkopf and tête de nègre are standard items in European patisseries. The easy shift between Turk, Moor and Black, like that between turban and the anthropomorphic head, is instructive. The Turk's Head no longer serves an active commemorative function (few will identify the allusion to the Crusades or the Siege of Vienna), but it is no less key to an understanding of the complex racial and religious bigotry that underlies dominant Western ideology. Stigmatised as an object of both fear and fascination, the Muslim, reduced to a symbolic turban or a grinning face,[13] can be eaten. His supremacy in the medieval Holy Land, his incursion into the heart of Renaissance Europe, his threat to American hegemony is contained, imaginatively at least, when, transformed into something edible, he is ingested. In the endless reiteration of animosity, Israeli prime minister Ariel Sharon, in a candid moment during the 2001 election campaign, provides a salutary reminder that the line between the literal and the metaphoric is almost imperceptible: 'I am known as someone who eats Arabs for breakfast.'[14] Eating people then has very little to do with conventional morality, as 'wrong' implies; it is rather part – a legitimated one at that – of the complex way in which we, as individuals and communities, determine who we are. It has everything to do with who's cooking.

II

Richard Cœur de Lion, a romance whose medieval popularity is well attested, arrests modern readers with the spectacle of its man-eating king. Duped into mistaking a cooked Saracen for pork, the ailing Richard devours a dish of boiled flesh, faster than his steward can carve, and gnaws on the bones. Once revived, he demands a second meal and, when confronted with a detached and grinning black head, he laughs. Richard then invites a party of Saracen ambassadors to dinner and serves the cooked heads of his aristocratic Muslim captives as a first course; each head is placed face-up on a platter; its lips are splayed and on its forehead is pinned a parchment tag displaying the victim's name. Richard again eats voraciously, pausing only to register his guests' horror. He finally orders them home armed with the gruesome message that he will not leave the Holy Land until all the Saracens are eaten up. 'Nonsense' decrees George Ellis, *Richard*'s first modern editor; 'absurd' concurs Sir Walter Scott. What rankles the early commentators – and what still impedes our appreciation of the poem – is the conviction that these 'monstrous' incidents, so blatantly fabulous, 'disfigure' or (as Finlayson puts it) 'contaminate' the historical record of Richard's chivalric career. 'True history', Finlayson asserts, is 'at the base of this work'; fictitious accretion has turned the 'rigorously heroic' into a mere romance, 'impenetrable' (as Barron insists) 'to the discriminations of historians'.[15] *Richard*'s reputation as a composite romance, mingling fact and fiction, leaves scholars, almost without exception, picking over its plot in pursuit of anything authentic or factual. Not surprisingly, it is found wanting.

Richard's anthropophagy is historically unproven and, despite Arab suspicions that he did eat his victims, it is doubtless unverifiable; but it is certainly not absurd.[16] As Geraldine Heng has recently demonstrated, Richard's consumption of the Saracen – in particular the racially marked head (the 'swarte vys' and 'blacke berd', the 'whyte teeþ' and 'lyppys ... wyde' (3211–13)) – symbolically corroborates his crusader ideology: 'aggressive territorial ambitions, the consumption and discipline of alien communities'.[17] Richard's 'black humor' – putting interpretive weight on Richard's extravagant laughter, Heng insists it is constructed as a joke – is not romance 'nonsense', but a function of the 'color politics' of both the poem and the Third Crusade. And Heng is more emphatic still: this joke is the interpretive key to *Richard*'s political logic. Like Heng, I want to insist on the logical centrality of Richard's repeated anthropophagy, but my interest is only tangentially political. What I will argue is that eating people is essential to, and underscored by, the text's narrative logic, that the poetic mechanism that initiates and sustains *Richard*, not only makes sense of, but demands his anthropophagy. The logic that governs *Richard* is alimentary.

To be fair, the ongoing critical interest in the historicity of *Richard Cœur de Lion* is in part a product of its extant manuscripts.[18] The earliest version of the poem – identified by both Gaston Paris and Karl Brunner as a translation of a now lost Anglo-Norman original[19] – is found in the Auchinleck manuscript (*c.* 1330); it charts the key military events of the Third Crusade (1189–92) with virulent nationalism. English identity is constructed not simply in opposition to the racially marked infidel, but also against the treachery of the French and their king, Philip Augustus. In response to a papal call-to-arms, Richard sets out for Jerusalem. He meets Philip in Messina and winters there; skirmishes between the Messinesi and English troops compel Richard to assault and take the city. He sets out again in late spring only to come ashore at Cyprus where some of his fleet have, a few weeks earlier, been wrecked and pillaged, their sailors murdered or imprisoned. Richard challenges the Cypriot emperor, defeats him, and takes control of Cyprus. He sets out again, intercepts and defeats a Saracen supply ship, and finally arrives at Acre. Richard learns of the deprivation suffered by the crusader armies camped at Acre and begins his attack on the Saracen city. At this point the fragmentary Auchinleck text breaks off, but it is not hard to guess what originally followed: Richard's victory at Acre and his slaughter of the Saracen prisoners; Philip's return to France; the decisive victory at Arsuf; the occupation of Jaffa; the removal to, and refortification of, Ascalon; the battle of Darum; the defence of Jaffa; and finally the three-year truce with Saladin guaranteeing free passage to Jerusalem for Christian pilgrims. In all likelihood, the original poem concluded with a short account of Richard's journey home and his death.[20]

This broad military narrative (from the crusade's inception to the truce, concluding with Richard's death) underlies all extant copies, in manuscript and print, of the Middle English romance. While Brunner divides the extant texts into two distinct groups – a shorter, more historical narrative and a longer version interpolated with fabulous romance material – the evidence is more complicated. No text of *Richard*, other than that found in Auchinleck, is wholly devoid of so-called romance material and it is impossible to tell – even if we believe the Paris/Brunner chronology (Anglo-Norman source, Middle English translation, Middle English elaboration) – whether the romance elaboration is the product of one or more redactors.[21] While most scholars are interested in going backwards to trace the shape of either the (hypothetical) Anglo-Norman source or the earliest Middle English version, I want to move in the opposite direction to look at how the romance narrative works and to examine how Richard's anthropophagy plays a logical, and fully integrated, role in that narrative. The text of *Richard* printed by Brunner (Cambridge, Gonville and Caius, MS 175/96 supplemented by the two Wynkyn de Worde prints) represents the fullest, the most 'contaminated' and most romance-like, version of the poem. It offers us the opportunity to explore the mechanics of romance logic, to think about how the internal narrative coherence that is crucial to romance is actually achieved.

The transformation of Auchinleck's 'history' of the Third Crusade into a full-blown 'romance' is primarily effected by the interpolation of a series of episodes, many of which draw on stock romance motifs. The crusade is prefaced by a 1200–line account of Richard's birth (to Henry II and a faerie queen Cassiodorien who, when compelled to remain in church for the duration of the mass, flies through the roof never to return), his secret sponsorship of a pre-crusade tournament (at which he fights three times in, alternately, black, red and white disguise) and a preparatory pilgrimage to the Holy Land with his right-hand men (Thomas Moulton and Fulk D'Oilly, two Lincolnshire knights – not otherwise known as famous crusaders – whose families may have patronised *Richard*'s poet). On his return from pilgrimage, Richard is imprisoned by the King of Almeyne and the King's son challenges him to an exchange of blows. Richard wins, killing the son and prompting the Duke to offer him up to the mercy of a starved lion. The King's daughter Margery falls in love with Richard and offers to help him. Richard rips out the lion's heart, gains his familiar sobriquet, and returns to England to launch his crusade. The narrative of the crusade itself is also expanded, but since Auchinleck is imperfect it is impossible to tell exactly how much is the product of later interpolation. In addition to a series of new (predominantly fictional) battles designed to exemplify the martial valour of Moulton and D'Oilly, the key 'meruayle[s]' (2683) include the following: Richard's first attack on the Saracens at Acre (he erects a multi-coloured, flaming mill that noisily emits a blood-like substance, terrifying the onlookers who assume it grinds Richard's victims); his unwitting consumption of Saracen flesh during the siege of Acre; his anthropophagic feast for the Saracen ambassadors after securing Acre; and his combat – astride a devil-possessed horse (a treacherous gift from the Saracens) – with Saladin.[22]

As I have just described it, Richard's anthropophagy comprises two discrete compositional units slotted into a pre-existing narrative. It is the blatant mechanics of this kind of plot construction that repeatedly draws critical contempt for romance and its audiences. What I want to demonstrate, however, is the extent to which these anthropophagic interpolations not only function in dialogue with other (interpolated) 'romance' episodes, but participate fully in the discursive, or poetic, logic that makes this text cohere. I remarked above that the logic that governs and sustains *Richard* is alimentary. By this I mean that the narrative, put crudely, is animated by Richard's hunger. As Fielding says of Homer's *Odyssey*, *Richard* is a great 'eating poem'.[23] Eating – from the culinary practicalities of food preparation to the symbolic resonance of the anthropophagic banquet – is here informed by two imperatives: feast and fast. Like other binaries, they are simultaneously opposite and contiguous. Feasting has long been recognised as a key feature of Middle English romance. Romance feasts, like their historic counterparts, are overdetermined sites of social (as well as political and economic) contestation: with their complex hierarchies of seating and food consumption (only those at the high table, for instance, enjoy the most expensive and elaborate dishes) they confirm social division while at the same time uniting all of the diners, at least for the duration of the meal, in a utopic experience of commensality. And implicit in the exhibitionist hospitality that characterises so many medieval feasts is the spectre of alimentary deprivation: alongside the liturgical cycle of fast and feast is the very real hunger that is the inevitable corollary of both widespread famine and a seasonal food economy.[24]

No matter where we look in *Richard* we are likely to find food – or, in its absence, hunger. The text is jammed with alimentary detail. Fluctuating food prices, methods of cooking, inventories of fish, fowl, meat and other edibles, the provision of tableware, and the slurps of hungry eaters repeatedly remind us of the vitality of food and its consumption. The poet knows that taste is a cultural construct, that it divides nations and races, and that it is subject to the vagaries of fashion; he knows the nutritive value of a balanced diet and the dangers of insufficient or spoiled food; and he knows too that food is a tool to seal friendship and confirm animosity. As is often the case in romance, the poetic formulae – the stock, reiterated phrases and motifs that are commonly dismissed as meaningless – provide a useful guide to the text's preoccupations and assumptions. More than twenty meals are recorded in *Richard* – over half of them formal feasts – but rarely do they merit more than a few lines: the board is set, the trumpets blown, and we are simply told 'þey eeten and drank and maden ham glade' (113). As the poet makes clear: 'knyȝtes seruyd þere good spede, / Off what to telle it is no nede' (157–8). Feasts mark key narrative incidents (like Cassiodorien's arrival at London, the start of Richard's crusade, and the victory in Cyprus), while more informal meals signal social cohesion (Richard's reconciliation with the King of Almeyne), erotic intrigue (Richard's liaison with Margery) and general well-being (Richard's shipmates celebrate their arrival at Acre with a round of drinks). Conversely, a meal interrupted (like the roast goose that is left unfinished when Richard and his companions are captured in Almeyne) inevitably presages a breakdown in order and hierarchy. In *Richard*, meals function as a form of narrative punctuation (they conclude or initiate action) and the poet expects his audience to understand their significance with only minimal textual prompting. What gives reson-ance to all of *Richard*'s eating is the threat of hunger.

Hunger kills: this is the inescapable reality of the crusaders' wars. On two separate occasions, Richard is directly confronted with the spectre of enforced starvation. At the start of his crusade, he travels to Almeyne to settle accounts with the king, Modard. When he arrives at Cologne, he is unable to buy fowl, the poet's shorthand for meat, and learns that all sales to the crusaders have been prohibited ('þe hye mayere off þat cyte / Comaundyd ... / No man selle hem no ffowayle' (1477–9)). Modard is identified as responsible and his motivation is clear: 'he wenes, sykyrly, / þat ȝe schal haue mete non; / þus he þynkes ȝoure men to slon' (1490–2). Richard's reaction to Modard's alimen-tary warfare is instructive; threatened with hunger, he commands his men to make do with whatever is available: fruit and nuts as well as wax, tallow and grease. This mixture of low status food and the conventionally inedible provides a model for survival that is reiterated when Richard reaches Acre. The archbishop of Pisa details the hard-ship suffered by the Christian troops camped outside the city. At the onset of winter, with their supply lines cut and local prices outrage-ously inflated, the men are forced to slaughter and eat their horses; the traditionally taboo flesh is rationed and everything is consumed: guts, head and blood (2837–76).[25] The poet insists on the necessity of the crusaders' alimentary solution – 'þey myȝte haue non oþir þyng' (2875) – and, in his reiteration of hunger's dire consequences ('ffor hungyr oure ffolk it slowȝ; / ffor hungyr we loste', 'oure folk vnwexe, /

and dyede for hungyr and ffor woo' (2842–3, 2864–5)), he confirms the merit of a pragmatic diet. But the spectre of hunger is more pervasive still. The provision of food supplies, essential to a well-managed military campaign, is the kind of functional detail that is often elided in romance narrative, yet in *Richard* it is part of the formulaic fabric of the text. [26] Key supplies, like meat, bread or simply *vitayle*, are as much a part of the poet's martial vocabulary as armour (and other military effects) and treasure or booty; indeed, as the formulaic homology makes clear, food is both military effect and treasure. Richard's ships leave England 'wel vitailid, / wiþ flour, hawberkes, swerdys, and knyuys' (1390–1); they are 'chargyd' the poet reiterates 'wiþ armure, drynk, and mete' (1662); when the crusaders raid a Saracen camp they win 'whete, bred, and wynes, / gold, and syluyr, and bawdekynes' (2797–8); similarly the victory at Acre explicitly promises 'ryche tresore': 'helmes and hawberkes ... / And oþer ryhchesse ... / Whete jnowȝ and oþir tresore' (3310–13); and these are not isolated examples. What strikes *Richard*'s reader is the way in which food saturates every level of the narrative, informing and giving dimension to a whole range of (apparently trivial) textual detail.

I want now to return to the question of Richard's anthropophagy and its logic. The two occasions on which Richard explicitly consumes human flesh are not, as commentators often imply, isolated or aberrant incidents of dietary transgression. They are embedded in a narrative that is acutely aware of the practical and symbolic function of food and whose alimentary code, oscillating between the competing demands of fast and feast, is resolutely pragmatic. Modern readers are affronted by the narrative's endorsement of Richard's barbarity: some ascribe it to the imagined temper of the times, blood-thirsty and cruel; for others it simply defies comprehension. Yet neither of these explanations is very satisfactory. In section I of this essay I argued that eating people (contrary to basic assumptions) is not in fact uniformly taboo, that the anthropophagic act can be – and is – a standard, even legitimate, feature of medieval and modern cuisine. I want to propose that Richard's anthropophagy is likewise licensed. Although Richard's consumption of the Saracen is shocking (for fellow crusaders and the romance audience), it neither elicits narrative censure nor, I would argue, the opprobrium of its original audience. The fact that both Saracen and French (the anti-types against whom the English Christian is measured) do censure Richard (explicitly and implicitly, respectively) only serves to confirm the narrative's endorsement of his diet. [27] The romance narrative embraces the taboo inherent in anthropophagy while, at the same time, insisting that eating people makes culinary and cultural sense. What I will explore below is precisely how this 'sense' is achieved.

If, for a moment, we ignore the cultural taboos that prohibit anthropophagy, eating people is an inspired resolution of the crusaders' military ambitions and their alimentary needs. Anthropophagic annihilation (the total consumption of a people) not only mirrors the crusaders' political and religious aspirations, as Heng argues, but fuels those aspirations (it provides the crusaders with the alimentary sustenance that is otherwise in short supply), and – if successful – guarantees the impunity of Christian hegemony. All eaten up, the threat of the infidel is eradicated. Richard's strategy of anthropophagic annihilation is horrifically brilliant. And it is this brilliance that the romance endorses: 100 per cent. Richard is foiled only because he has to return to England to quell his brother's attempted usurpation of the throne; neither the narrator nor Richard's fellow crusaders ever doubt the efficacy or appropriateness of the anthropophagic solution. Eating people makes an awful lot of pragmatic sense.

Yet, *Richard* does not simply demand that we ignore the taboos. Instead, it purposefully makes eating people an identifiable and legitimate feature of the culinary system that prevails not only in this romance but in late medieval Europe. The insertion of 'Saracen' into a known culinary world, subject to the alimentary codes that structure everyday dining, renders what is otherwise alien and forbidden a familiar, and thus edible, food; it effectively diffuses the taboo that makes man-eating, if not unthinkable, unpalatable. Significantly, in order to effect its legitimation of eating people, *Richard* exploits the anthropophagic potential already present in medieval cuisine.

The incorporation of human flesh (the meat itself) into the familiar medieval culinary system is first, and not surprisingly, achieved by means of the cooking process. The initial proposal to eat human meat (offered in response to the ailing king's insatiable hunger for pork) immediately establishes the pattern of what I will call culinary accommodation: 'Takes a Sarezyn ȝonge and ffat', demands one of Richard's trusted companions,

> Jn haste [see] þat þe þeff be slayn,
> Openyd, and hys hyde off fflayn,
> And soden fful hastyly,
> Wiþ powdyr, and wiþ spysory,
> And wiþ saffron off good colour. (3088–93)

The old knight's command, right from the opening (and near obligatory) 'take', precisely mimics not only the lexis and syntax of conventional medieval recipes, but their imperative mood and abbreviated style. Only the designation 'þeff' and the twice-repeated request for 'haste' signals that 'Sarezyn', a term current in medieval cookery books to denote exotic foods of Eastern origin, is not a standard English dish.[28] The transformation of a young Muslim into a plate of pork (the meat that is the ubiquitous mark of a Christian diet) is achieved by subjecting the unfamiliar flesh to the normal rules of English cooking. Boiled, flavoured with spices and coloured a popular saffron yellow, Richard's fresh portion of Saracen neither looks nor tastes any different from the meat to which he and the crusaders have been culturally accustomed. This is in marked contrast to conventional depictions of the man-eater in romance and elsewhere that preserve the physical integrity (and sometimes even the vitality) of the human meat in order to insist on the transgression that its consumption necessarily entails. The giant of Mont St Michel recorded in Geoffrey of Monmouth's life of King Arthur, for instance, eats vanquished knights half alive (*semiuiuos*) and, in the *Alliterative Morte Arthure*, he barbecues infants whole.[29] Likewise in Matthew Paris' illustrated *Chronica Universale* (Cambridge, Corpus Christi College, MS 16), the Tartar's feast is a riot of severed heads and disassembled limbs; one Tartar bites into a blood-drenched leg (its pair held in eager anticipation) while a second turns a full-length skewered boy over the hot embers of a roasting pit. [30]

When Richard articulates his anthropophagic solution – eating up the enemy – to the English crusaders, he carefully links pragmatism ('Schole we neuere dye for defawte, / Whyl we may ... / Slee Sarezynys' (3219–21)) with gustatory satisfaction: does Saracen really taste *this* good? ('is Sarezynys flesch þus good?' (3216)). He reiterates the recipe formula – 'take' 'þe flesch' (3221) – and proposes a complete programme of culinary accommodation: 'Seþen, and roste hem, and doo hem bake' (3222). Boil, roast, and bake: all of the ordinary things English people do to their meat. By the time the English sit down to dinner with Saladin's messengers, 'Sarezyn' is accorded the status of a national dish; its privileged position in the formulaic list of meat that's good to eat (the kind of list we always find in descriptions of feasts, real and imagined)[31] is intended, not I think to single it out as an alimentary abomination, but to confirm its legitimate place in the English diet:

> Þer is no fflesch so norysschaunt
> Vnto an Ynglyssche Cristen-man,

Partryck, plouer, heroun, ne swan,
Cow ne oxe, scheep ne swyn,
As is þe flesshe of a Sarezyn. (3548–52)

The alignment of Saracen (as something edible) with the established linguistic and culinary codes of English cuisine is a consistent feature of the way the romance depicts Richard's (and by extension English) anthropophagy. Yet, I don't finally want to give the impression that this process of accommodation wholly neutralises anthropophagy. Culinary acculturation renders eating people acceptable (it no longer provokes the horror or disgust associated with the consumption of a taboo food), but it does not make it any less effective as a tool for social and political negotiation.

The spectacle of severed Saracens' heads, stripped of hair, cooked, and laid out, face up and grinning, on serving platters is certainly designed to shock Richard's dinner companions (both Saracen guests and crusaders) and, with them, the romance audience. Richard's subsequent and hearty consumption of a steaming head must elicit a gasp of disbelief and it is no doubt disturbing. The anthropophagic banquet, detailed at length and recounted twice (once by the narrator and a second time, immediately afterwards, by a messenger on his return to Saladin), does not seem, to the modern reader, to fit the process of culinary acculturation, and with it accommodation, that I have documented so far. The head, furnished with an identifying and personalising name tag, remains resolutely human; its upturned, grinning face openly flouts the taboos that conventionally prohibit anthropophagy. I began this essay with a fourteenth-century recipe for Turk's Head, a meat pie shaped to resemble a Turk's (or Saracen's) face that functions as a kind of comestible entertainment. As far as medieval party tricks go, the Turk's Head is pretty tame. A grotesque caricature of someone few English diners will have ever seen, its consumption confirms inherited racial and religious prejudice; there is nothing inherently difficult about its preparation and the required ingredients are all readily available. Yet, ultimately its success as a dinnertime diversion depends on the way that it, much like the real Saracens' heads served at Richard's banquet, counters the diner's culinary expectations: we don't expect meat pies to look like people, to stare back at us as we cut into them, but when they do eating them is bound to provoke a shiver of excitement, our acknowledgement that we are flirting with the forbidden.

This fascination with the unexpected, with flouting the rules that traditionally govern food and its consumption, is not unique to the

Turk's Head. I mentioned above the medieval penchant for illusion, or counterfeit, food, a feature of both aristocratic and bourgeois dining that serves simultaneously to entertain guests and impress them with the status and resources of their host. The appeal of many late medieval *entremets*, like the *appraylere* (ground meat moulded and painted to resemble a clay pitcher) and *yrchoun* (a hedgehog of pork spiked with almond quills), lies precisely in their power to disturb the neat divide between what is and what isn't edible.[32] Evidence, from recorded aristocratic banquets as well as sources like the Turk's Head, and its close counterpart Priest's Head (*tête de cure*), indicates that these illusions include feigned anthropophagy. To the extent that *entremets* function as an assertion of the host's lordship (the authority that goes hand in hand with social magnificence), they also serve to remind the guest of the risk that inheres in dining out; this is usually illusory but, in the case of royal or other politically motivated events, it doubtless has very real implications.[33] One recipe demands that a roasted peacock be returned to its plumed skin (skilfully removed before cooking) and served 'as if it were alive'; a second provides instructions for a mercury concoction that causes a cooked fowl to jump animatedly in its dish; a third recommends hiding live birds inside a pie shell so that they fly out when the pie is cut open.[34] These dishes and others like them force the diner to acknowledge that the host, even if apparently only in jest, has the power to conjure life itself and, by implication, death. When a pie shell contains not simply birds but a complete orchestra of musicians, as it did at Philip the Good's extravagant Feast of the Pheasant held at Lille in February 1454, we are necessarily impressed not only with the enormity of the pie but the magnitude of the host's prerogative.

If we think about Richard's Saracen's Head as a conventional *entremets*, as the narrative, scrupulously attentive to the naturalistic detail of the feast, encourages us to do, then there is nothing absurd about it at all.[35] Like other successful *entremets*, it articulates, with inescapable clarity, the nature and extent of the host's authority; it asserts his hegemony and in its blatant exhibitionism confirms his ability to enforce it. What distinguishes these Saracens' Heads from other recorded *entremets* is, of course, that they demand not illusory but actual anthropophagy. I have already argued, given the ambitions of the crusaders and those who share their fantasy of Christian dominion, that there is scant difference between the illusory and the actual. Key to my reading of the Turk's Head (in section I) is my conviction that the familiar binaries edible and inedible are not so much opposed categories of meaning as points on a continuum that can – and do –

move toward one another. Eating a meat pie that looks like a Turk's head is just a step away from eating a real Turk's head. Conventionally, we understand the difference between these two acts of ingestion in terms of another pair of binaries: metaphoric and literal. Eating a Turk's Head is permissible because it is simply metaphoric; eating a Turk, because literal, is on the other hand prohibited. But, as I discussed above, these binaries too prove to be inadequate. When metaphoric consumption (eating a Turk's Head) symbolises literal consumption (the fantasy of Muslim genocide) we cannot be content with the security – the impunity – of the metaphor. I want now to consider how this shift from the metaphoric to the literal, evident in Richard's presentation and consumption of real Saracens' heads, is consistent with the poetic (and not just alimentary) logic of the romance.

III

Ambroise, author of the *Estoire de la guerre sainte* and putative eye-witness to the events of the Third Crusade, provides the earliest extant reference to Richard's cognomen 'quor de lion', but it is certainly not original to him. Bernard Itier, a Benedictine monk at Limoges records in his memorandum on the king's death in 1199 that Richard was known as 'Cor Leonis' and William the Breton, a chronicler in the retinue of Philip Augustus, likewise designates Richard 'corde leonino' (lionhearted).[36] The popularity of the epithet, standard in references to Richard by the mid-thirteenth century, confirms his reputation, already well established in his lifetime, as a fierce and noble warrior. 'Lionheart', as the chroniclers (and we) understand it, is a metaphor: it works by means of an implied *figurative* comparison between Richard and the lion. Richard is not a lion; his heart is not a lion's heart; the metaphor, in fact, tells us nothing about lions at all. Rather, Richard, celebrated for his martial valour, exhibits certain qualities (might, courage, ferocity, nobility) that we (and the medieval bestiaries) con-ventionally attribute to the lion. What distinguishes metaphor – according to the classical definition – is precisely its interruption or violation of the mimetic codes that govern literal expression.

In *Richard*, however, 'lionheart' is transformed into a narrative event. At the court of Almeyne Richard wins his famous cognomen by wrenching the heart out of a ferocious lion. The romance undoes the violation inherent in the metaphoric epithet and renders it mimetically coherent.[37] Richard is 'cœur de lion' not on account of his figurative likeness to a lion but because he *literally* wins a lion's heart. The manuscripts (with the exception of Auchinleck which omits it entirely) record two slightly different versions of the episode. In the more 'historical' version (the version which omits his magical birth and consumption of the Saracen), Richard strangles the lion and then, cutting it open with a knife, removes the heart. In the inflated 'romance' text (the version of *Richard* that I am interested in) the knife is omitted; Richard thrusts his arm down the animal's throat, rips out its heart and (to the surprise of the King of Almeyne in whose salt cellar he dips the bloody meat) eats it. That Richard's identity is contingent on an act of ingestion accords with the narrative's alimentary logic. The figurative analogy implicit in the chroniclers' designation of Richard as 'lionheart' is rendered baldly literal; it is recast as a simple act of (alimentary) cause and effect: you are what you eat. Equally important, however, is what this episode – and its successive transformations – tells us about the poetic code that operates in *Richard*. 'Lionheart' as narrative event is effectively a spelling out – a clarification and explanation, achieved by actualising a metaphor – of Richard's cognomen. Here (and I would argue elsewhere in the romance) *Richard* rejects the metaphoric as a mode of both discourse and action and embraces instead the literal. As modern readers, we have learned to privilege the metaphor; literal signals to us something naive or crude and indeed critics of popular romance regularly dismiss the genre as just that. The kind of spelling-out that the lion heart episode effects is, in fact, remarkably consistent with what scholars identify as fundamental to the genre: a stripped-down narrative, comprised of a sequence of linearly coherent events, that moves with singular purpose toward a self-evident resolution. Popular romance is distinguished by the way in which it prioritises plot, what Peter Brooks calls the 'organizing line and intention of narrative'.[38] The result is an enormously satisfying, event-filled story, but one that achieves satisfaction at the expense of what we, as academic readers, have been trained to value in a literary text: structural complexity, ambiguity, resistance to closure, and a sophisticated use of metaphor (among other things).

There is of course nothing necessarily second rate about literal, or mimetic, discourse. On the contrary, to the extent that it refuses the mediation inherent in metaphor – the distance that, for instance, separates the sweet-and-sour Turk's Head pie from Muslim genocide – it provides an uncompromising immediacy, a bluntness that demands that we confront head-on events or ideas that elsewhere remain camouflaged in indirection. The kind of spelling out that we find in

Richard forces us to acknowledge the presence of a fully legitimated anthropophagy, real and imagined, in Western culture. I want to conclude this essay by suggesting that Richard's anthropophagy derives meaning from (and disturbs our understanding of) not only the conventions of late medieval cuisine, but a blatantly literal eucharistic theology. Eating people – literally – is the prerogative of the virtuous Christian.

The textual history of *Richard* is complex (the product not only of translation but at least two revisions), but I am confident that the redactor who transforms Richard into a man-eater also rewrites the lion heart episode to include his consumption of the heart. Likewise, the same redactor substitutes Cassiodorien, a fairy princess, for Richard's historical mother Eleanor of Aquitaine and invents the episode in which she flees the mass through the roof of the church. That all of these incidents are the product of a single redactor is not coincidental. The Cassiodorien episode, added to the start of the romance, not only provides Richard with the kind of mythical parentage common to romance heroes, but effectively initiates the narrative that follows. A beginning, as Edward Said reminds us, is a 'formal appetite'; it signals narrative desire, a 'hunger' (as Said sees it) for a particular kind of story.[39] Popular romance tends to have sharply demarcated beginnings and endings. The insistence with which it signals its parameters is key to understanding the logic of the story: romance does not so much demand a 'willing suspension of disbelief' as create its own system of belief. Romance logic, like its morality, is self-reflexive. This is not to say that romance cannot reflect broader cultural realities, but simply that within its parameters (from the 'hic incipit' through to 'Amen. Explicit' of each individual romance) the audience is invited to participate in – to believe in – the narrative system that makes that romance cohere. The Cassiodorien episode, interesting precisely because it is a late addition to the romance, stands out for the way in which it is purposefully productive of the hunger that, as we have seen, drives *Richard*.

Like many progenitors of romance heroes, Cassiodorien has a touch of the diabolical; and, as we might expect, she passes this on to her son. *Richard*, much like *Sir Gowther*, is in effect a narrative of exorcism: an account of how Richard successfully purges himself of his devilish inheritance. Significantly, Richard's anthropophagy, far from being a sign of that inheritance, not only marks, but produces, his return to the Christian community. Cassiodorien's alterity is a function not of her obscure origins, her otherworldly beauty, or her exotic attire, but of her inability to sit through the mass. On her first visit to church she faints just before the consecration of the host, is carried away to her chamber and only returns, fifteen years later, when a powerful earl challenges Henry with his wife's impiety. On this second occasion, her reaction is more definitive: at the moment of consecration, she flies out through the roof and never returns. The narrative is careful to locate Cassiodorien's alienation from the mass in the 'sakeryng' (222), the precise moment at which the bread and wine of communion, elevated for the congregation to see, is transformed into the body and blood of Christ; as she says herself, 'I dar neuere see þe sacrement' (194). Cassiodorien, like the witches, Jews and heretics (all familiar host abusers) of popular eucharistic miracles, is outed, so to speak, by the *corpus verum*, the wheaten disc that once consecrated (so late medieval theologians insist) is the actual flesh and blood of Christ in all of its materiality. Cassiodorien is unable to participate in the ritual of theophagy, the holy anthropophagy that binds Christian communicants into a harmonious community of believers; she is prohibited from seeing the eucharist – an act considered sufficiently analogous to literal consumption that even Alexander of Hales (who denies its sacramental nature) speaks of 'eating by sight' (*manducatio per visum*) – and so she is expelled from the community.[40]

Although Cassiodorien is never mentioned again, we understand that Richard, judged by more than one knight as 'a deuyl' (500) or 'pouke' (568), takes up arms in direct response to the taint of impiety that necessarily, after his mother is exposed as an unbeliever, adheres to him.[41] Crusading is well known in romance as a sure means to salvation and the Pope is explicitly cited as promising Richard eternal 'paradys' (1326) in exchange for his assault on the Saracen-controlled Holy Land. Richard flaunts the trappings of piety (his tournament disguises, for instance, all sport elaborate devices that align him against his mother's kin – heathens, unbelievers, and God's enemies) and he sets about crusading with a palpable urgency. His anthropophagy is positioned at the mid-point of the narrative and divides it into two distinct halves. A thirteen-line invocation to May (flowers, birdsong, and amorous couples (3759–71)) immediately follows the Saracen Head banquet and, precisely because it is abrupt and contextually inappropriate, confirms the formal rupture that the anthropophagy effects. Structurally speaking, the first half of the romance finds its resolution in Richard's consumption of the Saracen. Richard does not yet gain the promised paradise (that awaits his combat with Saladin in the second half of the romance) but what he does achieve, in overt contrast to his mother, is an assured identity as a Christian. For the first time in the romance, Richard can assert, with impunity, 'j am kyng, Cristen, and

trewe' (3514) because his holy anthropophagy (Saracen flesh consumed in the service of God) performs the same function as conventional Catholic theophagy. Like the eucharist, it is authorised by Christ
as a sign of 'hys grace and his vertu' (3067); it replicates the sacrament's
power to restore the communicant to health (the medicinal quality of
the Host is a commonplace of eucharistic verse), successfully rendering
Richard 'hool and sounde' (3118); it forges a corporate Christian
identity ('þer is no fflesch so norysschaunt / Vnto an Ynglyssche
Cristen-man' (3548–9)) that is defined as much by purposeful exclusion as inclusion (the Saracens report to Saladin 'Non off vs eet morsel
off bred, / Ne drank off wyn' (3635–6)); and, for one extraordinary
instant, it demands that man eat man.[42]

The extent to which late medieval Christians both recognise and
embrace the anthropophagy inherent in the sacrament of the eucharist
is well attested.[43] The doctrine of the Real Presence – the belief that
Christ is literally present, in flesh and blood, in the consecrated host –
is made manifest in an iconography (verbal and visual) of food and
eating that is at once homely and outrageous. Hungry communicants
not only feed on 'Crist in a cake', the 'soþefast mete' that is commonly
received 'in fourme of bred' or as 'rosted' flesh, they do so with
enthusiastic 'smackyng', marvelling at its 'deliciows' flavour or distinctive 'swetnes'; at times Christ is 'oure sugre', at others he is simply
'foode'.[44] Culinary metaphor transforms the crucifixion into an exercise
in baking: the wheat is 'þresschen', the 'curnel[s]' pounded into
'meole', 'knede[d]' and 'molded' into loaves, and finally, in an extraordinary rendition of the entombment, 'don in þe ouene'.[45] Sin, on
the other hand, renders the host 'raw flessch bledyng': a woman who
denies the sanctity of something as mundane as bread, for instance,
finds in its place a bleeding finger.[46] Even more arresting, however, are
those eucharistic *exempla* in which a priest, sometimes having slaughtered him first, eats a small boy. These narratives commonly depict the
anthropophagy as a god-sent vision (designed either to reward the
virtuous believer or to incite the unbeliever's conversion), but there is
nothing ephemeral about the way they figure the communicant as a
man-eater.[47] At the moment of elevation, the priest raises up not a
white disk but a bloodied infant – 'a ffeir child, I-woundet sore', 'a
child blodie', as one fifteenth century English sermon describes it –
and proceeds, in the company of the other mass-goers, to eat his gory
meal: '[he] ete þe child / þat he bi-twenen his hondes held / And al þat
weore in þe churche þermide / … so heo dude'.[48] More gruesome is
Robert of Brunne's account of the doubtful religious: at the moment

of consecration, a living child 'in feyr forme, of flesshe & blode' is hacked to pieces on the altar; chunks of his bloodied flesh ('Morselles of þe chyld al newe sleyn / ... / Wyþ al þe blode þer on al fresshe') are offered to the communicant and, awe struck, he believes.[49] What these so-called miracles demonstrate, as they flout the taboos against infanticide and anthropophagy, is the audacity of medieval eucharistic piety.

The requirement that Christ be literally present in flesh and blood – real to see, touch and taste – on the altar, in the priest's hands and in the communicant's mouth liberates us to imagine the unimaginable and, more significantly, forces us to record these fantasies in words and images. Acts conventionally deemed transgressive no longer elicit opprobrium; indeed they incite, and license, other fantastic acts. [50] When Hugh of Lincoln, for instance, is rebuked by the abbot of Fécamp for gnawing like a dog on the arm bone of Mary Magdalene, he dismisses him with eucharistic logic: 'If, not long ago, we have touched the most sacred body of the Lord of the saints with our fingers, however unworthy, and having touched it with our teeth and lips absorbed it in our stomach, why should we not ... confidently handle in the same way the body parts of his saints.'[51] Eating people, that inveterate Christian taboo, is simultaneously one of its most potent fantasies. The ideology of Christian communion, the desire of individual and community to forge their identity around the shared ingestion of a man-god's flesh, is an enormously productive ideology of licensed anthropophagy, literal and metaphoric. Richard's consumption of the Saracen, constructed as both an alimentary necessity and an act of sacral devotion, provides the romance audience with a convenient focus for its own fantasies of religious supremacy, political dominion, nationalism and a good meal. *Richard*, like so many popular romances, is resolutely logical; driven by hunger (for the body of Christ, foreign lands, and material sustenance) it finds satisfaction in the literal ingestion of the Saracen, the alien other whose annihilation Western culture demands. *Richard*'s logic is disturbing (it's meant to be) but it is certainly not, any more than Ariel Sharon's 'Arabs for breakfast', absurd.

Notes

Thanks are due to Ann Rycraft and Hélène Tronc for innumerable conversations about food, medieval and modern, and anthropophagy and to Victoria Stavely for her culinary experiments.
1 *Diuersa Cibaria* in *Curye on Inglysch*, eds C. Heiatt and S. Butler, EETS s.s. 8 (London, 1985), p. 48. The recipe is extant in three manuscripts, one

Anglo-Norman (British Library, MS Royal 12 C. xii, fol.12v (*c.* 1320–40)) and two English (British Library, MS Additional 46919, fol. 20v (before 1333); British Library, MS Cotton Julius D. viii, fol. 105v (*c.* 1450)).

2   Michael Flanders, 'The reluctant cannibal', *The Songs of Michael Flanders and Donald Swann* (London, 1977), pp. 64–6.

3   The word 'cannibal' derives from *Caniba*, a variant of *Carib*, the term used by the both the islanders and Spanish colonists to designate the natives of the Caribbean islands. Columbus promoted the belief that the *Canibales* were savage man-eaters; their reputed dietary transgressions were quickly exploited by the colonists as a justification for the decimation of native culture and its practitioners. Peter Hulme argues that '"cannibalism" is a term with no application outside the discourse of European colonialism', *Colonial Encounters* (London, 1986), p. 84. See also F. Lestringant, *Cannibals: The Discovery and Representation of the Cannibal from Columbus to Jules Verne*, trans. R. Morris (Berkeley and Los Angeles, 1997), pp. 15–17.

4   The Psalter (British Library, MS Additional 28681, *c.* 1250), Ebstorf (thirteenth century), and Hereford (*c.* 1300) *mappaemundi* all relegate anthropophagi to the far south of the world, on the edges of Africa and at Christ's extreme left; John Mandeville locates his anthropophagi in the east, in the vicinity of Ynde, in places like Sumatra, the Andaman Islands and Tibet. The Mongols (or Tartars) were routinely stigmatised as man-eaters and when they invaded Eastern Europe in the thirteenth century, Western fear conjured ever more graphic images of their reputed loathsome diet; Matthew Paris, for instance, depicts Tartar practice in a gruesome illumination in his *Chronica Universale* (discussed below in section II). Accusations of domestic, European anthropophagy were directed against Jews (and closely linked to the accusations of ritual murder discussed by Miri Rubin in *Corpus Christi: The Eucharist in Late Medieval Culture* (Cambridge, 1991) and *Gentile Tales: The Narrative Assault on Late Medieval Jews* (Yale, 1999)) and witches (see Richard Kieckhefer, *European Witch Trials: Their Foundations in Popular and Learned Culture, 1300–1500* (London, 1976), *passim* and Reay Tannahill, *Flesh and Blood: A History of the Cannibal Complex* (London, 1975), pp. 92–107), as well as the *Tafurs*, a troop of hungry desperadoes who, at Antioch and Ma'arat-an-Nu'man, gorged on the rotting corpses of the Muslim enemy. See L. A. M. Sumberg, 'The "Tafurs" and the First Crusade', *Medieval Studies*, 21 (1959), 224–46 and J. Tattersall 'Anthropophagi and eaters of raw flesh in French literature of the Crusade period: myth, tradition and reality', *Medium Aevum*, 57 (1988), 240–53.

5   The fourteenth-century *Forme of Curye* (compiled by Richard II's chief cook) includes a recipe for *cokantrice* (*Curye on Inglysch*, eds Hieatt and Butler, p. 139); similar recipes are found in the fifteenth-century: *Two Fifteenth-Century Cookery-Books*, ed. T. Austin, EETS o.s. 91 (London, 1888), pp. 40, 115. Instructions detailing 'how somme mete schalle seme raw' are found among other 'slyʒtes of cure' in the *Liber Cure Cocorum*, ed. R. Morris (Berlin, 1862), p. 5.

6 See Terence Scully, 'The medieval French e*ntremets*', *Petits Propos Culinaire*, 17 (1984), 44–56; Danielle Queruel, 'Des Entremets aux intermedes dans les banquets Bourguignons', in *Banquets et manières de table au Moyen Age* (Aix-en-Provence, 1996), pp. 143–57; and Bridget Ann Henisch, *Fast and Feast: Food in Medieval Society* (University Park, PA, 1976), pp. 206–36 for an introduction to the origin and history of the *entremets*.

7 The mock battle is illustrated in the *Grandes Chroniques de France*, Paris, Bibliothèque nationale, MS. fr. 2813, fol. 473v (*c.* 1379). See L. H. Loomis, 'Secular dramatics in the royal palace, Paris, 1378, 1389, and Chaucer's "tregetoures"', *Speculum*, 33 (1958), 242–55; also Henisch, *Fast and Feast*, p. 234.

8 Claude Lévi-Strauss first coined the terms 'good to eat' (*bon à manger*) and 'good to think' (*bon à penser*) in his analysis of the totemic value of animals (*Totemism*, trans. R. Needham (London, 1964), p. 89); the terms were quickly extended to the study of food by anthropologists sympathetic to Lévi-Strauss's structuralist ideology.

9 *MED*, eten (v.) 4c; devouren (v.) 3b; swolwen (v.) 2d; glotoun (n.) 1b; feste (v.) 1a.

10 *Richard Cœur de Lion. Der Mittelenglische Versroman über Richard Löwenherz*, ed. Karl Brunner (Vienna, 1913), lines 5489–91. All quotations from *Richard* will be from this edition and will be cited by line number in the text of the essay.

11 For a summary of Catholic doctrine on the eucharist (including transubstantiation and the 'Real Presence') see *The New Catholic Encyclopedia*, 15 vols (Washington, DC, 1967): 'Eucharist', vol. 5, pp. 594–615; 'Transubstantiation', vol. 14, pp. 259–61. Miri Rubin outlines key medieval debates on the nature and substance of the eucharist in *Corpus Christi*, pp. 14–35.

12 Sally Kevill-Davies, *Antique Pocket Guides: Jelly Moulds* (Guildford, 1983) reproduces a selection of eighteenth-century moulds as well as an illustrated page of earthenware blancmange moulds from Copeland's 1902 catalogue (see especially pp. 11–12, 27). The 1881 catalogue for Simmons Hardware Company in St Louis, Missouri advertises large and small metal Turk's head pans; the relevant page is reproduced in R. Barlow (ed.), *Victorian Houseware, Hardware and Kitchenware: A Pictorial Archive with over 2000 Illustrations* (Mineola, NY, 1992), p. 109. Current popularity of the distinctive mould is suggested by baking guru Rose Levy Beranbaum; 'my favorite mold [for fruitcake] is a … Turk's head': *The Cake Bible* (New York, 1988), p. 68.

13 See Nabil I Matar, 'Renaissance England and the turban', in D. Blanks (ed.), *Images of the Other: Europe and the Muslim World Before 1700* (Cairo, 1997), pp. 39–54 for an informative account of the politics of turbans and Turks' heads in Renaissance England; Matar's argument has clear implications for medieval representations of Islam and the Arab world.

14 Quoted during the 2001 Israeli election campaign in *Independent on Sunday*, 28 January 2001; Jean Marie Le Pen, leader of France's ultra rightwing Front National, makes a similar claim: 'Je mange du musulman

tout cru à mon petit déjeuner comme ne l'interdit pas le Prophète'; cited
in 'Les bons mots oubliés du chef', *Le Canard enchaîné*, 30 April 2002.

15 George Ellis, *Specimens of Early English Metrical Romances*, 2 vols (London,
1805), vol. 2, p. 174; Sir Walter Scott, 'Introduction' (dated 1832) to *The
Talisman*, ed. W. M. Parker (London, 1991), p. 3; John Finlayson,
'*Richard, Cœr de Lyon*: romance, history or something in between?',
Studies in Philology, 87 (1990), 156–80 (pp. 161, 165, 161); W. R. J.
Barron, *English Medieval Romance* (London, 1987), p. 180.

16 *Cronicon Richardi Divisensis de Tempore Regis Richardi Primi. The Chronicle
of Richard of Devizes of the Time of King Richard the First*, ed. and trans. J. T.
Appleby (London, 1963), p. 77.

17 Geraldine Heng, 'The romance of England: *Richard Cœr de Lyon*, Saracens,
Jews, and the politics of race and nation', in J. J. Cohen (ed.), *The Post-
colonial Middle Ages* (New York, 2000), pp. 135–71 (p. 137 and *passim*).

18 *Richard* is extant in seven imperfect manuscripts conventionally divided
into a longer, more fabulous, A version – Cambridge, Gonville and Caius
College, MS 175/96 (*c.* 1400); London, British Library, MS Additional
31042 (*c.* 1440) – and a shorter, more historical, B version – Edinburgh,
National Library of Scotland, MS Advocates 19.2.1, the so-called Auchinleck manuscript (*c.* 1330); London, College of Arms, MS Arundel 58 (*c.*
1400–50); London, British Library, MS Egerton 2862 (*c.* 1390); London,
British Library, MS Harley 4690 (fifteenth century); Oxford, Bodleian
Library, MS Douce 228 (late fifteenth century). *Richard* was printed by
Wynken de Worde in 1509 and 1528; the printed text is very close to the
so-called A version manuscripts. Karl Brunner's 1913 edition of *Richard*
(which remains the most recent and only readily available edition) uses
Cambridge, Gonville and Caius, MS 175/96 as its base text, supplemented by Wynkyn de Worde's prints for the following lines missing
from the Cambridge manuscript: 227–449, 679–796, 1736–2468, 6864–
992. A new edition is long overdue, but since all manuscripts are imperfect
no edition, with a readable complete text, can ever be wholly satisfactory.

19 Gaston Paris, 'Le Roman de Richard Cœur de Lion', *Romania*, 26 (1897),
353–93 (pp. 361–2); Brunner, *Der Mittelenglische Versroman über Richard
Löwenherz*, Introduction 1.4: pp. 17–23.

20 John Gillingham, *Richard I* (New Haven, 1999) provides the most up to
date and thorough account of Richard's life and reign.

21 The longer A version of *Richard* is conventionally distinguished from the
shorter B version by its inclusion of fabulous romance-like material
which disrupts B's historicity; Finlayson, '*Richard, Cœr de Lyon*: romance,
history or something in between', attempts to identify, episode by
episode, the historically verifiable core that underlies the romance. Yet,
as even Finlayson notes (p. 161), all extant manuscripts, other than
Auchinleck, contain some non-historical 'interpolated' material.

22 The defective nature of *Richard*'s manuscripts makes it difficult to assert
with confidence exactly how much fabulous material each extant text

originally contained. I have, however, noted that those manuscripts (Arundel 58, Harley 4690 and Douce 228) that identify Eleanor of Aquitaine as Richard's mother and Berengaria of Navarre as his wife (2040b: 1–13), thereby maintaining a modicum of historical accuracy, omit not only the fabulous Cassiodorien (as we might expect), but also Richard's anthropophagy and his consumption of the lion's heart. There is no reference to Eleanor or Berengaria in Auchinleck, but it is deficient at the relevant point in the text so we can draw no firm conclusions; since it omits Cassiodorien there is no reason why it should not include Eleanor. Gonville and Caius 175 and Additional 31042 start with Cassiodorien as Richard's mother, omit Eleanor and Berengaria, and include both his anthropophagy and his eating of the lion's heart; Egerton 2862 is illegible at the start (so it is not possible to confirm its inclusion of the Cassiodorien episode) but both Richard's anthropophagy and his eating of the heart are included. See section III below for a discussion of the significance of these additions (and omissions).

23 Henry Fielding, *Tom Jones*, eds F. Bowers and M. C. Battestin, 2 vols (Oxford, 1974), vol. 1, p. 509.

24 See W. C. Jordan, *The Great Famine: Northern Europe in the Early Fourteenth Century* (Princeton, 1996) for a comprehensive account of late medieval European famine.

25 For fruit and vegetables as peasant food see C. Dyer 'Did the peasants really starve in medieval England?', in M. Carlin and J. T. Rosenthal (eds), *Food and Eating in Medieval Europe* (London, 1998), pp. 53–71 (p. 63). For horse flesh as a taboo meat see F. J. Simoons, *Eat not this Flesh: Food Avoidances from Prehistory to the Present*, 2nd edition (Madison, 1994), pp.79–86; for an account of both horse flesh and inferior foods as a sign of famine see J. Marvin, 'Cannibalism as an aspect of famine in two English chronicles' in Carlin and Rosenthal (eds), *Food and Eating in Medieval Europe*, pp. 73–85.

26 Susan E. Farrier underlines the general absence of any practical reference to food in Middle English romance in her essay 'Hungry heroes in medieval literature', in Melitta Weiss Adamson (ed.), *Food in the Middle Ages: A Book of Essays* (New York, 1995), pp. 145–59 (pp. 145–6).

27 The enraged Saladin, learning that his compatriots have been eaten, condemns Richard as a 'deuyl' (3664); Philip of France's censure is implicit in his decision, when hungry and ailing, to eschew the English king's restorative diet of cooked Saracen, choosing instead to return to Europe (5467–80, 5913–30).

28 Dishes like *Bruette Sareson* (a type of beef stew) and *Saunc Sarazine*, alternately called *Sawse Sarzyne*, (an almond flavoured sauce commonly coloured red) use ingredients, cooking techniques and colours imported from and associated with Eastern cuisine; all three can be found in *Curye on Inglysch*, eds Hieatt and Butler, pp. 72, 86, 117. C. Anne Wilson provides a survey of the Arab flavour of medieval cuisine in a pair of articles:

'The Saracen connection: Arab cuisine and the medieval West: part 1' and 'The Saracen connection: Arab cuisine and the medieval West: part 2', *Petits Propos Culinaire*, 7 (1981), 13–22 and 8 (1981), 19–28.

29 Geoffrey of Monmouth, *The Historia Regum Britannie of Geoffrey of Monmouth I: Bern, Burgerbibliothek, MS. 568*, ed. Neil Wright (Cambridge, 1984), p. 165; *Alliterative Morte Arthure* in *King Arthur's Death*, ed. L. D. Benson (Exeter, 1986), lines 1049–52.

30 Suzanne Lewis, *The Art of Matthew Paris in the Chronica Majora* (Aldershot, 1987), fig. 180.

31 See for instance, *The Seege or Batayle of Troye*, ed. M. E. Barnicle, EETS o.s. 172 (London, 1927), lines 2052–6; *Havelok*, ed. G. V. Smithers (Oxford, 1987), lines 1725–30; *Of Arthour and of Merlin*, ed. O. D. Macrae-Gibson, EETS o.s. 268 (London, 1973), lines 3117–23. See also *Two Fifteenth-Century Cookery-Books*, ed. Austin, pp. 57–64 and pp. 67–9 for a selection of historic menus; these unelaborated documents simply list the meats and dishes served.

32 A recipe for *yrchouns* is included in the *Forme of Curye* (*Curye on Inglysch*, eds Hieatt and Butler, p. 139); recipes for both *yrchouns* and *appraylere* are edited by Austin (*Two Fifteenth-Century Cookery-Books*, pp. 38, 39).

33 Felicity Heal reminds us that for the guest, or outsider, the unfamiliar household was a 'potentially hostile environment'; the guest's 'very security' is dependent on the 'belief that [the] host will obey the laws of hospitality: *Hospitality in Early Modern England* (Oxford 1990), p. 192. In an informative study of table manners that insists on the violence inherent in eating, Margaret Visser proposes that '[b]ehind every rule of table etiquette lurks the determination of each person present to be a diner, not a dish', *The Rituals of Dinner: The Origins, Evolution, Eccentricities and Meaning of Table Manners* (Harmondsworth, 1992), p. 4.

34 A recipe for *Pecock rosted* is edited by Austin, *Two Fifteenth Century Cookery-Books*, p. 79; Albertus Magnus provides instructions for the preparation of a leaping chicken: 'If thou wilt that a Chicken or other thing leap in the dish', *The Book of Secrets of Albertus Magnus*, eds M. R. Best and F. H. Brightman (Oxford, 1973), p. 98; and the recipe for 'De pastillo auium uiuarum' is found in the *Liber de Coquina*: 'Deux traités inédits d'art culinaire médiéval', ed. Marianne Mulon, *Bulletin philologique et historique (jusqu'à 1610) du comité des travaux historiques et scientifiques* (1968), vol. 1, pp. 368–435 (p. 405).

35 Key details suggest that for Richard (and the narrator) the Saracen's Head is purposefully designed to function as an *entremets*: it is piped in with a characteristic flourish of music; it is served one dish between two diners in conventional aristocratic fashion; and a parchment name-tag, effectively explaining its political as well as culinary significance, is affixed to each head. For a useful comparison with historical *entremets* see Scully, 'The medieval French *entremets*', Queruel, 'Des Entremets' and Henisch, *Fast and Feast*.

36 Ambroise, *L'Estoire de la Guerre Sainte*, ed. G. Paris (Paris, 1897), line 2310; Bernard Itier, 'Obitus Richardi Regis', *La Vérité sur la mort de Richard Cœur-de-Lion Roi d'Angleterre*, ed. L'Abbé Arbellot (Paris, 1878), p. 61; William the Breton, *Philippidos*, in *Oeuvres de Rigord et de Guillaume le Breton*, ed. H. F. Delaborde, 2 vols (Paris 1885), vol. 2, p. 396.

37 *Richard* provides the first extant account of 'lion heart' as a narrative event. Loomis has suggested, on the evidence of the Chertsey tiles, that the story, however, predates *Richard*. For the purpose of my argument, it does not matter if *Richard*'s poet invented the story or not, but simply that he embraced it in all of its literalness. See R. S. Loomis, '*Richard Cœur de Lion* and the *Pas Saladin* in medieval art', *PMLA*, 30 (1915), 510–20.

38 Peter Brooks, *Reading for the Plot: Design and Intention in Narrative* (Cambridge, MA and London, 1984), p. 37.

39 Edward Said, *Beginnings: Intention and Method* (New York, 1975), p. 76.

40 Alexander of Hales's distinction *manducatio per gustum* and *manducatio per visum* is cited by Édouard Dumoutet in what is still the most complete study of the doctrine and practice of 'sacramental viewing', *Le Désire de voir l'hostie et les origins de la devotion au saint-sacrement* (Paris, 1926), p. 20. Rubin, *Corpus Christi*, pp. 49–63; Eamon Duffy, *The Stripping of the Altars: Traditional Religion in England 1400–1580* (New Haven, 1992), pp. 95–102 and Leah Sinanoglou, 'The Christ Child as sacrifice: a medieval tradition and the Corpus Christi plays', *Speculum*, 48 (1973), 491–509 all provide accounts of popular, sometimes frenzied, devotion to 'seeing God'. As the laity was increasingly distanced from the touch and taste of the host, sight (signalled by the ringing of the sacring-bell and the elevation of the host) became paramount and the elevation provided the climax of the mass; see T. W. Drury, *Elevation in the Eucharist: Its History and Rationale* (Cambridge, 1907), p. 125 and *passim*.

41 Richard's brother John is likewise tainted with diabolical blood – 'Jhon,/ þat was the fendes ffflesch and bon' (6335–6) – but for him, of course, there is no redemption.

42 See John Bossy for his classic account of the mass as productive of corporate identity and social integration, 'The Mass as a social institution, 1200–1700', *Past and Present*, 100 (1983), 29–61; also relevant is Miri Rubin, 'The eucharist and the construction of medieval identities', in David Aers (ed.), *Culture and History 1350–1600* (Detroit, 1992), pp. 43–63; the mass is, of course, equally productive of social division, but in *Richard* the analogy of the eucharistic feast is employed to underline the king's participation in a Christian community, not his exclusion from it.

43 See Rubin, *Corpus Christi*, pp. 359–60 and *passim*. Sister Loretta McGarry, *The Holy Eucharist in Middle English Homiletic and Devotional Verse* (Washington, 1936) and Michele Theresa Priscandaro, *Middle English Eucharistic Verse: Its Imagery, Symbolism and, Typology* (New York, 1975) offer comprehensive surveys of vernacular English eucharistic verse; both include a selection of explicitly anthropophagic material.

44 These citations reflect only a tiny percentage of references to Christ as food; most are commonplace, repeated time and again in devotional literature, and the references below are by no means unique. 'Crist in a cake': 'Festivals of the church', *Legends of the Holy Rood*, ed. R. Morris, EETS o.s. 46 (London, 1871), p. 211, line 40; 'soþefast mete': Oxford, Merton College, MS 248, fol. 167, 'Caro mea vere cibum' (C. F. Brown, *A Register of Middle English and Didactic Verse*, 2 vols (Oxford, 1916–20), vol. 1, p. 148, vol. 2, p. 207); 'in fourme of bred': 'Welcome, Lord, in fourme of bred', *Minor Poems of the Vernon MS: Part I*, ed. C. Horstmann, EETS o.s. 98 (London, 1892), p. 24, line 1; 'rosted': Robert Mannyng, *Meditations on the Supper of our Lord, and the Hours of the Passion*, ed. J. Meadows Cowper, EETS o.s. 60 (London, 1875), line 82; 'smakyng': 'Ronde in schapyng', *Verses in Sermons: Fasciculus Morum ad its Middle English Poems*, ed. S. Wenzel (Cambridge, MA, 1978), p. 182, line 4; 'deliciows': Hoccleve, 'The song of graces of alle seintes upon Paske day', *Hoccleve's Works III: The Regement of Princes and Fourteen of Hoccleve's Minor Poems*, ed. F. J. Furnivall, EETS e.s. 72 (London, 1897) p. l, line 17; 'swetness': John Lydgate, 'The fifteen ooes of Christ', *The Minor Poems of John Lydgate*, ed. H. N. MacCracken, EETS e.s. 107 (London, 1911) pp. 238–50, line 209; 'oure sugre': 'The fifteen ooes of Christ', line 211; 'foode': 'The Magi', *The York Plays*, ed. R. Beadle (London, 1982), line 321.

45 'Whon grein of whete is cast to grounde', in 'Proprium Sanctorum: Zusatz-Homilien des Ms. Vernon fol. CCXV ff. zur nördlichen Sammlung der Dominicalia evangelia', ed. C. Horstmann, *Archiv für das Studium der Neueren Sprachen und Litteraturen*, 81 (1888), 83–5: lines 81, 82, 118, 115, 120, 126.

46 John Mirk, *Mirk's Festial: A Collection of Homilies*, ed. T. Erbe, EETS e.s. 96 (London, 1905), p. 173, line 23.

47 See Sinanoglou, 'The Christ Child as sacrifice: a medieval tradition and the Corpus Christi plays'. Miri Rubin argues that the importance of the child-on-the-altar topos, as well as its frequency of representation, rose markedly from the thirteenth century and she aligns its popularity with 'the same trends which portrayed increasingly gory images of the crucified Christ'; Rubin, *Corpus Christi*, p. 139.

48 'De festo corporis Christi', *The Minor Poems of the Vernon Manuscript: Part I*, ed. Horstmann, pp. 168–97, lines 143, 177, 153–6.

49 Robert Mannyng, *Handlyng Synne*, ed. Idelle Sullens (Binghamton, 1983), lines 10055, 10066–8.

50 Miri Rubin likewise argues that the eucharistic miracles produce 'sites for fantasy', *Corpus Christi*, p. 139.

51 'Si … ipsius Sancti sanctorum paulo ante corpus sanctissimum digitis licet indignis contrectauimus, dentibus quoque uel labiis attrectatum ad interiora nostra transmisimus, quare non etiam sanctorum eius menbra … fiducialiter attrectamus …?' (*Magna Vita Sancti Hugonis*, ed. D. L. Douie and H. Farmer, 2 vols, (London, 1962), vol. 2, p. 170.

7

The Siege of Jerusalem and recuperative readings

Elisa Narin van Court

Dismissed for years from serious critical attention, the fourteenth-century alliterative narrative *The Siege of Jerusalem*[1] has recently begun to generate the kind of interest associated with more canonical Middle English works. Scholarly studies have emerged to fill the lacunae of response and readings, and a new edition is forthcoming.[2] In this essay I will argue that this new attention to *Jerusalem* is well deserved and long overdue, inhibited more by scholarly distaste for the poem's perceived relentless and violent anti-Judaism, than by any intrinsic lack of literary or cultural value. The variety of new readings generated by this poem which once existed, as Ralph Hanna notes, 'on the suppressed margins of critical attention, unaccompanied by commentary',[3] testifies to its increasing importance in medieval studies. Yet even as a community of readers work to recuperate *Jerusalem* from its marginal placement, with few exceptions they continue to read the narrative as thoroughly anti-Judaic.[4] My argument concerning the poem is predicated on a recuperative reading in another sense of the word; I suggest that the virulent anti-Judaism from which scholars recoil is neither as unambiguous nor singular as is commonly claimed. Indeed, a full and nuanced reading of *Jerusalem* reveals that the poem does not deserve its 'reputation as the chocolate-covered tarantula of the alliterative movement',[5] and I will argue that the poem belies long-held critical assumptions both about this specific poem and about a conventional, monolithic anti-Judaism considered axiomatic in late fourteenth-century Middle English texts.

The Siege of Jerusalem was probably composed in the last decades of the fourteenth century in far west Yorkshire.[6] The nine surviving manuscripts testify to a wide popularity and the medieval collations indicate that the poem was 'capable of polyvocal recuperations' in the fourteenth and fifteenth centuries. Thus the alliterative narrative is, in some manuscripts, placed in contexts which suggest it be read as a 'quasi-scriptural narrative', another manuscript supports its being read as romance, while others suggest the poem's connection with, variously, crusade poetry, alliterative history, or learned classical history.[7] This lack of a uniform medieval interpretation anticipates the recent and widely different readings which have emerged from the study of this complex narrative.

Drawing on chronicles and legendary materials, including Josephus' first-century account of *The Jewish War*, the apocryphal *Vindicta salvatoris*, Higden's *Polychronicon*, the *Bible en françois* of Roger d'Argenteuil, and the *Legenda aurea*, *The Siege of Jerusalem* tells, with varied emphases and details, the story of the destruction of Jerusalem in 70 CE.[8] Titus and Vespasian, Roman leaders and recent converts to Christianity (conversions accomplished through miraculous cures and the Passion twice told), embark upon a crusade against the Jews of Jerusalem to avenge Christ's death. The Romans lay siege to the city and after a tremendous battle in which many Jews are slain, the Jews retreat within the city walls and the Romans assail the town. The poem relates the diverse details of both Roman and Jewish actions during the two-year siege, including detailed scenes inside the city walls where hundreds die daily for lack of food and water, culminating in the surrender of the Jews and their sale into slavery by the Romans. *Jerusalem* is informed throughout by a variety of sensibilities: religious, political, economic, and social. The Roman crusade against the Jews and Jerusalem is framed by Christian justifications; issues of empire and rule are played out within the Roman camp and between the Romans and the Jews; because the Jews have refused to pay tribute to Rome, the economics of revenge initiate, in part, the original impulse to besiege the city; the social dimensions range from the semi-chivalric Roman knights hunting and hawking outside the city's walls, to relations within the city and relations between individual Jew and Christian. The *Jerusalem* poet scripts a highly complex narrative which transcends accounts found in traditional siege literature.

In the 1970s and 1980s the poem received only brief and dismissive attention. Derek Pearsall charges the poem with morbidity and excessive violence and A. C. Spearing even more explicitly recoils from its 'horrible delight in the suffering of the Jews'.[9] The graphically violent and seemingly unambiguous bigotry of *Jerusalem* convinced critics that the work was a repellent model of late medieval sentiment about Jews about which there was little to say. Echoing these earlier assessments,

Ralph Hanna decries the poem's 'gratuitous' and 'cheerfully sanctioned violence'.[10] Yet in his 1992 essay Hanna begins a process of recuperative criticism when he proposes a fifteenth-century reception and Lancastrian reading of the poem in which flayed Jewish flesh is transformed into flayed Lollard flesh. Mary Hamel proposes another type of contextualisation for *Jerusalem* when she argues for the poem's identity as a crusading narrative composed in response to the briefly resurgent crusade fervour of the late fourteenth century.[11] Unlike earlier critics, both Hanna and Hamel construct detailed contexts for understanding the composition and reception of *Jerusalem*. Yet both scholars join the small but unanimous group of critics who are repulsed by the poem's anti-Judaism and they go further than earlier assessments when they propose that either in its reception or its composition the poem's anti-Judaism is a deviant tropological bigotry relocated onto other groups. In essence, they decry the poem's anti-Judaism and then suggest that the poem is not about Jews.

Readings of displacement in which Jews become tropes for other heterodox or heretical groups are understandable: there is no evidence for organised Jewish communities after the expulsion of 1290 (although Jews are never entirely absent from England[12]) and it is possible that in their material absence their presence in narratives becomes a kind of pedagogical category into which other sources of anxiety are displaced. Yet this kind of interpretive supersession elides the very real issues of Jewish presence in Christendom which continue to concern the Christian community even in the absence of Jews. The proliferation of mid to late fourteenth-century Middle English narratives which directly address the issues of Jew *qua* Jew in relationship to the Christian community indicates a significant and ongoing concern with Jews and Judaism.[13] And it is essential to understand that this ongoing concern is neither always nor universally expressed in univocal anti-Judaic forms. I fear we construct a monolithic and univocal bigotry when we invoke 'the' anti-Judaism as an inevitable and universal commonplace of medieval thinking and writing. Medieval anti-Judaism is common but neither universal nor inevitable and until we recognise this we enable readings of medieval works which exclude or elide the variety and instability of medieval Christian responses to Jews, even as we make it difficult to attend to those discursive moments which resist or temper what we consider a cultural given.[14] *The Siege of Jerusalem* offers many such discursive moments which invite audience and reader into active colloquy with the poem's complex representation of Jews.

The nature of the poem's anti-Judaism is again explored by Christine Chism who notes that the poem 'never loses sight of the sufferings of the Jews'.[15] Yet even as she notes the poem's emphasis on suffering and sympathy, Chism argues for the poet's 'delight in cruel inversion' in which pity and sympathy 'lead to more suffering for the Jews'.[16] And in the first full-length study of *Jerusalem*, Bonnie Millar contextualises the poem as a narrative that encourages its audience to reconsider the nature of Christian–Jewish relations.[17] Clearly *The Siege of Jerusalem* is more than just a particularly virulent example of anti-Judaism common but not universal in late medieval culture. As evidenced in the recent readings generated by *Jerusalem*, this is a narrative of polyvocal possibilities; something which was known in the fourteenth and fifteenth centuries. And while it is important not to claim more for this narrative than an informed reading will allow, it is also important not to focus so entirely upon the conventions of anti-Judaism that we do not recognise the real conflicts this poem presents and represents. The polyvocal interpretations which have recently emerged from readings of it signal a growing awareness of the complexities of the narrative and the stimulating nature of the debate which begins to surround the poem. Key to this debate, of course, is the nature and substance of its anti-Judaism.[18]

In order to understand the full contexts for the composition of *The Siege of Jerusalem* we need to glance briefly at the ecclesiastical traditions behind this fourteenth-century production; traditions which are, I think, the essential contexts for understanding the varied response to Jews we find in the narrative. For it is the *ambivalent* nature of Christian doctrine about Jews that best testifies to and prepares us for the equally conflicted response we find in *The Siege of Jerusalem* and other literary productions.[19] In the highly influential Pauline epistles, the dual injunctions of Romans 11:28–9, 'As concerning the gospel, indeed, they are enemies for your sake: but as touching election, they are most dear for the sake of the fathers',[20] initiate a division in Christian doctrine concerning Jews. This division is seen in its most simplistic form in medieval representations of Jews which are articulated through two paradigms of opposition: in the first, the Jews are the other ('enemies') vis-à-vis the Christians; in the second, given the exigencies of Christian claims to a Hebraic heritage ('fathers'), distinctions are made between scriptural Jews, who are revered as the possessors of the Old Law, and historical Jews, who are reviled as the killers of Christ. The division between scriptural Jews and historical Jews is played out in the sermon literature, the drama, poetic histories and narratives; yet this most basic of paradigms is considerably complicated as the double value of the Jews is complexly reconfigured or even collapsed in medieval narratives.

The Pauline division between historical ('they are enemies') and scriptural ('they are most dear') is preceded in Romans 11:15 by an equally significant statement concerning Jewish disbelief which adds another variable to the perception of the divided Jews: 'For if the loss of them be the reconciliation of the world, what shall the receiving of them be, but life from the dead?' That is, Jewish disbelief is part of the Divine plan ('that blindness in part has happened in Israel, until the fullness of the Gentiles should come in' (Romans 11:25)) – and once the world is reconciled under Christ, the conversion of the Jews, which is certain to follow, will augur the final days and the Second Coming of Christ ('life from the dead'). Romans 11 reconstructs the Jews as eschatalogically essential for Christian history, even as it divides Jews (scriptural and historical) and Christian response to Jews.

The dual perspective and eschatalogical role imposed upon Jews in the Pauline writings are developed by Augustine into what is called the doctrine of relative toleration. With a patristic reading of Psalm 58:12 ('slay them not, lest at any time my people forget') as its central proof text, the doctrine enunciates a theological formula in which Jews are accorded a role in Christendom: alive, but in servitude, socially and economically degraded, and with their value dependent upon their status as symbols of Christ's Passion and witnesses to the truth of Christ-ianity.[21] The complexities and ambivalent gestures of the Augustinian position, in which toleration is yoked inextricably with persecution, dominate most medieval Christian writing about Jews (at least until the later Middle Ages). The equivocal and at times contested toleration proposed by Augustine translates into ecclesiastical and civil measures for the protection *and* limitation of the rights of Jews, and into intel-lectual traditions transmitted from Augustine through the writings of other theologians.[22] It is important to emphasise that the Augustinian approach towards Jews and Judaism 'determined the basic stance of virtually all early medieval Christian polemics against the Jews'.[23] Unfortunately, in the thirteenth and fourteenth centuries the policy of toleration begins to come under increased scrutiny and in concert with increasing social, economic, and political pressures a new, more hostile ideology begins to shape ecclesiastical, secular, and popular writing about Jews.[24]

Given this theological context, *The Siege of Jerusalem* is a narrative which announces itself as an exemplar of Christian thinking about

Jews: not only is the poem framed at beginning and end with retellings of Christ's Passion but the destruction of Jerusalem and the dispersion of the Jews are a favourite theme of patristic literature offered as testimony to Jewish perfidy, the supersession of Judaism, and the triumph of Christianity.[25] Those who would read Jewish presence in *Jerusalem* as a trope for Lollards or Saracens overlook the extent to which this poem insists upon the very specific and conflicted relationship between Jew and Christian, Judaism and Christianity.[26] Yet what is noteworthy about *Jerusalem* is that at a time when the doctrine of toleration had almost entirely yielded to a more hostile ideological and practical treatment of Jews, the narrative's complications demonstrate the divided nature of its ideological origins. The poem is, on the one hand, outrageously violent and bigoted: fields run with blood and gore, and metal runs through 'vn-mylt hertes' (556); the Jews are 'þe heþen' (307), 'þe fals men' (551), 'þis faiþles folke' (481), who 'on no grace tristen' (515). When Titus and Vespasian set out for Judea, the narrative warns:

> Cytees vnder Syon, now is ʒour sorow uppe:
> Þe deþ of þe dereworþ Crist der schal be ʒolden.
> Now is, Bethleem, þy bost y-broʒt to an ende;
> Jerusalem & Ierico, for-juggyd wrecchys,
> Schal neuer kyng of ʒour kynde with croune be ynoyntid,
> Ne Jewe for Jesu sake iouke in ʒou more. (295–300)

Passages such as this, in which brutality against the Jews is justified as fitting revenge for Christ's death, frame the narrative and join with the inescapable and excessive detail of violence and bloodshed in the poem to produce an *almost* convincing demonstration of a straightforward and brutal anti-Judaic poetic. Yet, as is increasingly noted, there is another narrative strand which continually intrudes upon and complicates the seemingly unambiguous anti-Judaism. In the early scenes of the poem the Jews are 'þe faiþles' and 'þe heþen'. In the simile that describes their flight into Jerusalem from the Romans they 'Flowen, as þe foule doþ, þat faucoun wolde strike' (310), fall on the battlefield as 'hail froward heuen' (598), and 'wynnen with mychel wo þe walles with-ynne' (612). However, when the poet explains why there are so many Jews in Jerusalem (it is the Pesach holiday), he departs from his sources and enlists the rhetoric of individuation as he refers to 'Princes & prelates & poreil of þe londe, / Clerkes & comens of contrees aboute' (313–14). This rhetorical catalogue effectively differentiates the Jews –

they are not 'þe faiþles' but individuals. And in a related gesture the *Jerusalem* poet undermines the stereotypes of his sources. In Josephus' *Jewish War* and Higden's *Polychronicon*, the Jews are persistently characterised as acting in 'impetuosity and unbridled rage',[27] or *'furor cum temeritate'* – what Trevisa translates as 'woodnesse and folye'.[28] In *Jerusalem* the Jews speak 'mekly' (338), and in their fighting are 'ferce men & noble' (867), while the unbridled rage is transferred onto Vespasian, who is variously described as 'wroþe' (371), 'wode wedande wroþ' (381), and 'wroþ as a wode bore' (781).

One of the *Jerusalem* poet's sources, Flavius Josephus, is himself the focus of some curious revisions. The poet puts him in his place, as it were, by locating him in Jerusalem during the siege. This placement allows for the 'Jewe Josophus, þe gentyl clerke' (785) to be exceedingly active against the Romans in defence of Jerusalem, and to act the noble Jew: when Titus falls ill, no one can be found to cure him, 'Saue þe self Josophus, þat surgyan was noble, / & he graunteþ to go with a goode wylle' (1035–6). Historically, Josephus had been captured at the earlier battle of Jotapata; at Jerusalem he is outside the city walls, with the Romans, from which vantage point he will return to Rome and write his *Jewish War* as a pro-Roman *apologia*.[29] The apologetical motif of Josephus' work is apparent throughout: the Romans, in a manner of speaking, save the Jews from themselves (IV. 134; IV. 397; V. 256–7, etc.). The *Jerusalem* poet refuses to represent the Romans as the 'saviours' of the Jews; his Romans are intent upon the destruction of Jerusalem. With the Romans reinstated as aggressors, and Josephus repositioned within the walls of Jerusalem, the poet revises the dynamics of Josephus' historical account: Roman brutality against the Jews is unequivocal and leads us, finally, to sympathy for the Jews; Josephus, like his text, is reconstructed – no longer outside the walls of Jerusalem, he plays the part of the noble Jew in a revision of his own work where there are no noble Jews.

However striking, the revisions I note above are only partial accounts of the ways in which this poem complicates the issues of militant Christianity and conventions of anti-Judaism. Granted that *Jerusalem* is framed with retellings of Christ's Passion as traditional justification for brutality against the Jews, within this framework the poem inscribes complex alternative representations of Jews and Jewish suffering. There are numerous narrative strategies with which the poet restructures medieval response to Jews[30] and I will focus here on two key revisions in the poem: the first is a central passage or set piece in the siege of Jerusalem narratives and the second is the way in which the language of anti-Judaism fails in passages where the poet details the sufferings of the besieged Jews.

The central passage or set piece, in which a woman suffering from the siege-inflicted famine kills and eats her own child (1077–96), exemplifies the nuanced account of Jews which the *Jerusalem* poet offers. This extended passage is showcased in the various siege of Jerusalem narratives, significant both for its local effect and for the subtexts with which it is informed. In the poet's sources the act of infanticide and cannibalism is used as dramatic testimony to Jewish barbarity and the final rationale for their destruction.[31] The *Jerusalem* poet reworks the rhetoric of his sources and renders the act a result of desperation in a sympathetic account that invites not disgust but sorrow from the reader. In the sources, the scene is prefaced by a pointed rendition of 'you are what you eat' calculated to degrade and dehumanise the Jews. In Josephus, the starving Jews eat sewage, cow dung (V. 571), and 'objects which even the filthiest of brute beasts would reject' (VI. 197). The *Polychronicon*, in even more explicit fashion, lists shield leather, filth which clung to stinking walls, vomit, cow dung, snake skins, and horse carcasses among the foodstuffs. Only the *Golden Legend* shows restraint as it reports that the Jews ate shoes, but it shares with the other narratives a second set of prefatory remarks in which children snatch food from parents, parents from children, husbands from wives and wives from husbands.[32] All this is by way of introducing the infanticide and cannibalism. Josephus begins the scene with the claim that 'I am here about to describe an act unparalleled in the history whether of Greeks or barbarians, and as horrible to relate as it is incredible to hear' (VI. 199). In his version, the mother is a woman of fortune who has lost her wealth in the siege. As a result, 'the fire of rage was more consuming even than the famine' and she kills and eats her child 'impelled by the promptings alike of fury and necessity' (VI. 204). Her act is called an 'abomination'; when news of it spreads to the Romans 'the effect on the majority was to intensify their hatred of the nation' (VI. 214) and to fuel Titus' resolve to destroy the city: he would 'bury this abomination of infant-cannibalism beneath the ruins of their country, and would not leave upon the face of the earth, for the sun to behold, a city in which mothers were thus fed' (VI. 217). The *Golden Legend*, with its usual economy, merely reports that the townspeople ran 'trembling and terrified' away (276). In Trevisa's translation of the *Polychronicon*, however, this 'infamous' and 'horrible' act impels Titus to exclaim: 'We come to a bataille of men, but now I see þat we fiȝteþ aȝenst bestes; ȝit bestes rampaunt spareþ her owne kynde, be þey nevere so nedy, and helpeþ her owne children; but þese men devoureþ here owne children: þanne destroye we hem, for alle hir dedes stinkeþ'.[33] There are striking similarities between this passage and a passage in John Chrysostom's *First Homily Against the Jews*:

> What tragedy, what kind of wickedness, did they not outstrip in their bloodlust? ... Wild beasts often lay down their lives, disregarding their own safety in order to protect their young; but the Jews, without any necessity whatever, slaughtered their progeny with their own hands to serve the accursed demons, who are enemies of our life.[34]

Chrysostom's passage occurs in a section of the *First Homily* entitled 'Proof that Demons Inhabit the Jews', just one of the many polemical proofs Chrysostom offers to his Christian audience to encourage them to avoid both Jews and Judaising. Chrysostom's influence on later polemical writings against Jews is well attested, although whether there is a precise transmission of this particular passage into Higden's chronicle is not known.[35] What *is* known is that the *Jerusalem* poet, drawing on Higden's narrative, chose not to include this particularly virulent example of Jewish inferiority even to wild beasts. Thus the poet is not only selective when he borrows and revises from Josephus' secular Roman text, but is similarly particular when he draws on chronicles written with a specifically Christian ideological agenda.

In *Jerusalem* the infanticide scene follows one in which Josephus, the 'noble' surgeon, has cured Titus and refused all reward. What follows upon this scene of the exemplary Jew is itself exemplary. The poet introduces the scene by noting the trouble and 'hard hunger' (1063–5) that has befallen the city. The elaborate detail of disgusting foodstuffs is deleted and replaced with an account of what they *do not* have: neither fish, nor flesh; bread nor broth; water nor wine 'bot wope of hemself' (1068–70) – they drink their own tears.[36] Even when the narrative notes that they ate old shields and shoes, it is not, as it is in Josephus, 'the shameless resort to inanimate objects' (VI. 199), but another reason to pity them – the shields are difficult to chew ('þat liflode for ladies was luþer to chewe' (1072)). The poet also deletes the prefatory remarks in which children and parents and husbands and wives snatch food from one another, and although he replaces this with the observation that they acted like wolves, even this is qualified by the first half-line: 'wo wakned þycke' (1075).

In the *Jerusalem* poet's account the mother is a 'myld wyf' (1077) who addresses her child with 'rewful wordes' (1079); she is 'þat worþi wif' who confesses to the Jewish townspeople that 'in a wode hunger' she roasted her own child (1089). It is in the townspeople's response especially that the poet radically revises his sources. Their response is essential to the episode; it sets the interpretative spin with which audience and reader are encouraged to concur. The poet deletes the harsh Roman response; only the townspeople hear what the mother has done and

> A-way þey went for wo, wepyng echone,
> & sayn: 'Alas, in þis lif how longe schul we dwelle?
> ȝit beter wer at o brayde in batail to deye,
> Þan þus in langur to lyue, & lengþen our pyne.' (1093–6)

They make a decision 'þat deil was to hure' (1097), to kill all non-combatants 'that vitelys destruyed': those who cannot fight (women, the aged, the weak) are to be sacrificed because of the siege-induced hunger. There is no literary source for this self-massacre – in the *Vindicta salvatoris* eleven thousand Jews kill each other to prevent the enemy from claiming the glory of their deaths, but here in *Jerusalem* the slaying is prompted by moral imperative. Significantly, Jewish self-massacre had assumed for Jewish communities, by the thirteenth and fourteenth centuries, the dimensions of a spiritualised martyrdom as the *Kiddush ha-Shem*, or Sanctification of God's Name, through which each victim commits an 'act of ultimate piety'.[37] In a narrative whose purported object is vengeance for Christ's perfect sacrifice, the *Kiddush ha-Shem* of the Jews is a persuasive counterpoint to the source narratives' (and contemporary) accounts of the bestial Jews. Clearly, the local effect of this episode is radically different from that of its sources: there the act of cannibalism heightens the hatred and disgust directed at the Jews; here, disgust is transformed into sorrow and pity. Yet there are two subtexts here which resonate beyond the local moment. When Josephus introduces this scene in his *Jewish War* with the claim that he will describe an act unparalleled in history, he is being more than a little disingenuously dramatic. This cannibalistic act, particularly when enacted by parent upon child, is part of the literature of prophetic warnings found throughout the Hebrew Scriptures. Leviticus, Deuteronomy, Kings, Jeremiah, Baruch, and Lamentations all contain versions of cannibalism either prophesied or threatened in consequence of disobedience to God.[38] Chrysostom draws on these biblical passages when he accuses the Jews of cannibalism in his *Fifth Oration*

Against the Jews: 'The like of what does he mean? The eating of little children by their mothers! Moses foretold it, and Jeremiah reported its fulfilment.'[39] When the source narratives showcase this episode by making it central and emphatic, they demonstrate that scriptural prophecy has been fulfilled. In recasting this episode, the *Jerusalem* poet not only transforms a local moment, he comments, if only indirectly, on the fulfilment of Scripture which his entire narrative signifies.

The second subtext which informs the infanticide/cannibalism scene relates to the scriptural subtext, in so far as it originates from it, but it addresses with more immediacy a late fourteenth-century audience. To tease out the logic of this second subtext it is necessary to summarise briefly the mythologies of ritual murder and host desecration in the Middle Ages. Early Christians were accused of cannibalism, a charge which Christian apologetics quickly transferred onto the Jewish community.[40] Drawing on scriptural prophecies such as those cited above, and on writers like Chrysostom, medieval Christian polemic against the Jews transmitted the idea of the Jews as cannibalistic from the 'logical' supposition that if the Jews were capable of deicide, they were capable of any abomination imaginable.[41] The charge of cannibalism against the Jews informs the two most heinous accusations against medieval Jewry – ritual murder and host desecration.[42] While it is difficult to determine the precise psychological function these narratives fulfilled for the Christian community, there is some consensus that the ritual murder charges, accompanied or preceded as they were by pogroms against the Jews, were a projection of Christian guilt about Christian violence against Jews.[43] With regard to host desecration charges, many scholars agree that their primary function was a projection onto the Jews of Christian doubt about transubstantiation.[44] In both charges, importantly, *body* is central: in ritual murder charges it is usually the body of a Christian child; in host desecration charges it is the *Corpus Christi*, or body of Christ which is defiled. Yet as Kenneth Stow notes, 'the Eucharistic host was often visualised not only as Jesus incarnate but also as a child, and sometimes as Isaac, the perfect sacrifice'. Thus cannibalistic anxieties concerning the consumption of the host, both as the body of Christ and the body of a child, figure in some repressed form in the host desecration narratives. Stow further suggests that 'cannibalistic anxieties may have been at work' as part of ritual murder accusations.[45] Thus we have cannibalistic charges against the Jews transmitted from antiquity to the Middle Ages, which in turn serve as the point of origin and substantiation, as it were, for contemporary charges of ritual murder and host desecration, which are themselves, in turn, the transference of Christian anxiety about their own act in the consumption of the host and the host fantasised as child.

This trajectory of repression, transference, and accusation leads us back to *The Siege of Jerusalem*. The infanticide/cannibalism scene in the siege narratives is the centrepiece of the action, that most horrific of acts which provides substantive proof that Jews are bestial, and verifies, in a narrative otherwise devoid of ritual murder or host desecration charges, that Jews do, indeed, cannibalise young children. Drawn from the pages of scriptural prophecy, this scene gives local habitation and a name to the sometimes ephemeral accusations against medieval Jews. Yet at this most dramatic of moments, where the other siege narratives exploit the scene to heighten the anti-Judaic polemic of their tales, the *Jerusalem* poet diminishes the impact (and contemporary applications) by revising the context within which this scene is enacted and inter-preted. Rendered with nuance and sympathy, the scene is transform-ative as the poet unwrites the Jew as cannibal, in a subtext with both historical and contemporary applications.

The second key revision with which the *Jerusalem* poet compli-cates his narrative is the extent to which the language and ideology of anti-Judaism fail in passages where the poet details the sufferings of the besieged Jews. Even a few examples will suffice to demonstrate the poet's sympathetic account of Jewish suffering. After the Romans execute Caiaphas (the High Priest of the Jews) and his scribes: 'Þe Jewes walten ouer þe walles for wo at þat tyme, / Seuen hundred slow hem-self for sorow of her clerkes' (709–10). The poet's rendering of Jewish sorrow is uncompromised by the commonplace suggestion that their hardship is deserved and justified; there is no subtextual sneer to mar this straightforward and emotional account of the Jews' reaction to the death of their priests. In later passages, the poet lingers over graphic descriptions of the starving and defeated Jews, who were a 'pite to byholde' (1243):

> Wymmen falwed faste & her face chaungen,
> Ffeynte & fallen doun, þat so fair wer;
> Some swallen as swyn, som swart wexen,
> Som lene on to loke, as lanterne-hornes. (1143–6)

There is so much death that the citizens do not know what to do with the bodies (1147–50) and when the Jews finally yield to the Romans they seek mercy in their 'bar chertes' (1238); the poet's powerful artistry includes such details as:

Þe peple in þe pauyment was pite to byholde,
Þat wer enfamyned for defaute whan hem fode wanted.
Was noȝt on ladies lafte bot þe lene bones,
Þat wer fleschy byfor & fayr on to loke;
Burges with balies as barels or þat tyme,
No gretter þan a grehounde to grype on þe medil. (1243–8)

What is particularly striking about these passages detailing the emaci-
ated and suffering Jews is the failure of the vocabulary of anti-Judaism
we find earlier in the poem: not once does the poet invoke 'þe fals
men' as the Jews are individuated in these passages as, variously,
'Jewes', 'wymmen', 'ladies', 'man', 'burges', and 'peple'. As the level of
suffering increases, so too does the humanising impulse with which
the poet has throughout, sometimes lightly and sometimes emphatically, complicated his narrative.

As is the case with many narratives of medieval England, *The Siege
of Jerusalem* reveals the fissures inherent in ecclesiastical traditions: Jews
are simultaneously 'enemies' and 'fathers', 'other' and 'self', and their
representation has as much to do with the problematics of Christian
identity as it does with Jewish. *Jerusalem* is often a violent and militant
narrative, but it is fully aware of the terrible practical consequences of
its own Christian militancy and relentless in detailing (with uncommon sympathy) the sufferings of the Jews. Clearly the poem is more
than just a particularly virulent example of 'the' anti-Judaism long
thought to form and inform Christian writings about Jews in medieval
England; indeed, in its representation of Jews the poem goes far to
debunk the myth of a univocal, universal medieval anti-Judaism, not
an insignificant contribution to medieval studies. Compounded of
unequal measures of assertive bigotry and melancholy apologetic, the
poem holds in unrelieved tension two competing ideologies concerning Jews in Christendom, even as it invites audience sympathy for
Christianity's most complex 'other'. If we accept that a univocal anti-
Judaism is not inevitable in medieval English writings, we can (and
should) scrutinise specific historical, cultural and theological ideologies
to account for the mutability of Jewish representation. In the case of
Jerusalem, the poem's demonstration of the divided ideology of doctrinal
ambiguities, coupled with its nuanced and sympathetic account of
Jews, suggests a specific ecclesiastical tradition. I would like, in conclusion, to contextualise briefly *The Siege of Jerusalem* and its representation
of Jews by placing the anonymous *Jerusalem* poet and his narrative in a
particular tradition of English historical writing.

Drawing on manuscript evidence, Hanna locates the most likely site of composition for the *Jerusalem* poem at Bolton Augustinian Priory.[46] If the poet was writing at Bolton (and considering the learned source-texts this seems probable), he was most likely an Augustinian canon and his religious affiliation is key to contextualising the conflicts of representation we find in his poetic narrative. Long after the attenuation of the doctrine of toleration had led to a more hostile response to and representation of Jews, Augustinian writers demonstrate a humane moderation in their chronicle entries concerning Jews. From William of Newburgh's detailed accounts of the anti-Jewish riots of 1189–90, to Thomas Wykes's late thirteenth-century condemnation of anti-Jewish violence and the 1290 expulsion, to Walter of Guisborough's early fourteenth-century histrionic account of the brutality against Jews upon their expulsion from England, we can trace a long-standing and well-established Augustinian tradition which holds in balance the claims of Christian polemic and the claims of humanity.[47] The *Jerusalem* poet and his narrative participate in this particular tradition of English historical writing which is generally framed by conventional Christian justifications for Jewish suffering but falters in the face of violence against Jews. Newburgh's chronicle entries are an exemplar of this historical tradition as the chronicler first justifies Jewish suffering as fitting revenge for that 'perfidious' race, yet quickly invokes Psalm 58:12 ('Slay them not, lest at any time my people forget') – the standard proof-text of the Augustinian doctrine of toleration. As his narrative unfolds, Newburgh is unflinching in his detailed accounts of the violence against the Jews which swept England on the occasion of the crowning of Richard I. Indeed, as the level of violence increases, the chronicler becomes more and more sympathetic to the plight of the Jews, particularly those involved in the massacre of York,[48] until his sympathies lead him to fully expressed condemnation of the Christian communities responsible. In a manner strikingly similar to that of the *Jerusalem* poet, the Augustinian historian attempts to contextualise the violence with Christian justifications and anti-Judaic language, only to have both justifications and language fail when confronted with the practical consequences (massacres and violence) of his militant Christianity.

The relationship between the Augustinians and *The Siege of Jerusalem* will continue to be debated, as will the nature of the poem's complex representation of Jews. And this is precisely as it should be. The poem is technically brilliant, thematically dense, and reveals both the problematics of Christian identity in late fourteenth-century

England and the difficulties attendant upon a sympathetic representation of the materially absent but conceptually and theologically present Jews. *The Siege of Jerusalem* makes available an intriguing range of readings and the recuperative readings of *Jerusalem* which begin to retrieve the poem from the suppressed margins of critical attention accord the poem the distinction and commentary it so well deserves and so well repays.

Notes

1 *The Siege of Jerusalem*, ed. E. Kölbing and Mabel Day, EETS o.s. 188 (London, 1932). All quotations are from this edition, cited by line number.

2 Ralph Hanna and David Lawton are editing a forthcoming edition of the poem; I am indebted to both of them for generously allowing me pre-publication access to their introductory materials. For recent scholarly studies see Mary Hamel, 'The Siege of Jerusalem as a crusading poem', in Barbara N. Sargent-Baur (ed.), *Journeys Toward God: Pilgrimage and Crusade* (Kalamazoo, 1992), pp. 177–94; Ralph Hanna, 'Contextualizing *The Siege of Jerusalem*', *Yearbook of Langland Studies*, 6 (1992), 109–21; Elisa Narin van Court, '*The Siege of Jerusalem* and Augustinian historians: writing about Jews in fourteenth-century England', *Chaucer Review*, 29 (1995), 227–48; David Lawton, 'Titus goes hunting and hawking: the poetics of recreation and revenge in *The Siege of Jerusalem*', in O. S. Pickering (ed.), *Individuality and Achievement in Middle English Poetry* (Cambridge, 1997), pp. 105–17; Christine Chism, '*The Siege of Jerusalem*: liquidating assets', *Journal of Medieval and Early Modern Studies*, 28 (1998), 309–40; Bonnie Millar, 'The role of prophecy in the *Siege of Jerusalem* and its analogues', *Yearbook of Langland Studies*, 13 (1999), 153–78; Bonnie Millar, *The Siege of Jerusalem in its Physical, Literary and Historical Contexts* (Dublin and Portland, 2000); Elisa Narin van Court, 'Socially marginal, culturally central: representing Jews in late medieval English literature', *Exemplaria*, 12 (2000), 293–326.

3 Hanna, 'Contextualizing', p. 109.

4 For the exceptions see Millar, *The Siege of Jerusalem*; Narin van Court, '*The Siege of Jerusalem* and Augustinian Historians', and Narin van Court, 'Socially marginal, culturally central'.

5 Hanna, 'Contextualizing', p. 109.

6 *Ibid.*, pp. 113–15; Hanna and Lawton, forthcoming edition.

7 Hanna and Lawton, forthcoming edition. For comprehensive discussions of the manuscripts see this edition; Millar, *The Siege of Jerusalem*, pp. 15–41.

8 Flavius Josephus, *The Jewish War*, trans. H. St J. Thackeray, Loeb Classical Library (Cambridge, 1928; rpt. 1990); *Vindicta salvatoris*, in Constantin

Tischendorf (ed.), *Evangelia apocrypha*, 2nd edn (Leipzig, 1876), pp. 471–86; Ranulph Higden, *Polychronicon, Together with the English Translation of John of Trevisa and an Unknown Writer of the Fifteenth Century*, ed. Churchill Babington and Joseph R. Lumby, 9 vols, Rolls Series 41 (London, 1865–91); *Jacobi a Voragine Legenda aurea*, ed. Th. Graesse (Leipzig, 1850), in translation, *The Golden Legend: Readings on the Saints*, trans. William Granger Ryan, 2 vols (Princeton, 1993); *The Middle English Prose Translation of Roger d'Argenteuil's Bible en français*, ed. Phyllis Moe, Middle English Texts 6 (Heidelberg, 1977). See Phyllis Moe, 'The French source of the alliterative *Siege of Jerusalem*', *Medium Aevum*, 39 (1970), 147–54. The *Jerusalem* poet's use of Josephus' *Jewish War* was never seriously considered until Hanna and Lawton's recent investigations. In the introduction to their forthcoming edition they make a strong case for the poet's access to Josephus' classical history. The work was well known in England with at least fifteen copies produced there surviving.

9   Derek Pearsall, *Old English and Middle English Poetry* (London, 1977), p. 169; A. C. Spearing, *Readings in Medieval Poetry* (Cambridge, 1987), p. 167. Spearing specifically appeals to 'modern readers' when he writes about *Jerusalem*: 'It is not only strongly and credulously in favour of the Christians, it is also permeated by the antisemitism that was so common in the Middle Ages', p. 167.

10   Hanna, 'Contextualizing', pp. 111, 110.

11   Hamel, '*Siege of Jerusalem* as a crusading poem', p. 179.

12   The long-held assumption of a *judenrein* England after 1290 is a subject of scholarly debate. James Shapiro notes that 'despite the blanket claims of Victorian historians (and their modern successors) that there were few or no Jews in Shakespeare's England, archival research over the past hundred years makes it clear that small numbers of Jews began drifting back into England almost immediately after the Expulsion', *Shakespeare and the Jews* (New York, 1996), p. 62.

13   Writing about the English obsession with Jews in the sixteenth and seventeenth centuries, Shapiro makes a point that could easily refer to the late medieval period: 'If Jews were just not that important to English culture, it is hard to make sense of their frequent appearance not only in Tudor and Stuart drama but also in English chronicles, travel narratives, and sermons, let alone in the various works on trade, millenarianism, usury, magic, race, gender, nationalism, and alien status. Even as the Elizabethans have something to tell us about the Jews, their obsession with Jews tells us even more about the Elizabethans (and again, I might add, those who write about them)' (*ibid.*, p. 88). In the mid- to late fourteenth century we find Jews not only in the drama, but in Chaucer, Langland, Gower, sermon literature, chronicles, poetic narratives and histories, devotional works and various other genres.

14   In her recent book, *Gentile Tales: The Narrative Assault on Late Medieval Jews* (New Haven and London, 1999), historian Miri Rubin traces out the

origins and development of host desecration narratives, and examines in some detail those places and circumstances under which resistance, doubt, or disbelief defuse the power of the narrative. Rubin's study demonstrates the ways in which social pathologies like anti-Judaism are complicated systems which tend to resist essentialising definitions. See also David Nirenberg, *Communities of Violence: Persecution of Minorities in the Middle Ages* (Princeton, 1996).

15 Chism, 'Liquidating assets', p. 327.

16 *Ibid.*, 337, n. 26, 327–8. While I am indebted to Chism's reading which acknowledges the poem's sympathy for the Jews, I disagree with her argument concerning the poem's 'delight in cruel inversion'.

17 Millar, *The Siege of Jerusalem*.

18 Much of what follows derives from my previous work on *The Siege of Jerusalem*: Narin van Court, 'Critical Apertures: Medieval Anti-Judaisms and Middle English Narrative' (PhD dissertation, University of California at Berkeley, 1994); Narin van Court, '*The Siege of Jerusalem* and Augustinian historians'; Narin van Court, 'Socially marginal, culturally central'.

19 For a fuller discussion of the ecclesiastical traditions see Narin van Court, 'Critical Apertures'; Marcel Simon, *Verus Israel*, trans. H. McKeating (Oxford, 1986); Rosemary Ruether, *Faith and Fratricide: The Theological Roots of Anti-Semitism* (New York, 1974); A. Lukyn Williams, *Adversus Judaeos: A Bird's-Eye View of Christian Apologiae Until the Renaissance* (Cambridge, 1935); Jeremy Cohen, *The Friars and the Jews: The Evolution of Medieval Anti-Judaism* (Ithaca, 1982); Jeremy Cohen (ed.), *Essential Papers on Judaism and Christianity in Conflict* (New York and London, 1991); Kenneth Stow, *Alienated Minority* (Cambridge, MA, 1992); Gavin Langmuir, *Toward a Definition of Antisemitism* (Berkeley, 1990). Both Cohen and Stow provide comprehensive bibliographies.

20 All English Biblical citations are to the Douay-Rheims, rev. Bishop Richard Challoner (Rockford, 1971).

21 *Aurelii Augustini Opera Pars 14: De civitate Dei*, 2 vols, Corpus Christianorum Series Latina 47–8 (Turnholt, 1955), book XVIII, see especially chapter 46, lines 13–50. English translation by Marcus Dods, *The City of God* (New York, 1950), book XVIII, chapter 46. See also Augustine of Hippo, *In Answer to the Jews*, VI.8, in *Treatises on Marriage and Other Subjects*, trans. Charles T. Wilcox *et al.*, ed. Roy J. Deferrari, The Fathers of the Church: A New Translation, vol. 27 (New York, 1955), pp. 319–414.

22 There are many intellectual and ecclesiastical traditions concerning Jews and Judaism that develop over the centuries; some are more Augustinian than others and I focus here on the Augustinian because it was, in many ways the most influential.

23 Cohen, *The Friars and the Jews*, p. 20 and *passim*. On the topic of the place of Jews in Christendom see also Cohen (ed.), *Essential Papers*; Stow, *Alienated Minority*; Edward A. Synan, *The Popes and the Jews in the Middle Ages* (New York, 1965); James Parkes, *The Jew in the Medieval Community*,

2nd edn (New York, 1976); Salo Baron, *A Social and Religious History of the Jews* (Philadelphia, 1952); Mark Cohen, *Under Crescent and Cross* (Princeton, 1994); Solomon Grayzel, *The Church and the Jews in the XIIIth Century* (Philadelphia, 1933).

24 Cohen, *The Friars and the Jews*, *passim*; see also Cohen, 'The killers of Christ in the Latin tradition, from Augustine to the friars', *Traditio*, 39 (1983), 1–27. There are numerous explanations for the deterioration in the position of the Jews in the thirteenth and fourteenth centuries. Cohen argues that mendicant orders established a new and more virulent form of missionising among the Jews and a corresponding transformation in Church doctrine, specifically the Augustinian tradition, *Friars and Jews*, *passim*. Robert Chazan suggests that the attenuation of rights and tolerance is the logical conclusion to centuries of ambivalent Church doctrine, *Daggers of Faith: Thirteenth-Century Christian Missionizing and Jewish Response* (Berkeley, 1989), p. 180. Others claim that the erosion of Jewish rights began with the crusades of the eleventh century when Jewish communities were massacred by crusaders and others on their way to the Holy Land (see, for example, Léon Poliakov, *The History of Anti-Semitism: Volume 1: From the Time of Christ to the Court Jews*, trans. Richard Howard (New York, 1965), pp. 41–56). Still others attribute it to economic conditions: the rise of the profit economy and the competition between Jews and Christians in the marketplace and in the political sphere; see Lester K. Little, 'The Jews in Christian Europe', in Cohen (ed.), *Essential Papers*, pp. 276–97. See also R. I. Moore, *The Formation of a Persecuting Society* (Oxford, 1987), pp. 33–4, 136–40. In my view the most compelling interpretations continue to be those that focus upon theological considerations because it is the fundamental theological differences between Jew and Christian that contribute to Christian self-definition and cultural identity.

25 For a comprehensive summary of this theme in patristic literature see Ruether, *Faith and Fratricide*, pp. 117–82; see also Simon, *Verus Israel*, pp. 65–8.

26 For a more comprehensive discussion than can be accommodated here that demonstrates the poem's specifics vis-à-vis Christians and Jews see my '*The Siege of Jerusalem* and Augustinian historians'.

27 Josephus, *The Jewish War*, ed. and trans. Thackeray, VI.159. All citations are by book and line number.

28 Higden, *Polychronicon*, vol. 4, p. 429.

29 See Menachem Stern, 'Josephus and the Roman Empire as reflected in *The Jewish War*', in Louis H. Feldman and Gohei Hata (eds), *Josephus, Judaism, and Christianity* (Detroit, 1987), pp. 71–80. Stern argues that Josephus' text is not pro-Roman, yet admits that 'its very title, *The Jewish War*, shows that it was written from the Roman standpoint', p. 71. Josephus' treatment of the Jews in his history is harsh, and as Marcel Simon notes, 'there is no doubt whatsoever that Josephus was led to place

[his] interpretation on events by political opportunism and in the interests of his own preferment', *Verus Israel*, p. 5.

30 In one strikingly appropriate departure from his sources, the *Jerusalem* poet has the Romans not only blockade the water sources for the city, but attempt to contaminate both atmosphere and water with carcasses and filth, lines 681–8. This attempt to infect water supplies is, of course, one of the more insidious accusations against Jews during the plague years – they are said to have intentionally contaminated wells and water supplies to poison all of Christendom. See Joshua Trachtenberg, *The Devil and the Jews* (New Haven, 1943), pp. 97–108; Stow, *Alienated Minority*, pp. 231–2; Little, 'Jews in Christian Europe', pp. 276–97.

31 See Higden, *Polychronicon*, vol. 4, pp. 438–46; Josephus, *Jewish War*, V. 571–VI. 217; Jacobus de Voragine, the *Golden Legend*, trans. Granger Ryan, vol. 1, chapter 67. Further citations of the *Golden Legend* are to the page numbers of this volume.

32 Higden, *Polychronicon*, vol. 4, pp. 438, 442; Josephus, *Jewish War*, VI. 194; the *Golden Legend*, pp. 275–6.

33 Higden's Latin: 'Ad bellum hominum venimus; sed, ut video, contra beluas dimicamus. Quin etiam ferae rapaces a propria specie abstinent, etiam in summa necessitate suos foetus fovent; sed isti proprios devorant. Ipsos ergo deleamus, quorum foeda sunt omnia', *Polychronicon*, vol. 4, pp. 446–7.

34 John Chrysostom, *Chrysostom's Homilies Against the Jews*, trans. C. Mervyn Maxwell (PhD dissertation, University of Chicago, 1966), p. 28.

35 Simon, *Verus Israel*, pp. 217–21; Ruether, *Faith and Fratricide*, pp. 130–1, 173.

36 Tears as a sign of sanctity and piety are a common motif in both orthodox and mystical Christian writings. There is copious weeping by the Jews in *Jerusalem*, and this drinking of their own tears suggests a sanctified self-consumption to anticipate and counter-balance the later cannibalism.

37 Stow, *Alienated Minority*, pp. 116–18. The *Kiddush ha-Shem*, as detailed in rabbinic commentaries, fulfils the command of Leviticus 22:32: to sanctify the divine name through self-immolation.

38 Leviticus 26:27–9; Deuteronomy 28:52–7; 2 Kings 6:24–30; Jeremiah 19:9; Baruch 2:2–3; Lamentations 4:10.

39 Chrysostom, *Eight Homilies Against the Jews*, trans. Marvyn Maxwell, p. 133.

40 Simon, *Verus Israel*, pp. 205–21, 470 n. 16; Ruether, *Faith and Fratricide*, pp. 117–82; Langmuir, *Toward a Definition of Antisemitism*, pp. 263–81. See also R. Po-chia Hsia, *The Myth of Ritual Murder* (New Haven, 1988); Alan Dundes (ed.), *The Blood Libel Legend* (Madison, 1991); Rubin, *Gentile Tales*.

41 Cecil Roth, 'The medieval conception of the Jew', in Cohen (ed.), *Essential Papers*, p. 308. Stow, *Alienated Minority*, pp. 238–9.

42 The ritual murder accusation, popularised and developed by Thomas of Monmouth, proliferates during the twelfth and thirteenth centuries in

England and on the Continent. Charges of host desecration, like those of ritual murder, are widely circulated and both become rationales for massacres of Jews and both have either implicit or explicit implications of cannibalism by Jews. See Rubin, *Gentile Tales*, and her 'The Eucharist and the construction of medieval identities', in David Aers (ed.), *Culture and History, 1350–1600* (Detroit, 1992), pp. 43–63.

43   Little, 'Jews in Christian Europe', p. 287; Hsia, *The Myth of Ritual Murder*, passim.

44   Rubin, 'The Eucharist', pp. 54–7; Rubin, *Gentile Tales, passim*; Langmuir, *Toward a Definition of Antisemitism*, pp. 307–8; Little, 'Jews in Christian Europe', p. 287; Stow, *Alienated Minority*, pp. 236–7. For a comprehensive historical and cultural analysis of the doctrine of transubstantiation see Miri Rubin, *Corpus Christi* (Cambridge, 1991).

45   Stow, *Alienated Minority*, pp. 237–8.

46   Hanna, 'Contextualizing', pp. 115–16. Simultaneously, and working separately, Hanna and I came to the same conclusion regarding the poem's provenance. The manuscript evidence includes the presence at Bolton Priory of a copy of the *Bible en françois* and a scribal copy of *The Siege of Jerusalem*. I based my conclusions on the striking similarities between the poem's sensibilities regarding Jews and those of the Augustinian order.

47   William of Newburgh, *Historia rerum anglicarum*, in *Chronicles of the Reigns of Stephen, Henry II, and Richard I*, ed. Richard Howlett, 4 vols, Rolls Series 82 (London, 1884–9). In translation, *The Church Historians of England*, vol. 4, part II, trans. Joseph Stevenson (London, 1856). Thomas Wykes may be found in *Annales Monastici*, ed. Henry Luard, 5 vols, Rolls Series 36 (London, 1864–9), vol. 4. See also Antonia Gransden, *Historical Writing in England, c. 550 to c. 1307* (Ithaca, 1974); *The Chronicle of Walter of Guisborough*, ed. Harry Rothwell, Camden Society, 3rd series 89 (London, 1957). For a fuller account than I can accommodate here see my 'Critical Apertures' and 'The Siege of Jerusalem and Augustinian historians.' It is of some interest to note that Wykes cites Newburgh in his introduction, and that Guisborough draws heavily on Newburgh's chronicle for his own accounts of the English Jews.

48   See especially R. B. Dobson, *The Jews of Medieval York and the Massacre of March 1190*, Borthwick Papers, 45 (York, 1974).

8

Story line and story shape in *Sir Percyvell of Gales* and Chrétien de Troyes's *Conte du Graal*

Ad Putter

Introduction

The romance of *Sir Percyvell of Gales* (henceforth *Percyvell*) was probably composed in the north of England early in the fourteenth century but obviously enjoyed widespread popularity in medieval England.[1] Geoffrey Chaucer, who quoted two lines of it in his parody of popular romance *Sir Thopas*, evidently knew it well, and the anonymous poet of the *Laud Troy Book* (*c.* 1400) included Percyvell in a catalogue of famous heroes celebrated by 'gestoures … at mangeres and grete festes';[2] the other heroes in his list – Bevis, Guy, Tristrem – suggest that the poet was thinking of the English Perceval story rather than Chrétien's *Conte du Graal* (*c.* 1180), on which it is loosely based.[3] But while (according to the *Laud Troy Book*) the romance was once popularised by professional entertainers, it has come down to us only in a single manuscript, Lincoln Cathedral, MS 91, copied around the middle of the fifteenth century by the Yorkshire gentleman Robert Thornton.[4] In 2288 lines of extended tail-rhyme, *Percyvell* tells the following story:

> King Arthur's sister Acheflour flees with her only child to the forest after her husband Percyvell, Arthur's favourite knight, has been killed in a tournament by the Red Knight. The child, named Percyvell after his father, is thus brought up in the wilderness, ignorant of his lineage and the world of chivalry. One day Percyvell, dressed as usual in goat's skin, meets in the forest three knights of the Round Table (Gawain, Ywain and Kay). When they explain they are Arthur's knights, Percyvell decides that he also wants to be knighted by Arthur. He hurries home to his mother, who initiates him into the rudiments of courtly behaviour. The

next morning she gives him a ring, and he leaves for Arthur's court.

On his way he comes across a damsel in a castle, and clumsily puts his mother's advice into practice. After exchanging rings with the maiden, he continues his journey to Arthur's court, making his entry on horseback. His curt order that Arthur should knight him forthwith brings tears to Arthur's eyes, for the king recognises in the young Percyvell the features of his own dead brother-in-law. The latter's killer, the Red Knight, still terrorises Arthur's court; that very moment he rushes in and steals Arthur's golden cup. Percyvell goes after him to retrieve the cup and kills the Red Knight with a well-aimed throw of his javelin. Unable to get his victim's armour off, Percyvell kindles a fire and is just about to set the corpse alight when Gawain intervenes to help him into the Red Knight's armour. Percyvell rides off on his victim's war-horse. *En passant* he also dispatches the Red Knight's mother, a witch, whom he skewers on his lance. Further adventures unite Percyvell with his uncle, and lead him to Maidenland, where he liberates the castle of lady Lufamour from the Sultan (Gollotheram) and wins her hand in marriage. Arthur and his knights arrive in time for the wedding and Percyvell is knighted by Arthur, who reveals Percyvell's lineage.

A year later Percyvell remembers his mother and sets out to find her. On the way, he meets again the maiden with whom he exchanged rings. She has been bound to a tree by her jealous lover, who suspects her of infidelity. Percyvell defeats the lover in combat and demands his ring back, but it has been given away to appease a cruel giant. Percyvell seeks out the giant (Gollotheram's brother), kills him, and learns from the porter the strange story of the ring: the giant had taken it to a lone widow in the forest to win her love, but she went mad with grief, believing her son to be dead. Percyvell returns to the forest and restrains his mother, who is restored to health by the porter. Together with his mother, Percyvell rejoins his wife and finally makes a good end by dying on crusade. Amen.

In an excellent discussion of medieval popular literature, Rosemary Woolf justly described this as 'a crude piece of work compared with the French and German analogues'.[5] Much the same could be (and has been) said for other Middle English romances based on French originals (*King Horn*, *Sir Tristrem*, for example), for comparisons tend to show that the French romances are subtler and more sophisticated.

Fortunately, it is not always conscious artistry that attracts us in literature, and the most obvious way of reconciling the often-observed crudeness of Middle English popular romance with the satisfaction it has given to many is that 'crude' – or, less pejoratively, 'simple' – stories have powers of their own. 'Crude', as critics like to call popular romance,[6] is a culinary metaphor, deriving from Latin *crudus* 'bloody, raw'. In a narrative, the *crudités* are a story line with a beginning, middle and end. These may be 'cooked' by authors in various ways: the linear order of events may be scrambled by 'anachronies',[7] it may be distorted by the use of point of view, interrupted by descriptions and digressions, and complicated by means of subplots and interlaced stories. Such devices enable authors to create the impression that the events presented are determined not simply by the logic of actions and sequence, the 'proairetic code', as Roland Barthes called it,[8] but by various other codes. We ask not 'what happens next?' but 'what does it mean'? Is the author telling us something about the psychology of a 'character' (the semic code); is he developing a 'theme' (the symbolic code); is there a mystery or enigma to be solved (the hermeneutic code); or does he appeal to our sense of verisimilitude (the cultural code)?

What the Middle English romances show is that this process of artistic elaboration that turns 'story' into 'plot' (*fabula* into *siuzhet*)[9] could be reversed by poets sensitive to the direction and shape of a story. While this reverse process has previously been considered as degeneration, it might be described more precisely as the reconversion of 'plot' to 'story' and the foregrounding of the proairetic code at the expense of all others. How does such jargon help? It emphasises, firstly, that the Middle English romancers adapted material purposefully (and not just haphazardly); and, secondly, it emphasises that the impoverishment of some codes in popular romance is compensated for by the reinforcement of another. For instance, because the proairetic code is end-oriented, its dominance produces little description yet powerful closure, and it is no coincidence that in this respect many English romances (e.g. *Amis and Amiloun*) are more decisive than the French.

The *Percyvell*-poet is, as I hope to show, a master of the proairetic code: he is clear about where the story is going, and makes sure that we are clear about it too. The importance of that clarity in a work that was once recited by professional entertainers cannot be overemphasised today, when we know popular romances only from reading them in private. In the fourteenth century, however, *Percyvell* owed most of its popularity not to being read, but to being told and re-told, possibly from memory.[10] This makes a real difference to the structure of narratives. As Nancy Mason Bradbury has argued, tellers and hearers need 'to perceive the tale's structure in workable segments. The "seamlessness" or "structural tautness" prized in the novel discourages reshaping by denying its readers a foothold, so to speak.'[11] By contrast with the modern novelist, the *Percyvell*-poet has sought rather to multiply the 'footholds' that facilitate retellings and memorisations and so ensure the story's survival.

The aural reception of *Percyvell*, which the *Laud Troy Book* describes for us, offers a functional context for my argument that the poet set out, systematically, to expose the 'crude' ingredients of narrative: that is, the story line with its beginning, middle and end. My related claim is that he produced a very satisfying ending. This is no mean achievement: Chrétien de Troyes never finished his *Conte du Graal*, and even by line 8960, Chrétien's last, the happy ending is nowhere in sight. Not only has the plot got thicker (especially after Gawain has been launched on a parallel quest), but after a comic start Perceval is overtaken by misfortune: he learns that he has killed his mother and left a king crippled and without a realm. For these 'sins', committed unwittingly, the romance extorts a huge emotional price from the hero, without offering him the chance to redeem himself. Perceval's past mistakes retain their devastating finality in the *Conte du Graal*. Providing a happy ending, which means resolving the past in the present, thus involved the *Percyvell*-poet in a drastic overhaul of Chrétien's design; and when we look at the English poet's free adaptation of Chrétien's *Conte* we should, like the poet, always have that happy ending in mind.

My discussion of the poet's reshaping of his source is in two sections. The first deals with the *Percyvell*-poet's 'unscrambling' of Chrétien's plot, and considers how this affects the mood of the story. The second deals with the poet's happy ending and asks what makes it, in all senses of the word, fulfilling.

From siuzhet *to* fabula

Middle English romances are unusually emphatic when signalling the basics of the story. Both beginnings and endings are commonly indicated by extra-diegetic discourse (a prayer, an address to the audience) and by a range of other signals – titles, incipits and explicits; display script for opening and closing lines, initials, etc. – which appear far more frequently in Middle English romances than in pieces that accompany them in the medieval codex.[12] Chrétien's *Conte du Graal* and *Percyvell* both begin with extra-diegetic discourse – a lengthy prologue in Chrétien and a plea for attention in *Percyvell* – but the greater clarity of the story line in *Percyvell* becomes evident if we ask the question: where does the story begin? In *Percyvell* the natural order of events in the story (story order) and the poet's presentation of these events (text order) cannot readily be distinguished. The story commences with what may well be the hero's biological beginning, namely the wedding of Percyvell the elder and Acheflour (16–48). We then hear, in chronological order, of the nuptial tournament, in which Percyvell senior defeats the Red Knight, who vows vengeance; of the birth of Percyvell junior and the tournament proclaimed on his birthday; of the father's death at the hands of the Red Knight, and the consequent flight of the widow to the forest.

In the *Conte du Graal*, story order and text order pull in different directions. Chrétien opens with a morning in spring, when '*the* son of *the* widowed lady of *the* Waste Forest' ('*li filz a la veve dame / de la Gaste Forest*', 74–5) rises early.[13] The deliberately 'irregular' use of the definite article to introduce unknown characters and places (which normally require the indefinite article) warns us that we have entered the story late; the discourse proceeds *as if* we had encountered them before and no introductions were needed. On this spring morning, Chrétien continues, the boy (not named Perceval till much later in the narrative) goes hunting and meets a group of Arthur's knights, who remain nameless. Determined to become a knight also, he hurries back to his mother to tell her of this meeting. Horrified, she explains why she has kept him away from the chivalric world. The explanation takes us back in time to the reign of Arthur's predecessor, Uther Pendragon: the boy's elder brothers (whom he never knew he had) were violently killed and his crippled father (whom he never knew either) died of grief. To protect her remaining son, the mother fled with him to the forest. Chrétien has plunged us *in medias res*, restoring Perceval's past to us in a vivid retrospect. Even then the past returns in the obscure form of an enigma. What, for example, is the meaning of the gruesome mutilation of the elder brother: 'Awesome wonders befell the elder, for crows and rooks pecked out his eyes, and that is how people found him dead'? The significance of this is at once asserted (for these are *mervoilles*, 475) and withheld. The disruptions of sequence and sense sound the first ominous note of the romance – loud enough to worry anyone but the hero, who has better things to do than listen to his mother. And since no elucidation of these mysteries is asked from the mother, none needs to be given by the poet. Enter the hermeneutic code.

The main effect of the *Percyvell*-poet's alternative prehistory and re-ordering of events is to make the past immediately accessible to us and to the hero, since the line that connects the past with the present is direct and unbroken. Compare for example how differently the deaths of the fathers impinge on the protagonists. In Chrétien the father is said, again in the mother's distancing retrospect, to have been wounded in the leg and crippled by a stranger (which gives him an uncanny similarity to the lame Fisher King in the Grail Castle). What is Perceval to make of this? In *Percyvell* the father is treacherously killed on the son's birthday by the Red Knight, who thereby revenges a humiliating defeat. And what Percyvell is to make of *that* is no mystery: he must now in turn avenge his father's death, as prophecies predict: 'The bokes says that he mon / Venge his fader bane' (567–9). In short, the meaning of these events is constituted solely by the proairetic code (defeat → murder → vengeance).

Even where the *Percyvell*-poet follows his source closely, he tends to naturalise the sequence and de-activate the hermeneutic code. Consider the events that lead the hero into Arthur's court. In Chrétien the sequence is as follows: on his way to the court, Perceval catches sight of a stranger with handsome red armour, who clutches a golden cup. (Hermeneutic code: who is this knight?) Perceval rides on into Arthur's court, finding the king oblivious to his presence. Only when he turns his horse so close to the king that he sends Arthur's hat flying does he emerge from his reverie. The king's explanation again gives Chrétien an opportunity to relay part of the *fabula* in an analepsis: Arthur has been vexed by the Red Knight, who, some time before Perceval's arrival, had rushed in to steal his cup, and spilled the wine all over Guinevere, who has now left her husband in a huff. Always impatient with retrospects, Perceval wonders with growing irritation what all this has to do with him, and soon departs to claim the Red Knight's coveted armour. He kills the Red Knight with a javelin and is helped into his armour by Yvonet, who alone has witnessed the scene.

The *Percyvell*-poet rearranges the sequence to avoid an 'anachrony' and the complication of Chrétien's sub-plot (the Red Knight's taunting of Arthur), which has no immediate connection with the hero and takes place in the protagonist's absence. Thus Percyvell does *not* pass a Red Knight with a stolen cup on the way to Arthur's court, but the villain conveniently postpones his appearance in the narrative – or rather his re-appearance (for he earlier featured as the slayer of Percyvell's father) – in order that Percyvell may be present to witness the outrage for himself. All Percyvell then has to do is to pursue the Red Knight and rid the narrative simultaneously of his father's murderer and Arthur's arch-enemy. A further saving on the cast of characters is effected when the person to help Percyvell into his new armour is not a lowly servant (Yvonet), but Gawain, one of the knights (anonymous in Chrétien) whom Percyvell has already met in the Wild Forest.

All this adds up to a remarkable exercise in narrative economy, though I am not sure that it makes *Percyvell* a 'closer knit *and better* narrative' than Chrétien's, as Arthur Brown claims.[14] For these enhancements of narrative transparency evidently leave *Percyvell* poorer in other ways – in terms of, for example, the 'cultural code' that governs verisimilitude. It may be uneconomical to field Chrétien's lavish cast of characters, including household names, minor characters, as well as various unnamed folk, but, to be world-like, a fictional world too must be populated, ideally with characters who, as regards their familiarity to us, exhibit the same gradations as do real people: some we know well (like Arthur, Gawain, Kay, etc), some we know barely (the Yvonets of this world), and some are seen only once (like Chrétien's nameless knights in the forest). The same applies to Chrétien's unparsimonious plot, which consists of two initially unrelated story lines: the first concerning a hero who comes to court, and the second, over which Perceval accidentally trips, concerning Arthur's stolen cup. Untidy perhaps, but then so is the world, which contains many life stories totally unrelated to ours; and when these intersect they usually do so in the same unrehearsed manner as that in which Perceval collides with the Red Knight. In terms of the symbolic code, too, Chrétien's choice of Yvonet is significant, since Chrétien portrays a hero who, for as long as he is a 'nobody', can only be known by characters who are themselves 'nobodies':[15] by 'little Yvo' the messenger boy (Yvonet is a diminutive), by the Maiden-Who-Never-Laughs, and by the court fool who welcomes the simpleton as a hero-in-the-making. The function of identifying the messianic hero is predictably demystified in *Percyvell* and, to save on the character cast, reallocated to Gawain and Arthur, the former helpfully confirming that he has seen this bumpkin earlier in the forest, and the latter recognising in Percyvell the likeness to his father.

Is *Percyvell* better? I think not. But Brown is surely right to consider it a tidier narrative, for all the changes made to Chrétien's *Conte* improve the continuity of the *fabula*. We have already considered in

this light the realignment of story-order and text-order, and the redis-
tribution of narrative functions to just a handful of main characters like
Gawain and the Red Knight, who, simply by dint of reappearing and
being related to other characters,[16] become, as it were, the very
embodiments of narrative continuity.

There are also other, apparently bizarre, changes in detail that
work purposefully to the same end. The naming of Percyvell after his
father, unique to this story, is an example of such a change, as is the
father's motive for holding a tournament to mark his son's birth:

> For he wolde his son were gette
> In the same wonne. (119–20)

The father has expressed his will, and because his untimely death con-
secrates that wish as his last, the rest of the narrative effectively unfolds
under its influence. The premise of the narrative (and the name-
sharing between father and son) is thus that Percyvell will find his place
in the symbolic order and assume, in the name of the father, the
heritage of the past from which his mother had tried to cut him off.

In her effort to thwart the father's last wish, the mother actually
provides her son with the means to bring it to fruition. In a small but
significant departure from Chrétien, she gives to her son his father's
spear, which she pretends to have found in the forest, lest it should
give the son a clue to the past:

> Of all hir lordes faire gere
> Wolde scho noghte with hir bere,
> Bot a lyttill scotte-spere[17]
>   Agayne hir son yode.
>
> And when hir yong son yode,
> Scho bade hym walke in the wodde;
> Tuke hym the scote-spere gude
>   And gaffe hym in hande.
> 'Swete modir,' sayde he,
> 'What manere of thyng may this bee
> That ye nowe hafe taken mee:
>   What calle yee this wande?'
> Than byspakke the lady,
> 'Son,' scho sayde, 'sekerly,
> It es a dart doghty:
>   In the wodde I it fande.' (189–204)

But despite the mother's attempt to purge the object of any paternal residue, the spear comes to objectify the link between father and son, and nothing could be less of a coincidence than the fact that the young Percyvell should revenge his father's death by throwing this dart at the killer.

Thus form and content in *Percyvell* join forces to emphasise the continuity of the story line. While it would obviously be misleading to say that such continuity is wholly absent from the *Conte du Graal*, Chrétien's *fabula* plainly does not unravel as perspicuously as *Percyvell*'s, either in terms of presentation (witness the temporal distortions) or content. Specifically, compared with Percyvell's mother, Perceval's has been strikingly more successful in erasing the boy's family history. The hero has no name apart from her appellation 'fair son', and no heirloom materialises the affinity between father and son. All that remains of the past are mysterious traces: a brother with his eyes pecked out, a father wounded in the thigh, and so on.

As Chrétien's *Conte* unfolds, the hero collects, analeptically, more debris from the past. To give an example: after Perceval has visited the Grail Castle, where (obeying his mentor's orders not to talk too much) he did not ask about the grail, Perceval chances upon a damsel under an oak tree, who is holding the corpse of her decapitated lover. The damsel elicits from Perceval a rehearsal of his adventures at the Grail Castle and a confession that he did not ask who was served by the grail. At this point Perceval mysteriously guesses his own name (*Perceval li galois*), and is then rebuked by the maiden:

> 'Your name is changed, good friend.'
> 'To what?'
> 'Perceval the wretched. Oh, luckless Perceval! How unfortunate you are to have failed to ask all this! You would have healed the good king who is crippled, and he would have regained the use of his limbs and the rule of his land – and you would have profited greatly. But know this now: many ills will befall you because of the sin against your mother [*por le pechié … de ta mère*, 3580–1], for she has died of grief on your account. I know you better than you know me; you don't know who I am, but I was brought up with you at your mother's house for a long time: I'm your cousin and you are mine.'

No sooner has Perceval recovered his name than it is changed by the maiden, who, instead of making sense of the story so far, provides a retrospective 'explanation' that flouts any normal understanding of cause and effect: *because* Perceval has failed to ask the question, a king languishes without a realm (since when can a question produce such results?); and he failed to ask the question *because* he deserted his mother who died of grief (since when does the one entail the other?).[18] Missing pieces of *fabula* are retrospectively filled in: Perceval grew up with his cousin, his mother is dead, the crippled king has been waiting to be delivered by a question, but the *fabula* has become more, not less, enigmatic in the process. As to the future, all Perceval knows is that he is jinxed by a mysterious agency that was set in motion when he left his mother, and that punishes him for obeying his destiny and the laws of the genre (since the hero must leave for there to be a story): 'Many ills will befall you because of the sin against your mother.'

We are far from the cosy world of *Percyvell*, where the son is bound, in the name of the father, to take after him. The *Conte du Graal* bodies forth a spookier world, where processes of 'normal' signification are sabotaged and the hero's progress is thwarted by the spectre of the mother who, like the father in *Percyvell*, seems to influence her son's life more profoundly from beyond the grave. The most effective way of protecting the impetus to narrative progression, of ensuring that the son takes his father's place, would therefore be to keep the mother harmlessly alive. And that, of course, is what *Percyvell* does.[19]

Happy ending

The unstoppable forward impetus, proleptically anticipated by the prophecy that the son will avenge the father, by the father's name and last wish, the heirloom, and so forth, makes *Percyvell* superior to the *Conte du Graal* at least in terms of the resoluteness of its direction and the clarity with which this direction is signposted to the audience. However, I believe that *Percyvell* is more strongly coded not only for sequence but also for overall shape. To make good the second part of that claim I want to examine the ending, in which the story folds back on itself by reverting to the beginning.

In bringing that pattern to our attention, *Percyvell*'s overtly segmented structure, particularly its strong *sense* of an ending, makes a crucial contribution. The fitt divisions, probably lost in scribal transmission, may have helped to signal the approach of the end. Thornton copied only the first of these fitt divisions ('Here es a ffytt of Percyvell of Galles', after line 432), presumably because, in a book intended for private or family reading, such aids to oral performance had ceased to be meaningful.[20] But even in the absence of performance-related instructions, the beginning of the end is so well marked in the narrative that we can make a good guess about where the last fitt (or possibly the penultimate one) would have commenced. After Percyvell has achieved his worldly ambitions (having married Lufamour and become king), the story suddenly loses its forward momentum and halts on a portentous 'Now than':

> Now than yong Percevell habade
> In those borowes so brade,
> For hir sake that he hade
>   Wedd with a ryng.
> Wele weldede he that lande;
> Alle bewes to his honde –
> The folke that he byfore fonde
>   Knewe hym for kyng.
> Thus he wonnes in that wone
> Till that the twelmonthe was gone,
> With Lufamour his lemman. (1760–70)

'Now' and 'then' typically introduce new fitts;[21] when we get both we know we must be making a fresh start. There are other telling signs. For as Percyvell uncharacteristically sits still, the narrative abruptly shifts gear, skipping over a non-eventful year in a single stanza, having devoted many previous stanzas to a couple of days. The accelerating pace is the narrative equivalent to a 'fast forward' to the ending, and is effective not only because it announces an impending finale but also because it allows poets to foreshorten the middle, and, by doing so, to juxtapose beginnings and endings in a contrastive diptych.

As Karl Kroeber observes, 'discrete narrative segments permit effective repetitions of diverse kinds, because only the distinctness of some "unit" (person, act, place, or even phrase) allows sharp recognition of recurrence'.[22] *Percyvell's* obvious segmentation has precisely this virtue of highlighting a pattern of recurrence. Especially noticeable, thanks to the spareness of the poem's time-place coordinates, is the recurrence of a season and a setting. I quote the lines that follow on directly from the passage quoted above:

> He thoghte on no thyng
> Now on his moder that was –

How scho levyde with the gres,
With more drynke and lesse,
   In welles there thay spryng.

Drynkes of welles ther thay spryng
And gresse etys, withowt lesyng –
Scho liffede with none othir thyng
   In the holtes hare.
Till it byfelle appon a day,
Als he in his bedd lay,
Till hymselfe gun he say
   (Syghande full sare):
'The laste Yole day that was
Wilde wayes I chese;
My modir all manles
   Leved I thare.'
Than righte sone saide he,
'Blythe sall I never be
Or I may my modir see,
   And wete how scho fare!'

Now to wete how scho fare
The knyght busked hym yare;
He wolde no lengare duelle thare,
   For noghte that myghte bee!
Up he rose in that haulle;
Tuke his lefe at tham alle,
Both at grete and at smalle,
   Fro thaym wendis he.
Faire scho prayed hym even than,
Lufamour his lemman,
Till the heghe dayes of Yole were gane,
   With hir for to bee –
Bot it served hir of nothyng! (1771–1804)

The significant place is the well, with which the poet had associated
Percyvell in the notorious opening salvo of his romance:

Lef, lythes to me,
Two wordes or thre,
Off one that was faire and fre

> And felle in his fighte:
> His righte name was Percyvell;
> He was ffosterde in the felle,
> He dranke water of the welle –
> And yitt was he wyghte. (1–8)

It is difficult to forget that Chaucer parodied these lines in *Sir Thopas* – 'Hymself drank water of the well, / As did the knyght sire Perceyuell'[23] – and hence tempting to believe that they are bad, one 'of the more creaky features of this poem'.[24] But the well is a familiar medieval icon of primitive life, as Chaucer must have known, for in *The Former Age* he described the Golden Age as follows:

> A blisful lyf, a paisible and a swete,
> Ledden the peples in the former age ...
> They eten mast, hawes, and swich pounage,
> *And dronken water of the colde welle.* (1–2, 7–8)

It seems harsh, then, to fault the *Percyvell*-poet's beginning, which through the *topos* of the well evokes the world before culture of the hero's 'former age'. To this setting, still inhabited by the mother who has in all senses been left behind, the story now returns us mentally, in advance of the hero's actual return.

The significant time is Christmas day. For by another coincidence ('Till it byfelle appon a day') that is not one, it happens that Percyvell's thoughts return to his mother on the very day he left her. Why now? Because the hero is required to fulfil a pattern of repetitions that the poet must have planned from the very beginning, when he boldly altered Chrétien's springtime setting to Christmas:

> Tomorne es forthirmaste Yole day,
> And thou says thou will away.... (393–4)

As a result of that change, both the beginning and the ending unfold at the same time, at Christmas, not so much in a 'before' and 'after' but quasi-simultaneously along the parallel tracks of cyclical time.

The poet's emphasis on repetition makes it difficult to read Percyvell's rare moment of retrospection as a sign of change, as at least one critic has done: 'Perceval's second quest shows him to be motivated by a deep and positive love rather than by reckless impetuosity.'[25] It may be more to the point to note the blatant subservience of the semic code (constitutive of 'character') to the logic of sequence (the proairetic code), which demands that the ending must retrieve the past by repeating it.[26] Thus Percyvell must leave Lufamour on exactly the same day (and with the same reckless impetuosity) that he left his mother; Lufamour must try to make him stay, because Percyvell's mother did likewise; and Percyvell must disregard her pleas because he earlier ignored his mother's: 'Till on the morne he wolde away − / For thyng that myghte betyde' (419–20). Of course, much has changed: Percyvell has become knight and king and can now recognise the wildness of his former ways, but behind these differences the poet makes visible a reassuring continuity, a sense that the past is not irretrievably lost, as in the *Conte du Graal*, but even now being fulfilled in the present.

This sense is deepened by the curious adventitiousness of Percyvell's homeward journey, which the poet presents as the haphazard quest of an adventurous knight, even though the trajectory is destined to take us back to the beginning:

> Now fro tham gun he ryde;
> There wiste no man that tyde
> Whedirwarde he wolde ryde,
>   Ne whedir he wolde lende. (1808–11)

There is no good reason why Percyvell should should keep his mission secret from everyone, but the poet seems less interested in the postulates of ordinary life than in those of romance, where the knight errant 'carries within himself a mysterious purpose, known to him alone, which he will in fact realise, but in a roundabout way − governed not by the logic of cause and effect but by … the logic of the *adventure*'.[27] In keeping with this logic, Percyvell happens by chance upon a distressed maiden, who, needless to say, turns out to be the maiden with whom he exchanged rings a year ago:

> Bot forthe thus rydes he ay,
> The certen sothe als I yow say,
> Till he come at a way
>   By a wode ende.
> Then herde he faste hym by
> Als it were a woman cry;
> Scho prayed to mylde Mary
>   Som socoure hir to sende. (1816–23)

Percyvell, that is, arrives as if in answer to a prayer. The connectives (thus rydes he ... *Till* he come ... *Then* herde he) admit only to a temporal relationship between Percyvell's search and what he finds, but the contingencies are organised into a pattern specified by the spare geography ('By a wodes ende'): we must be back on the threshold of Percyvell's past, at the same point where, on the outward leg of the journey, he had found the maiden in the hall.

In Chrétien's *Conte du Graal*, Perceval's second encounter with the maiden is preceded by the episode of the Grail Castle, in which he fails to ask the question and then meets his cousin who tells him his mother is dead. This pre-history made it impossible for Chrétien to follow up Percyval's reunion with the maiden with a homecoming. Since his mother is dead, Perceval no longer has a home to go back to; when, in some of the later *Perceval Continuations*, he does return to the Wild Forest of his youth he poignantly finds not a 'home' but his mother's gravestone. But while Chrétien condemned his hero to a life of endless wandering, in *Percyvell* the hero's fortunate meeting with the maiden is clearly meant to inaugurate the hero's fated return to the beginning. To this end, the *Percyvell*-poet again altered the chronology of the *Conte du Graal* (where Perceval meets the damsel on the *second* day of his travels, one ordinary day ('un jor', 3827), and meets her again some eight days later)[28] so as to emphasise the 'coincidence' that Percyvell and the maiden's paths had crossed exactly a year ago, on what in *Percyvell* was the *first* day of the hero's travels, Christmas day:

> 'Now to the I sall say:
> Appon my bedd I lay,
> Appon the laste Yole day –
>   Twelve monethes es gone.
> Were he knyghte, were he kyng,
> He come one his playnge:
> With me he chaungede a ryng
>   The richeste of one.' (1844–51)

Unlike secular time, which is irreversible (Chrétien's 'one day' must inevitably be followed by 'another day'), liturgical time is cyclical and so ideally suited to suggest the circular progression of the story to its beginning. That reversibility of time also makes meaningful the maiden's apparent throwaway line 'Were he knyghte, were he kyng', which, though it *is* a mistake (a year ago Percyvell was neither knight nor king), predicts precisely what Percyvell was destined to become, and so reveals a miraculous conjunction between the remembered past and actual present. The maiden's account of the last Christmas makes this Christmas Day the fulfilment of a promise:

> He *was* bothe kyng and knyght;
> Wele he helde that he highte:
> He loused the lady so brighte,
>   Stod bown to the tre. (1872–5; italics mine)

And there are yet other promises, still unfulfilled, that make Percyvell's second encounter with the maiden indispensable to the ending, for Percyvell cannot go back without the ring which the mother (uniquely in this version of the Perceval legend) gave him as a token at the start of his adventures:

> His moder gaffe hym a ryng
> And bad he solde agayne it bryng:
> 'Sonne, this sall be oure takynnyng,
>   For here I sall the byde.' (425–8)

But when, after freeing the lady, Percyvell asks to have his ring back, the poet introduces a complication: the 'takenynng' has been given away to a giant, and so Percyvell must go after it and kill the giant. When the porter of the giant's castle gives back the ring, he tells Percyvell a remarkable story: with this very ring his master had tried to court a lady, but on seeing it she went mad with grief, accusing the giant of killing her son.

From the perspective of verisimilitude (Barthes's cultural code) the significance of this 'recognition token', a standard device in Middle English popular romances,[29] may seem tenuous, as Mills scornfully re-marks: 'Since the hero is almost fully grown, it might seem unnecessary to provide the mother with a token by which he can be identified.'[30] However, the code that makes sense of recognition tokens in popular romances is not so much the cultural as the proairetic code. They function as emblems of and cues to associated actions (separations) and actions-to-come (reunions), and as such they encode, and provide mnemonic support for, the story's subsequent unravelling. The poet's final twist to the story of the ring – its presentation by a giant to Percyvell's mother, who mistakes it for a sign that her son is dead – is also too quickly dismissed by Mills as 'tortuous', for we need only imagine the flat-footedness of an ending without it (Percyvell and the maiden exchange rings and the former returns to his mother) to appreciate why it is needed. Happy endings need unhappiness to put an end to, which is why, as Rosemary Woolf noted, the Middle English popular romances 'seem so often to be potential tragedies, which the poet, by ostentatious contrivance, nevertheless brings to a fortunate issue'.[31] By such contrivance, the ring produces the potential tragedy that might have been: a son killed by a giant (whom Percyvell indeed gets to fight) and a mother insane with grief.

And just as Middle English romancers understood the necessary implication of tragedy in happy endings, so they appreciated that the eventual recognition promised by 'tokens' (rings, cloaks, cups, and so on) is predicated upon prior misrecognition. The dramatic potential of recognition scenes lies in the oscillation between the loss and the recovery of identity, and, by precipitating the oscillation, the 'recognition tokens' of Middle English romance unleash this potential. Take some examples. Orfeo, disguised as a minstrel, returns home with his 'token', the harp; the faithful steward sees it and collapses because the 'recognition device' confirms his belief that his master is dead. Horn returns with his ring to his wife Rymenhild, who nearly commits suicide when she infers from it that her husband is dead. Amiloun, disfigured by leprosy, turns up on the doorstep of his old friend Amis, but is attacked by the latter, who thinks the leper has killed Amiloun and stolen his cup.

Only when we realise that so-called 'recognition devices' serve in the first place to provoke misrecognition, to bring about the imagined loss that makes the final recognition so jubilant, can we admire how loyally the *Percyvell*-poet continues the tradition. Like Rymenhild, Orfeo's faithful steward, and Amis, Percyvell's mother sees the recognition token and is convinced that her son is dead:

> 'At the firste bygynnyng,
> He wolde hafe gyffen hir the ryng,
> And when scho sawe the tokynyng
>   Then was scho unsaughte.
> Scho gret and cried in her mone;
> Sayd, 'Thefe, hase thou my sone slone
> And the ryng fro hym tone
>   That I hym bitaughte?'
> Hir clothes ther scho rafe hir fro
> And to the wodd gan scho go;
> Thus es the lady so wo,
>   And this is the draghte.

> For siche draghtis als this,
> Now es the lady wode, i-wys,
> And wilde in the wodde scho es,
>   Ay sythen that ilke tyde.
> 'Fayne wolde I take that free,
> Bot alsone als scho sees me,
> Faste awaye dose scho flee:
>   Will scho noghte abyde.' (2148–67)

The 'tortuous' incident follows logically from what the 'tokenyng' in Middle English romance is meant to do, namely to provide the hero, not with a means 'by which he can be recognised' (Mills), but with one by which the culminating moment of revelation can be deferred in the interest of a gratifying climax. In Aristotle's terminology, the token does not provoke *anagnorisis* (the climactic recognition) but blocks it, by prompting *paralogismos* (the plausible but false inference).[32]

It might be objected that the digression of the ring spoils the symmetry between the beginning and the ending, but for this the *Percyvell*-poet makes ample amends. For, as if prompted by the fate of his mother – 'Now es the lady wode, iwys, / And wilde in the wodde scho es' (2161–2) – Percyvell responds by regressing to his own wild ways, when, dressed in a goat's skin, he used to outrun the animals in the forest (341–2, 722–8), as he must now chase his 'wild' mother. And so he abandons his horse, dresses once more in a 'gayt skynne' (2197), and vows to catch the lady, whom he reveals to the porter to be his mother:

> 'I will assaye full snelle
> To make that lady to duelle,
>   Bot I will noghte ryde;
> One my fete will I ga
> That faire lady to ta:
> Me aughte to bryng hir of wa –
>   I laye in hir syde.'
>
> He sayse, 'laye in hir syde;
> I sall never one horse ryde
> Till I have sene hir in tyde:
>   Spede if I may!
> Ne none armoure that may be
> Sall come appone me
> Till I my modir may see,
>   Be nyghte or by day.' (2169–83)

Percyvell's recognition of his duty is movingly simple, and so it should be. For the debt that we owe our mothers is indeed basic – 'we lay in their sides' – and Christmas seems the right time to remember this. And because Percyvell's duty is primal, I cannot help feeling that the hero's response to his mother's altered state, to become, as far as he can, the little boy he once was, is utterly convincing, not only because of the perfect narrative symmetry that is thereby created (this really *is* an ending that was implicit in the beginning), but especially because at this juncture the narrative continuities and their limits (Percyvell cannot in other ways regain his youth) express something simple but true about the continuities and discontinuities of life, about how we are and are not the little ones we were, and about how our mothers are and are not what they were when we left them.

As for the final reunion between Percyvell and his mother that follows, it would be hard to find a passage that better illustrates the undemonstrative beauty of Middle English popular romance. So here it is in full:

> His armour he leved therin;
> Toke one hym a gayt skynne
> And to the wodde gan he wyn,
>   Among the holtis hare.
> A sevenyght long hase he soghte;
> His modir ne fyndis he noghte,
> Of mete ne drynke he ne roghte,
>   So full he was of care.
> Till the nynte day byfell
> That he come to a welle
> Ther he was wonte forto duelle,
>   And drynk take hym thare.
>
> When he had dronken that tyde,
> Forthirmare gan he glyde;
> Than was he warre, hym besyde,
>   Of the lady so fre.
> Bot when scho sawe hym thare
> Scho bygan forto dare
> And sone gaffe hym answare,
>   That brighte was of ble.
> Scho bigan to call and cry:
> Sayd, 'Siche a sone hade I!'

His hert lightened in hye,
   Blythe forto bee.
Be that he come hir nere,
That scho myght hym here
He said, 'My modir full dere:
   Wele byde ye me!'
Be that so nere getis he
That scho myghte nangatis fle;
I say yow full certeynly,
   Hir byhoved ther to byde.
Scho stertis appon hym in tene:
Wete ye wele, withowtten wene,
Had hir myghte so mekill bene,
   Scho had hym slayne that tyde!
Bot his myghte was the mare,
And up he toke his modir thare:
One his bake he hir bare –
   Pure was his pryde! (2196–235)

Could any Old French romance have done this better? Well, it so happens that a comparison is available in the *Second Continuation* of Chrétien's *Conte du Graal*, where Perceval's 'homecoming' is handled, very competently, as follows:

> He journeyed on till evening, but could find no house where he could take lodging; he slept out in the forest, and had nothing to eat all night and was in great discomfort. His horse grazed on the grass around him, which was heavy with dew, until morning came and the sun began to shine. Then Perceval mounted without delay, and rode on until about nine o'clock [*tierce*] … He rode swiftly through the forest, following the paths and tracks which he had come to know so long before, until he came to open ground and saw the house that had been his mother's.[33]

There are perhaps readers who think this passage shows up all the inanities of the corresponding one in *Percyvell*, and they seem to have an excellent case. A year ago, the mother had promised that she would wait for him at home, but it never occurs to Percyvell to look for his mother there. Instead he wanders aimlessly, as if he were a stranger to the forest where he lived for fifteen years. And could not the *Percyvell*-poet have avoided hackneyed formulas ('A sevenyght long', 'holtes hare') and been as precise about time and setting as the French poet, who acknowledges that Perceval knows the forest well? And to those readers I recommend the *Continuations* (all 58,000 lines of it).

But since there is only one forest in *Percyvell*, no lengthy descriptions are required to inform us that, when Percyvell 'to the wodde gan ... wyn, / Among the holtis hare', he has gone back to the forest of his youth:

> Fyftene wynter and mare
> He duellede in those holtes hare. (229–30)

True, 'holtes hare' is formulaic, but the recurrence of the formula is not pointless, for narratives can communicate a sense of déjà vu by what they *do* (by repeating) as well as *say*. The numbers too – *fifteen* years in the forest, *seven* nights of searching, the *ninth* day of deliverance – are wholly conventional, but resonate precisely for that reason. Fifteen is the age when noble youths become knights,[34] and so the poet need only mention Percyvell's age to tell us that he will soon be off. Seven is the number that represents a long period of trial and tribulation;[35] while nine, the last number in an incomplete decimal series, signals a turning point (hence Percyvell finds the well on day nine).[36]

And yes, it would make sense for *Percyvell* to take the shortest route home, but perhaps it is realism of a higher order to consider that the success of human enterprises depends not only on our wit (on knowing the way) but also on the cooperation of forces outside our control that must ultimately reward our endeavours. All this is implied by the concatenation of circumstances that leads Percyvell to his mother, circumstances at once wholly fortuitous – Percyvell does not even know where to look for her – *and* wholly deserved. For surely it is right that Percyvell should become aware of his mother *after* he has drunk again from the well that served him as a child: 'His righte name was Percyvell /... / He dranke water of the welle' (5–7). No wonder Chaucer remembered these lines when the romance commemorates them so deliberately. And is not it also right that Percyvell should find the well after nine days of fasting: 'Of mete ne drynke he ne roghte, / So full he was of care'? (Would Percyvell have found the well if he had not fasted?) The romance deflects such 'what ifs' by organising events into a pattern of poetic justice, which generously rescues the hero from the gaping holes in cause and effect, and casts accident and potential failure as destiny and heroic achievement.

And could any poet outside the popular tradition have given us the poignant words that mother and son speak to each other in *Percyvell?* The fugitive mother, whom no one had been able to catch ('Faste awaye dose scho flee', 2166), stands transfixed when she sees a man looking just like her son when he left her: 'Scho bygan forto dare' (2213). Used of animals, *dare* means to 'cower', of humans 'to be overwhelmed', of a madwoman possibly both. Then she shouts 'Siche a sone hade I' and is caught by Percyvell before she knows it. (Again we wonder: would Percyvell have managed to catch her if he had not returned as his former self?) Her five words sum up the story as it might have ended, were it not that Percyvell is alive and that, even in her madness, the mother is not changed so irrevocably that she cannot remember him, and, by remembering him, momentarily remember herself. Hence Percyvell's relief on hearing her desperate cry: 'His hert lightened in hye, / Blythe forto bee'. To him this cry means something special: his old mother is still dormant in the madwoman before him.

As Mills observes in a perceptive editorial note (to line 175), the reversal of roles has at the end of the romance become very marked: mother has become 'wild', while Percyvell has become king; he must look after her, carry her on his back, as she once did him; but under-lying such reversals is the reassurance that the past and our former selves are not lost forever; that we can, much as this narrative does, return to the beginning. Appropriately therefore, Percyvell speaks his last words of the romance in homage to the tenacity of the human soul:

> He said, 'My modir full dere:
> Wele byde ye me!'

The phrasing acknowledges the promise that Percyvell's mother made at the beginning ('here I sall the byde', 428), and which she has clung to by an instinct stronger than her mind. Of course, the acknowledge-ment is lost on the insane woman; but it is not just for her that it is meant: this is the poet's compliment to those readers who have kept the mother's promise in *their* hearts, and who have waited with her for this moving moment of fulfilment.

These 'crude' qualities, a sense of direction and a sense of narrative shape, make for good stories and happy endings. In my view, the strengths of this and other popular romances lie in this area, in sequence and in shape, contiguity and pattern, and their mutual tensions and accommodations – in short, in the domain of the proairetic code, which, together with the hermeneutic code, imposes its order on the passing of time. (By contrast, the semic, cultural and symbolic codes 'establish permutable, reversible connections, outside the constraints of time'.[37]) About the kinds of meaning that can be encoded by story lines and the shapes in which they are gathered up, literary criticism has had little to say; but, as my remarks about *Percyvell* will have suggested, I believe that story lines and patterns do speak to us, and can indeed speak more powerfully than non-temporal forms of narrative configuration about the things bound up with the passing of time: about what does and does not persist through change; about contingencies and the structures, including our identities, that can survive and comprehend them. Regrettably, the condition of narrative that brings it closest to the human condition – the fact that narrative, like life, must be 'lived forwards and understood backwards' (Kierkegaard) – has also interested critics least. Perhaps if our respect for stories pure and simple improves – and there are some encouraging signs that this is happening[38] – Middle English popular romances will become popular with medievalists again.

Notes

1 I cite the slightly modernised text in *Ywain and Gawain, Sir Percyvell of Gales, The Anturs of Arther*, ed. Maldwyn Mills (London, 1992), but have indented all tail-lines.

2 *Laud Troy Book*, ed. J. Ernst Wülfing, EETS o.s. 121–2 (London, 1902–3), lines 39–40.

3 I assume that the *Percyvell*-poet knew Chrétien's version (probably from memory). This position has been ably defended by David C. Fowler, '*Le Conte du Graal* and *Sir Perceval of Galles*', *Comparative Literature Studies*, 12 (1975), 5–20, and by Keith Busby, '*Sir Perceval of Galles, Le Conte du Graal* and *La Continuation-Gauvain*', *Etudes Anglaises*, 31 (1978), 198–202, and 'Chrétien de Troyes English'd', *Neophilologus*, 71 (1987), 596–613. The implausible alternative is that *Percyvell* goes back to a primitive version of a Perceval-legend that can be reconstructed from the earliest extant versions (Chrétien's *Conte du Graal*, Wolfram's *Parzival* (*c.* 1210), and *Peredur* (thirteenth century)). This case is argued at length by Reginald Griffith, *Sir Perceval of Galles: A Study of the Sources of the Legend* (Chicago, 1911), and Arthur Brown, 'The Grail and the English *Sir Perceval*', *Modern Philology*, 16 (1918–19), 553–68; 17 (1919–20), 361–82; 18 (1920–21), 201–28, 661–73; 22 (1924–25), 79–98, 113–32; some errors of fact, based on their misunderstandings of the text, are corrected in my article 'The text of *Sir Perceval of Gales*', *Medium Aevum*, 70 (2001), 191–203.

4 The Thornton manuscript, one of the most important repositories of Middle English romance, is available in facsimile: *Thornton Manuscript*

(Lincoln Cathedral MS 91), eds D. S. Brewer and A. E. B. Owen (London, 1975). For a codicological study see John J. Thompson, 'The compiler in action: Robert Thornton and the Thornton romances in Lincoln Cathedral MS 91', in Derek Pearsall (ed.), *Manuscripts and Readers in Fifteenth-Century England: The Literary Implications of Manuscript Study* (Cambridge, 1983), pp. 113–24.

5 Rosemary Woolf, 'Later poetry: the popular tradition', in W.F. Bolton (ed.), *The Middle Ages*, Sphere History of Literature 1 (London, 1970, repr. 1986), pp. 267–312 (p. 279).

6 E.g. Dorothy Everett on *Percyvell*, a 'crude romance': 'A characterisation of the English medieval romances', in her *Essays on Middle English Literature*, ed. Patricia Kean (Oxford, 1955), pp. 1–22 (p. 12).

7 The term is taken from Gérard Genette's classic study of time in *Narrative Discourse*, trans. Jane E. Lewin (Oxford, 1980).

8 Roland Barthes, *S/Z*, trans. Richard Miller (Oxford, 1996), p. 19.

9 The distinction is usually attributed to Boris Tomashevski, 'Thematics' (1925), in Lee T. Lemon and Marion J. Reis (eds), *Russian Formalist Criticism: Four Essays* (Lexington, 1965), pp. 61–98.

10 On the memorial transmission of popular romances see especially Murray McGillivray, *Memorisation in the Transmission of the Middle English Romances* (New York, 1990). Some critics doubt the importance of oral transmission; for assessments of the debate see Nancy Mason Bradbury, 'Literacy, orality, and the poetics of Middle English romance', in Mark C. Amiodo and Sarah Gray Miller (eds), *Oral Poetics in Middle English Poetry* (New York, 1994), pp. 36–96; and my 'Historical introduction', in Ad Putter and Jane Gilbert (eds), *The Spirit of Medieval English Popular Romance* (Harlow, 2000), pp. 1–15.

11 Nancy Mason Bradbury, *Writing Aloud: Storytelling in Late Medieval England* (Urbana, 1998), p. 59.

12 See Murray Evans, *Rereading Middle English Romance: Manuscript Layout, Decoration, and the Rhetoric of Composite Structure* (Montreal, 1995).

13 Citations from the French text are from *Le Conte du Graal*, ed. F. Lecoy (Paris, 1984). Translations from Chrétien's *Conte* and the later continuations are taken from *Perceval: The Story of the Grail*, trans. Nigel Bryant (Cambridge, 1982).

14 Brown, 'The Grail' (n. 3 above), p. 554; my italics.

15 Cf. Per Nykrog, *Chrétien de Troyes: romancier discutable* (Geneva, 1996), p. 190.

16 N. G. H. E. Veldhoen, 'I haffe spedde better þan I wend: some notes on the Middle English *Sir Perceval of Galles*', *Dutch Quarterly Review*, 11 (1981), 279–86, usefully observes that the *Perceyvell*-poet improves the internal consistency of the *fabula* by making almost everyone in this romance blood relatives. This is true also for the villains (the sultan and the giant are brothers) and for Arthurian characters who are not relatives in any other Arthurian texts. Thus Kay is presented, 'impossibly', as Percyvell's cousin. In medieval romance (cf. Malory's *Tale of Sir Gareth*) blood ties

readily do duty for what a realist aesthetic would conceive to be subtler ways of securing unity of action.

17 The manuscript reading 'Scottes spere' led Reginald Griffith to speculate about the 'Gaelic connections' of *Percyvell* – *Sir Perceval* (above, n. 3), p. 22 – but, as suggested by J. Campion and F. Holthausen in their editorial notes to *Sir Perceval of Gales* (Heidelberg, 1913), it is obviously a corruption of *scotte-spere* (cf. Old English *scotspera* 'dart, javelin'). Surpisingly, no editor has had the sense to emend it.

18 As Slavoj Žižek (writing about Wagner's version) shrewdly observes, the operation of a 'blind' causality shows up the weakness of the common interpretation of Perceval's failure as 'immaturity': 'It is here that the insufficiency of the Jungian interpretation which centers on Parsifal's "inner development" becomes manifest; by conceiving Parsifal's ability to ask the required question as the sign of spiritual maturity, this approach fails to take notice of the true enigma, which does not concern Parsifal but the other side, the Grail community: how can this single act of asking a question possess the tremendous healing power of restoring the health of the King and thereby of the entire community held together by the King's body?': *Tarrying With the Negative* (Durham, NC, 1993), p. 276, n. 41.

19 Hence the presence of the living mother does not, in my view, make *Sir Perceval* more 'matriarchal' than Chrétien's *Conte*, as F. Xavier Baron believes: 'Mother and son in *Sir Perceval of Galles*', *Papers in English Language and Literature*, 8 (1972), 3–14.

20 No further extra-narrative asides are found in the manuscript, nor are subsequent fitt divisions marked by large capitals. As Phillipa Hardman has suggested ('Fitt divisions in Middle English romances', *Yearbook of English Studies*, 22 (1992), 63–80), an alternative explanation for the fact that a number of Middle English romances preserve only the rubric for the first fitt division would be that, knowing the length of the first instalment, readers could easily estimate subsequent ones. However, in the case of the Findern copy (Cambridge University Library, MS Ff.1.6) of *Sir Degrevant*, the evidence of a half-copied *explicit* suggests that rubrics were lost in scribal transmission. On the relationship between fitt divisions and oral performance see Bradbury, *Writing Aloud*, pp. 114–23.

21 See Hardman, 'Fitt divisions', p. 72.

22 Karl Kroeber, *Retelling/Rereading: The Fate of Storytelling in Modern Times* (New Brunswick, NJ, 1992), p. 76.

23 *The Riverside Chaucer*, ed. Larry D. Benson *et al.* (Boston, 1987), *Canterbury Tales*, VII. 915–16.

24 *Sir Perceval of Galles and Ywain and Gawain*, ed. Mary Flowers Braswell (Kalamazoo, 1995), p. 69.

25 Baron, 'Mother and son', p. 12.

26 For a fuller analysis of 'redemptive' endings of this kind see Ad Putter, 'The narrative logic of *Emaré*', in Putter and Gilbert (eds), *The Spirit of Medieval English Popular Romance*, pp. 157–80.

27 Piero Boitani, *English Medieval Narrative in the 13th and 14th Centuries* (Cambridge, 1982), p. 54.

28 On the precise chronology, see J. G. Gouttebrooze, 'Sur l'étendue chronologique du premier mouvement du *Conte du Graal*', *Le Moyen Age*, 31 (1976), 5–24.

29 For a discussion of 'tokens' in Middle English romance see Richard Firth Green, *A Crisis of Truth: Literature and Law in Ricardian England* (Philadelphia, 1999), pp. 264–82.

30 *Ywain and Gawain*, ed. Mills, p. 194, note to line 425.

31 Woolf, 'Later poetry' (n. 5 above), p. 272.

32 I draw here on Terence Cave's *Recognitions: A Study of Poetics* (Oxford, 1988), pp. 39–43.

33 *Perceval*, trans. Bryant, pp. 148–9.

34 Thus Amis and Amiloun, Horn, and Chrétien's Cligés, are all knighted aged fifteen. The best gloss on this is a passage from the *Roman de Fauvel* (lines 3031–2), cited in J. A. Burrow, *The Ages of Man: A Study in Medieval Writing and Thought* (Oxford, 1986), p. 26: 'Le sanc veint demander sa rente /D'entour xv ans.' ('Blood begins to asks its due around the age of fifteen.')

35 Isumbras fasts for '*dayes seven*' (225) and is a pilgrim for '*sevenn yer*' (508): *Sir Isumbras*, in *Six Middle English Romances*, ed. Maldwyn Mills (London, 1973).

36 E.g. in *Athelston*, ed. A. Trounce, EETS 224 (London, 1951), lines 381, 571–3, 781–3, the bishop is on his *ninth* palfrey before reaching his destination; the blood-brothers walk across *nine* hot plough-shares, which the bishop blesses *nine* times.

37 Barthes, *S/Z*, p. 30.

38 Kroeber, in *Retelling/Rereading*, argues powerfully that professional critics have privileged 'plot' over 'story'; his book is a timely attempt to redress the balance.

9

Temporary virginity and the everyday body: *Le Bone Florence of Rome* and bourgeois self-making

Felicity Riddy

I

The earliest surviving representation of an English bourgeois family at prayer appears in a fifteenth-century book of hours, now known as the Bolton Hours, made for members of a York mercantile family.[1] The picture – one of a sequence of full-page illustrations – depicts a Crucifix-Trinity with four figures kneeling in front of it: a father and mother in the centre, flanked by a son and a daughter on the left and right. They all have scrolls issuing from their mouths, on which are written two Latin couplets.[2] The first couplet is spoken by the boy and the man, who share a rhyme. The boy says: 'O father, o son, you who are called the kind spirit' (O pater o nate tu spiritus alme vocate), and the father says: 'Grant what we seek from you through your com- passion' (Quod petimus a te concede tua pietate). The second couplet, which completes the prayer, is spoken by the woman and the girl. The mother says: 'Heavenly majesty, threefold god, one power' (Celica magestas trinus deus una potestas), and the girl says: 'You who dispense gifts, make us chaste and honourable' (Premia qui prestas nos castas fac et honestas). Her 'us' cannot refer to them all, though: the feminine plural endings of the Latin adjectives 'castas' (chaste) and 'honestas' (honourable) in the last line make it clear that it is the chastity and honour of the two women only, and not of the men, which is being prayed for by the family as a whole. What is at stake in 'castas' and 'honestas' is not only, or even primarily, a set of religious values, des- pite the religious context, but a social ethic. 'Chaste' and 'honourable' are part of a public discourse of female respectability in the fifteenth century. The family is represented as united around this issue: the sexual conduct and good name of its female members. And in this strongly ideological representation, it is the daughter who is made to speak these words: her aspirations are represented as not only hers but also her family's and those of her social group. The hope is, perhaps, that she will grow up to be like the 'honesta mulier' ('honourable woman'), Mary Brathwayt, widow of a former mayor of York, who 'out of her pure desire and devotion' had a cross built in the market place in York in 1421 in memory of her husband and all Christian souls, and who was probably known to the book's original owners.[3]

The family's whole prayer, cast as it is in that form of the future that imperatives bring into being – the future in which wishes, desires and fantasies are played out – opens up a space for narrative. 'Make us chaste and honourable' invites the reader/viewer to imagine a set of events in which the virtues of chastity and honour are brought into being (made), in which they are not states but forms of behaviour, not ways of being but ways of doing. Such an imagined set of events is not a scenario, like the picture I have been describing, but a story.

So we might link this bourgeois prayer with bourgeois narrative and this is, indeed, what I propose to do. There are many stories that survive from late-medieval urban milieux, including many romances. They are in well-known manuscripts, such as the Auchinleck manuscript, compiled in London in the 1330s,[4] or – a hundred and fifty years later – in less familiar books such as Cambridge University Library, MS Ff. 2. 38, written by a Leicestershire scribe, probably in the 1480s.[5] The latter is relevant here: commissioned perhaps a couple of generations later than the Bolton Hours, it is a paper manuscript containing nine romances alongside other kinds of stories – saints' lives and moral tales – as well as a courtesy text and rhymes on the essential articles of the faith. Like the Bolton Hours, it is provincial, and this is an important aspect of how both books have been regarded. The Bolton Hours is expensively illustrated, with forty-seven full-page illuminations. Nevertheless, the quality of the work, compared with books made in London for aristocratic patrons, has led art historians to treat it somewhat condescendingly. Likewise, CUL Ff. 2. 38, which emanates from a similar provincial milieu, has been described rather patronisingly as 'ideally suited to the instruction, edification and entertainment of well-doing, devout readers of modest intellectual accomplishments'.[6] We might compare the tone of this observation with that of comments made about a book that was apparently assembled to order in the 1440s, and which includes a range of courtly poems, especially love complaints and dream visions by Chaucer, Gower and Lydgate. Oxford, Bodleian Library, MS Tanner 346, we are told, 'forms an anthology of poetry that "reflects the social and literary refinements of the 'lettered chivalry' of the time'".[7] 'Modest intellectual accomplishments' and 'social and literary refinements': it is clear which is the approved group. But, of course, bourgeois romances in general have been treated patronisingly: they are the products, an influential critic has claimed, of 'a lower-middle-class audience, a class of social aspirants who wish to be entertained with what they consider to be the same fare, but in English, as their social betters'.[8] The implication is that the readers and commissioners of these works are people who aspire to the elite art-objects of their social superiors, but who lack the taste, cultivation or contacts to acquire the genuine article. There also seems to be an implication that the critic has a better eye for these things than they have.

This links, of course, to a larger debate over 'popular' culture, and to the extent to which the categories 'popular' and 'elite' (and the hierarchy of taste they assume) are themselves produced by the criticism that claims to be only describing them. It may be, however, that it is not only modern academic judgements that are at issue here, because the kinds of implicit distinctions and hierarchies being drawn in the twentieth century surely mirror practices from the fifteenth. The scribe of CUL Ff. 2. 38 was of Leicestershire origin and may have worked in Leicester itself.[9] The most obvious assumption is that the manuscript was commissioned for urban domestic use from a local professional. It was originally two unbound booklets, and presumably it has only survived at all because of the lucky decision of a later owner to bind the paper booklets together in leather. The book contains *The Adulterous Falmouth Squire, How a Merchande did his Wife Betray* and *A Gode Mater of the Merchand and his Sone*,[10] in a sequence starting about a third of the way into the first booklet. These are followed immediately by *The Erl of Tolous, Sir Eglamour of Artois, Sir Tryamour*, the northern *Octavian, Bevis of Hamtoun*, and the tale-collection, *The Seven Sages of Rome*, with which the first booklet ends. The second booklet follows on with four more romances: the so-called 'fifteenth-century' *Guy of Warwick, Le Bone Florence of Rome, Robert of Cisyle* and *Sir Degare*. If we dispense with our anyway tenuous modern generic boundaries, we have a long sequence of stories, starting with *The Adulterous Falmouth Squire* and ending with *Sir Degare*, most of which have to do with the closest ties of kinship: between husbands and wives, and between parents and children. The compilation, then, emphasises the idea of the nuclear family that is also discernible in the picture of the family at prayer in the Bolton Hours.

All these anonymous poems in CUL Ff. 2. 38 are, moreover, in tail-rhyme or four-stress couplets; there is nothing by Chaucer, Gower or Lydgate, and nothing written in the Chaucerian stanza forms – rime royal and five-stress couplets – that writers in the fifteenth-century courtly tradition adopted. Chaucer had made it clear in the 1390s that, as far as he was concerned, tail-rhyme was the medium of choice of the unrefined; his mockery of the stanza in 'The Tale of Sir Thopas' was a way of coding his own formal innovations, by contrast, as socially prestigious. His fifteenth-century followers understood this and many of them adopted Chaucerian modes. We find rime royal used by Osbern Bokenham and John Capgrave for saints' lives; by John Hardyng for a chronicle; by John Metham for a romance, and of course by all sorts of people for lyrics. Nevertheless, we cannot assume that the absence of Chaucer or his followers from CUL Ff. 2. 38 shows that the Chaucerian tradition had not spread to Leicestershire by the fourth quarter of the fifteenth century. It seems unlikely that by then people in the business of acquiring texts did not know about rime royal and what it meant, and did not know about Chaucer and what he meant. CUL Ff. 2. 38 is the product of a nationwide traffic in texts that was drawn on by different and overlapping readerships. Chaucer's poems were already part of this traffic by the mid fifteenth century. Contemporary with CUL Ff. 2. 38 is the Findern manuscript (Cambridge, University Library, MS Ff. 1. 6) compiled by members and associates of a gentry household in Derbyshire, including women, who must also have had access to the traffic in texts. The Findern manuscript contains poems by Gower, Lydgate and Chaucer, and many of its lyrics are in rime royal. The most striking feature of its contents by comparison with CUL Ff. 2. 38, however, is that there is so little narrative. It contains the romance of *Sir Degrevaunt* and an episode from the Alexander story, reduced to a static love debate. Much of what it contains is lyric; it is about states of mind and not events; about feeling rather than doing. This may help us to characterise CUL Ff. 2. 38, with its large collection of stories in non-Chaucerian modes, as something other than merely a compilation for 'well-doing, devout readers of modest intellectual accomplishments'. These are stories for people who do not care about 'literary' fashion, and whose tastes allow them to reject aristocratic forms as much as ape them. And so I come back to where I started: to the York book of hours, with its representation of the nuclear family and its strong sense of urban and provincial self-worth.[11]

Let us try to imagine these two books – the Bolton Hours and CUL Ff. 2. 38 – being read, not in a manor-house in the country, as the Findern manuscript was, but in a timber-framed urban house that was also a place of work: what Langland calls a 'burgeises place', as distinct from a 'beggers cote'.[12] We might think of a house like that owned by John Collan, a York goldsmith, who died in 1490: it had a hall, a parlour, a boulting-house (where flour was stored and sifted), a kitchen, a store-room, a great chamber, a second chamber and a work-shop.[13] It no doubt had at least one privy and was served by the network of public ditches that carried away waste and water. The bourgeois scene of reading was in a house like this: the goldsmith's, the tailor's, the grocer's; perhaps in the hall, or in the parlour, or in one of the chambers. There must have been a mixed readership of men and women, old and young, sons and daughters, as well as the para-family members who were servants and apprentices.

A house like this, though, was by the fifteenth century not only material but also ideological. By then an idea of domesticity had developed among what I am calling the bourgeoisie – that is, the fami-lies of the people who owned their own businesses, were members of the franchise and of the leading fraternities, and participated in town government.[14] The bourgeois home was where trade, manufacture, business, cooking, eating, sleeping – and reading – were all understood as interrelated but separate aspects of domestic life and ordered as such.[15] Managing this kind of domesticity entailed a particular con-ceptualisation of everyday space and time, locating the regimes of the body, which were its primary concern, inside the house and not, like the urban poor, outside it. The regimes of the body include getting the children up and putting them to bed; preparing the food and clearing it away; making a mess and tidying it up; looking after the sick, the old and the dying; the ordinary, daily repetition of life and death in all its materiality. One of the ideological tasks of bourgeois women, unlike their aristocratic counterparts, must have been the unmediated and intimate management of what I call the 'everyday body' in the home, to which I shall return later.

This home was the context, then, of reading and prayer – the kind of material found in CUL Ff. 2. 38, which simultaneously constituted and expressed urban domestic values. Of the 'family' narratives in CUL Ff. 2. 38 most, like most medieval narratives apart from saints' lives, have men as their protagonists. The exception is *Le Bone Florence of Rome*, which only survives here.[16] It concerns the adventures of Florence, daughter of the emperor of Rome, between the time when she is first sought in marriage and the time at which she conceives her first child. 'Make us chaste and honourable', is the daughter's prayer in the Bolton Hours, and the story of Florence can be read as a fantasy of that process of making.

II

Le Bone Florence of Rome is a much shortened version of an early thirteenth-century French poem, *Florence de Rome*, which circulated in England in the Anglo-Norman period: two of the three manuscripts in which it survives were copied by English scribes.[17] On the face of it, this looks like an example of what I am arguing against: the idea that Middle English romances are for 'social aspirants who wish to be entertained with what they consider to be the same fare, but in English, as their social betters'. But in fact this is no more true of *Le Bone Florence of Rome* than it is of *Troilus and Criseyde*: both poems are transformed by the shift to a new language and a new social milieu.

Florence, the heroine of the romance, is, as I have said, the daughter of the emperor of Rome. She is sought in marriage by the physically repulsive, one-hundred-year-old Sir Garcy, the emperor of Constantinople, whom she refuses. Florence's father is killed in the war that this refusal provokes, and Florence, lacking male protection, marries Sir Emere, the younger son of the king of Hungary. At Florence's request, however, Emere leaves Rome before the marriage is consummated in order to avenge her father's death on Sir Garcy. Florence is then subjected to a series of horrifying experiences: her brother-in-law Miles produces what he claims is Emere's dead body and tries to marry her, but she escapes; Miles then tells Emere that Florence has been unfaithful in his absence, abducts Florence, tries to rape her and hangs her up by her hair. She is rescued by Sir Tyrry, who takes her home with him, and she has to defend herself against an attempted rape by a knight of the household. The rejected knight cuts the throat of Tyrry's daughter, who shares Florence's bed, and leaves the bloody knife in Florence's hand. Cast out into the forest, she rescues a criminal from hanging and he becomes her servant. He conspires with a friend of his to sell her to a sea-captain who, along with all his men, tries to gang-rape her on board ship. Florence's prayers to the Virgin Mary produce a mass detumescence among the crew and a miraculous storm; she gets to shore, enters a nunnery and becomes a noted healer. Emere and all the people who have wronged her are by this time suffering from various kinds of illness; they all come to her without knowing who she is, rehearse their stories, and are healed. She is reunited with Emere and they finally consummate their marriage.

Le Bone Florence of Rome has been put alongside the stories of persecuted wives – Constance and Griselda – which emphasise, says Hornstein, 'the virtue of a meek Job-like faith'.[18] Nevertheless this poem is unlike those, and unlike Emare, which has another rare female protagonist, in that Florence, although technically married in the course of the narrative and therefore a persecuted wife, remains a virgin till the closing lines. In fact, it may already be clear that the poem places a particular value on the heroine's virginity and at the same time is unusually attentive to the body. These things are, as I shall show, related.

To take virginity first: we must bear in mind that there was more than one late-medieval discourse of virginity.[19] On the one hand, virginity was represented as a sacred vocation that was placed highest in the triad virginity-widowhood-marriage. This way of categorising female sexuality had been a commonplace of Christian thought since the fourth century. Religious virginity – the virginity of those who had committed themselves to lives of total sexual renunciation for the love of God – was held to be a form of perfection, 'the hyeste degree that is in this present lif', as Chaucer's 'Parson's Tale' has it: 'thilke precious fruyt that the book clepeth the hundred fruyt'.[20] This is a reference to the parable in Matthew 13.9 of the sower whose seeds fell on the ground and bore fruit, 'some a hundredfold, some sixtyfold, some thirtyfold'. Virginity earns the hundredfold reward, continent widowhood the sixtyfold, and chaste marriage the thirtyfold. Compared with the virginity of those who intend to remain continent for the whole of their lives, the temporary virginity of those who intend to marry does not rank at the top of this stern hierarchy; it is of an inferior order, no better than the chastely married.

There was, nevertheless, also another way of understanding virginity: as a phase in the life-course of women intending to marry, which produced the triad maid-wife-widow. Chaucer's Knight, for example, observes that 'A man moot nedes love, maugree his hede, ... Al be she mayde, or wydwe, or elles wyf'.[21] Here it is clear that the 'mayde' is not a consecrated virgin but a young unmarried woman, and the triad in which she occurs supposedly includes all women. By contrast, the religious triad, virgin-widow-wife, is not inclusive, but omits unmarried women who are sexually active. Since this is a hierarchy of states of virtue, the latter do not count at all. In one discourse, then, virginity is a religious value, in the other it is a social one, however much it may have been buttressed by appeals to religion. Heroines of saints' lives are usually virgins of the first sort; whether or not their virginity is at risk, it is an attribute of their sanctity. Heroines of romances are usually the second; they are wives in waiting and their virginity is an attribute of their marriageability.[22] The plots in which they figure are ones in which the goal is not a heavenly crown but a husband. The chastity of daughter and mother in the Bolton Hours illustration is of this second kind: they represent maid and wife, in the maid–wife–widow triad, not virginity and marriage in the virginity–widowhood–marriage hierarchy. Their chastity has to do with the management of fecundity in accordance with contemporary conventions of behaviour for women of their class.

Of course, these two triads blur and, of course, when young un-married women from elite families were considered as potential wives, there was a strong sense that they ought to be virgins, which was buttressed, as I have already said, by religious values. We can see this process at work in the Bolton Hours, where the young girl is repre-sented in a prayer book as praying for her own chastity. Nevertheless, the life-long virgin and the virgin-till-marriage were conceptually differentiated, as Florence's story shows. Much of the action consists of a concerted male alliance to put her virginity to the test, and although she spends time in a nunnery, at the end of the poem she is reunited in Rome with her husband, Emere. The reader knows that the religious life is not the goal of Florence's story – it is not about a consecrated virgin but about the other, temporary, kind. The nunnery is a detour *en route* to the wedding feast with which the poem ends.

So the story focuses on a particular phase in a woman's life: her maidenhood, defined as the point at which she becomes marriageable to the point at which she loses her virginity to her husband, quite a long time after the marriage ceremony. Florence at the beginning of the story is at least fifteen: she has been 'set to scole' (58), can read as well as being adept at harp and psaltery, and lives with her widowed father, the emperor of Rome. Nevertheless, maidenhood in this text is not coterminous with moving from her father's control to her hus-band's: that is, the story does not use yet another life-course triad which was available in late-medieval England: that of daughter-wife-widow.[23] The plot is shaped to allow Florence a period in which she is neither daughter, because her father is dead, nor wife, because she has not consummated her marriage. By having her tell Emere that she will not sleep with him until he has captured or killed Sir Garcy, Florence herself is made to create the narrative space in which she will occupy the ambiguous status of the virgin wife, and in which her 'maydenhedd' will be constantly under attack. The narrator does not describe Florence as Emere's 'wyfe' until after they have consummated their marriage at the end of the poem; in the meantime she is still called a 'maydyn'.[24] We might think of Florence's prolongation of her virgin state as the poem's way of decorously figuring a stage of pre-marital independence which we know existed for young women in late-medieval England, the semi-autonomous phase of service, in which the daughter has left her father's house but not yet entered her husband's and which daughter-wife-widow does not adequately map.[25] So what all this adds up to is the fact that the poem is interested, in a way that saints' lives are not, in virginity as a phase, as something that girls in particular are expected to grow into and out of. This is connected, as I have already suggested, with its focus on the body, and in particular with the body in time.

This latter focus is evident as soon as Florence's first suitor, Sir Garcy, is introduced at the beginning of the poem. He is a hundred years old, and possibly more:

> Hys flesche trembylde for grete elde,
> Hys blode colde hys body vnwelde,
> Hys lyppes blo forthy;
> He had more mystyr of a gode fyre,
> Of bryght brondys brennyng schyre,
> To beyke hys boones by,
> A softe bath a warme bedd,
> Then any maydyn for to wedd,
> And gode encheson why,
> For he was bresyd and all tobrokyn,
> Ferre trauelde in harnes and of warre wrokyn. (94–104)

This is in some ways a medicalised old man's body: cold and dry, as the theory of humours had it; a condition which cannot be reversed, only ameliorated by keeping warm, taking plenty of rest and avoiding sexual intercourse, as the best doctors advised.[26] It is the old body of the calendar illustrations that represent February as an elderly man sitting indoors by a fire. Garcy's fantasies of Florence's youthful body are the passive dreams of old age: 'Sche schall lygg be my syde, / And taste my flankys wyth hur honde' (108–9), he says. 'Taste' is a word that hovers between the medical, the erotic and the maternal: part caress, part healing touch.[27] He goes on to develop his strikingly unpenetrative, infantile dreams of reawakening to endless cuddles: 'Sche schall me boþe hodur and happe, / And in hur louely armes me lappe, / Bothe euyn and mornetyde' (112–14). When she hears of all this, Florence responds by invoking the grotesque old man's body of *fabliau*:[28]

> Sche seyde, 'Be God þat boght me dere,
> Me had leuyr þe warste bachylere,
>   In all my fadurs thede,
> Then for to lye be hys bresyd boones,
> When he coghyth and oldely grones …' (244–8)

From her point of view there is nothing infantile about this disgusting old person. He does not pose a sexual threat – those are to come later – and this is, of course, precisely why he is regarded with such contempt. Caring for the elderly is one thing, but marrying them is another. Florence knows the kind of virginity she represents: its whole point is that she is going to lose it. She also knows the plot she is part of: she is to marry a young man who can make her pregnant the first time they sleep together, as Emere will do. A coughing centenarian who wants to be cuddled will not.

Nevertheless, Florence's phrase, 'bresyd boones' (247), harks back to the earlier description of Garcy's body that I have already quoted: 'For he was bresyd and all tobrokyn, / Ferre trauelde in harnes and of warre wrokyn' (103–4). 'Bresyd' allows the fabliau perspective to shade into something different: it can mean simply 'decrepit' or 'exhausted', and elsewhere in Middle English it collocates with 'bones' in this sense.[29] It can also mean 'shattered', 'damaged' or 'injured', however, and is frequently used in these senses in contexts that have to do with fighting or warfare.[30] Lines 103–4 contain yet another view of the old man's body, as worn out by its own hard, male, soldiering life. This perspective sees the body as having a specific history that is something other than either the enfeeblement of medical discourse or the disgusting decrepitude of *fabliau*. It is picked up later when Garcy, having declared war on Rome, meets Florence's father on the field of battle. The two old generals realise that they are going to have to fight in single combat, despite their age and the fact that, as Garcy says, he has not worn armour for seven years: 'Wyth scharpe swyrdys faght þey þen, / They had be two full doghty men, / Gode olde fyghtyng was there' (679–81). This moment is shot through with a sense of what the two old men had once been and with nostalgia for what their style momentarily conflates: the way fighting was in the old days, and the way old men fight. These two old soldiers are their pasts, and their bodies tell their histories.

This curious moment hovers, as so much of the poem does, on the borders between nightmare and farce: in the course of their single combat Garcy hits Florence's father on the helm and issues the first of the many threats of rape that Florence is to receive: 'When þat Y haue leyn hur by, / And done hur schame and vylenye, / Then wyll I of hur no mare, / But geue hur to my chaumburlayne' (688–91). Old soldiers in late medieval culture – or at least in this product of it – do not retire, but carry on doing what young soldiers do: fighting, and raping the enemy's women. If this old soldier is his past, as I have suggested, these are what his past includes, and it is as much brutal as heroic. The poem's treatment of Garcy suggests that there is not a single fix on old age or a single way of talking about it: it is a mixture of energy and decay; of autonomy and dependence; of sexual impotence and a kind of Yeatsian desire for desire; simultaneously pathetic, contemptible, terrifying and absurd.

The poem does not only focus on the old body, however. Sick, deformed and wounded; needing to be fed, clothed, kept warm and given rest; eroticised, tormented and vulnerable; the corpse – all these varieties of the body in time are accommodated by the poem, and not as animal but as human. The representation of Florence and her experiences is strikingly corporeal. She is, we are told early on, 'þe feyrest þynge, / That euyr was seen wolde or ȝynge, / Made of flesche and felle' (307–9). In Middle English 'þynge' had a range of meanings, not all of them associated with materiality, and its use in line 307 seems to have been a way of signifying sympathy and tenderness.[31] Nevertheless another sense of 'þynge' as 'living, corporeal being'[32] is picked up in the next line in the brief allusion to human ageing ('wolde or ȝynge'), and made explicit in 'flesche and felle' in the line after. Florence's sufferings are inflicted on, endured by, and understood in terms of, the flesh as well as the will. She falls from her horse and is beaten with a sword (1425–6); wandering in a forest with her kidnapper, she 'hungurd wondur sare' (1451) and is given bread and water by a hermit – food which never tasted sweeter to her (1468–70); she is hung up by her hair from a tree and beaten on 'hur nakyd flesche' (1517); rescued, she is given a herbal bath that 'made hur sore sydes softe' and fed on rich food (1550–2); assaulted in her chamber, she picks up a stone and hits her attacker with it, so that he spits out his front teeth and his nose bleeds (1607–9); this attacker kills her bedfellow by gripping her throat and slicing through it while they sleep (1631–2); Florence wakes up in the morning to find a knife in her hand and the young girl, 'burlyng in hur blode' (1637), beside her in the bed; this is her third corpse: she has already seen the mutilated bodies of her father and – as far as she knows – her husband; a thief she has rescued from the gallows repays her by selling her for so much gold that 'hyt passyd almoost hur weyght' (1790); she is embraced so hard in the course of another attempted rape that 'Hur rybbes crakyd as þey breke wolde' (1850). In all this there is, it seems, no abjection: the body is not shrunk from and does not defile. It is multivalent: sometimes funny; at others appalling; at others no more than matter-of-factly there to be contended with: fed, rested, clothed. It is what the poem understands humans to be: what I call the everyday body.

III

The everyday body is the body at home; it is the product of the peculiar perspectives of close-quarters domestic living, of its intimacies and knowledge.[33] Home is the place where, as I have already said, the regimes of the body routinely take place: eating, sleeping, feeding, washing, defecating, caring for the sick, being born and dying. The ordinariness of these routines and of the home itself means that domestic perspectives on the body are for the most part unrecorded. Nevertheless, an unpretentious narrative such as *Le Bone Florence* of Rome, found in a manuscript assembled for bourgeois domestic reading and with a rare female protagonist, might be the kind of text where, if anywhere, such a perspective is to be found. We can find other kinds of evidence for the everyday body in the courtesy poems that were read in the bourgeois home, such as 'How the goode man taght hys sone' which is included in CUL Ff. 2. 38. Its sententious and commonplace advice includes dicta on daily routines: about praying before starting work in the morning, about getting enough rest, about not taking 'rere-sopers' (late-night suppers) that destroy the complexion, and so on. It is a text generated by the conditions of intimacy and offers guidance about living successfully in very close proximity with others. In other courtesy texts the everyday body is the subject of more intimate advice: about farting, scratching private parts, picking teeth, and wiping noses.

I am not arguing that the everyday body is somehow the body as it 'really' is – as a physical object outside history, a material ground of meaning. The body is always mediated; its 'natural' needs, for food, clothing, warmth and rest – needs that are primarily supplied by the home – are always also historical and social, and always seen from somebody's point of view. To use the everyday body as a tool of analysis, we need to specify it, to locate it in particular social contexts, and on grids of gender, class and age.

High culture did, of course, know the everyday body, but invoked it in order to dismiss it. We get a particularly jaundiced view of it in, for example, the rhetorical topos of the 'molestiae nuptiarum', or woes of marriage. This theme goes back to Ambrose and Jerome in the fourth century and, beyond them, to the Greek Fathers and classical literary tradition, and regularly occurs in writings aimed at discouraging the reader from forsaking celibacy for marriage.[34] A striking Middle English example occurs in *Hali Meiðhad*, a letter on virginity written in the West Midlands around the beginning of the thirteenth century.[35] This text, addressed to women, is an argument for virginity as the highest spiritual calling in the religious triad, virgin–widow–wife, which I have already discussed. In order to celebrate virginity, the author denigrates marriage in a variety of ways. There is, for example, a long passage on the bodily disfigurements and discomforts of pregnancy, which leads into the agonies of childbirth and the miseries of motherhood:

> Efter al þis, kimeð of þet bearn ibore þus wanunge andt wepunge, þe schal abute midniht makie þe to wakien … Ant hwet, þe cader fulðen, ant bearmes umbe stunde, to ferkin ant to fostrin hit se moni earm-hwile
>
> [After all this, there comes from the child born in this way, wailing and crying, which will keep you up in the middle of the night … And all the filth in the cradle, and in your lap sometimes, so many weary hours feeding and rearing it.][36]

By comparison with virgins, married women have

> of so heh se lahe iliht – of englene ilicnesses, of Iesu Cristes leof-mon, of leafdi in heouene, into flesches fulðe, into beastes liflade, into monnes þeowdom, ant into worldes weane.
>
> [descended so low from so high – from the likeness of angels, from the beloved of Jesus Christ, from a lady in heaven, into carnal filth, into the life of an animal, into servitude to a man, and into the world's misery.][37]

Here the life of the mind, whether religious contemplation or philosophy, is valorised and the bodily regimes of the home are represented

as a repugnant and sub-human bondage. The trope depends on accepting a series of familiar theoretical dualisms: between soul and body,
between heaven and hell, between purity and filth. Within the home,
however, the everyday body was apparently understood differently, as
something more like a practical unity of consciousness and materiality.
It was not, to this way of thinking, the lesser part of a body–mind
hierarchy.[38] Moreover, although much recent scholarship has argued
that medieval thought habitually equated the body with women, this
was not the everyday perspective.[39] To the home's way of thinking,
men – as *Le Bone Florence of Rome* acknowledges – are embodied too.[40]
The everyday body is vulnerable and needy, but it is not despised as
worthless flesh; its processes may be dirty and smelly but they are not
morally filthy; domestic living is not 'beastes liflade' (the life of an
animal), or at least not in the contemptuous sense in which this phrase
is used in *Hali Meiðhad*. As a concept, it is produced by the person who
cannot afford to be squeamish but just has to get on with cleaning up
the vomit on the floor. Coping, rather than recoiling, is the law of
domestic life. The mixture of perspectives on old age I have identified
in *Le Bone Florence of Rome* can be linked to this law: the everyday body
is not a thing but a bundle of attitudes, a way of thinking about the
body that makes it possible to get through the day, by turning distaste
into a joke and awe into pity, or allowing all these perspectives to co-
exist. The everyday body is tolerated, grumbled about, laughed at,
wept over and lived with. With all this in mind, we might interpret
Hali Meiðhad's depiction of the wearisome tasks of motherhood as
grounded in male bafflement at what women put up with, since it is
on women that the burdens of the home fall most heavily. And, to
return to an earlier point, the orderly domesticity of the late-medieval
'burgeises place' required the goodwife to take direct responsibility for
those burdens. *Le Bone Florence of Rome*, then, is more than a source of
evidence for the everyday body in late-medieval England, which is
what I suggested above; it is also a product of the ideological project of
bourgeois domesticity. *Hali Meiðhad* is written from the religious
perspective of the virgin–widow–wife hierarchy and presents domestic living and the management of the body in a hostile way, in order to
persuade young women to eschew them. *Le Bone Florence of Rome* is
written from the social perspective of the maid–wife–widow sequence
and presents domestic living and management of the body as something for which young women have special gifts.

This seems to be the point of the final part of Florence's story, in
which she reveals a hitherto unsuspected capacity for healing. After

escaping from a shipwreck through the protection of the Blessed Virgin, she fetches up in a nunnery where she is welcomed, given a nun's habit and lives the religious life. She becomes noted for curing the 'syke' and 'sare' (1927), and her fame spreads. Meanwhile, back in Rome, Florence's husband, Emere, has received an incurable head wound in battle, which 'was festurd wythowte delyte' (1943). Simultaneously, all those who have wronged her fall ill, and their illnesses have grotesque physical effects that are described with grim relish. Emere's brother, Mylys, who kidnapped Florence, has become a leper (a 'fowle meselle' (1965)), with 'pokkys and bleynes bloo' (2022), so hideous that he hides himself from public view; the knight who tried to rape Florence and cut her bedfellow's throat has the palsy 'and was crompylde and crokyd þerto' (1977); the captain of the ship who also tried to rape her hobbles on crutches, his eyes bulging and his limbs rotting 'Wyth woundys wanne and wete' (1992, 2027); while the thief she saved from the gallows has 'an euyll þat dud him grefe' (1994) and has to be trundled in a wheelbarrow because he 'Had no fote on to goo' (2031). This weird procession of the morally and physically deformed makes its way to Florence's nunnery, at the same time as Emere, in order to be healed. One reading of the poem's emphasis on all this corporeal bizarrerie is that it stresses the fact that Florence's enemies have been punished by God long before they receive human punishment at their final unmasking.[41] This does not exclude another reading: that it stresses the physical repugnance of the task of healing. This is not a job for the squeamish, any more than is the care of infants or the elderly incontinent. The language used here is not medical; what is at issue is the nurse's practical care, not the doctor's learned diagnosis. Although they do not know her in her nun's habit, Florence recognises them all straight away, and 'lyghtly at them loghe' (2018). Her laughter may be at the irony of their new situations, and what these reveal about the fragile basis of male power, resting as it has done for so much of the action on physical strength. The rapist, the murderer, the kidnapper – violence against women takes many forms in this poem – can only get away with it for so long, because their bodies will do for them in the end. This is the unspoken knowledge of the home, which sees patriarchy at its most vulnerable and from very close up. Florence insists that before she will heal them they must make public confession, and so one by one they tell the stories of their crimes which, patched together, are Florence's own horrific history. Then, unflinchingly, 'Sche handylde þem wyth hur hande' (2110) – the black sores, the shaking limbs, the footless legs – and they are made whole.[42]

We might, in conclusion, think about the function of this horrific history in the poem as a whole. It is a history in which the daughter proves herself chaste and honourable: after the wedding feast, the people thank God 'That þe lady was comyn agayne, / And kept hur chaste and clene' (2161–3). By the end of the poem Florence is the wife of the Emperor of Rome, as her mother had been, and is a mother herself. The only difference is that she does not die in childbirth, as her mother had done. In the orderly bourgeois household the daughter takes her mother's place and not her father's: in the Bolton Hours, mother and daughter together pray for an identical future. For the daughter to take the father's place is apparently unthinkable, even though Florence is her father's heir. When her father dies and Florence inherits all his 'brode landys' (829), his dukes, earls and barons all wring their hands and ask: 'Who schall vs now geue londys or lythe, / Hawkes, or howndys, or stedys stythe, / As he was wonte to doo?' (841–3) The expected answer is clearly not 'Florence, of course'. Florence may inherit but she cannot rule: in fact she is made to faint at this juncture as if to acquiesce in her own incapacity. And so the unequal distribution of public power between men and women perpetuates itself; the landless Emere acquires an empire, Florence sends him away and her nightmares begin. The period I have already identified in which she is neither a daughter nor a wife is the period of the horrific history that gets pieced together at the end of the poem. As bourgeois reading matter, *Le Bone Florence of Rome* is a parental fantasy, it seems, which allows the daughter a measure of freedom but teaches her that the world in which that freedom is exercised is nightmarishly hostile. It allows her to reject the unsuitable husband but obliges her in the end to take the suitable one for whom she has strenuously preserved her virginity; and of course it presents her with only one future, a future in which she will end up like her mother. Nevertheless, the representation of experience in terms of everyday corporeality also ensures that she has the measure of the world she lives in: the person who can cope with the body is the one who has the last laugh.

Notes

1 York, Minster Library, MS Additional 2; early fifteenth century. See Neil Ker and A. J. Piper, *Medieval Manuscripts in British Libraries*, 4 vols (Oxford, 1969–92), vol. IV, pp. 786–91, and Kathleen Scott, *Later Gothic Manuscripts, 1390–1490*, 2 vols (London, 1996), vol. II, pp. 119–21. See also Patricia Cullum and Jeremy Goldberg, 'How Margaret Blackburn taught her

daughters: reading devotional instruction in a Book of Hours', in Jocelyn Wogan-Browne *et al.* (eds), *Medieval Women: Texts and Contexts in Late Medieval Britain* (Turnhout, 2000), pp. 217–36.

2 The texts are transcribed by Ker, *Medieval Manuscripts*, vol. IV, p. 790. My translation.

3 *York Memorandum Book Part II (1388–1493)*, ed. Maud Sellers, Surtees Society 125 (Durham and London, 1914), p. 100.

4 Edinburgh, National Library of Scotland, MS Advocates' 19.2.1. See also *The Auchinleck Manuscript*, ed. Derek Pearsall and I. C. Cunningham (London, 1977). The most recent study is Ralph Hanna, 'Reconsidering the Auchinleck manuscript', in Derek Pearsall (ed.), *New Directions in Later Medieval Manuscript Studies* (Woodbridge, 2000), 91–102.

5 New watermark evidence has revised the slightly later date proposed in *Cambridge University Library MS Ff. 2. 38*, ed. Frances McSparran and P. M. Robinson (London, 1979), p. xii. See Friedrich Hülsmann, 'The watermarks of four late medieval manuscripts containing *The Erle of Tolous*', *Notes and Queries*, 32 (1985), 11–12. M. B. Parkes ('The literacy of the laity', in David Daiches and Anthony Thorlby (eds), *The Medieval World* (London, 1973), pp. 555–78, at pp. 568–9) regards it as mid-fifteenth century.

6 *Cambridge University Library MS Ff. 2. 38*, ed. McSparran and Robinson, p. vii.

7 *Manuscript Tanner 346: A Facsimile: Bodleian Library, Oxford University*, ed. Pamela Robinson (Norman, Oklahoma, 1980), p. xvii. The words in inverted commas are a quotation from *Bodleian Library MS Fairfax 16*, ed. John Norton-Smith (London, 1979), p. vii. We do not know who commissioned Tanner 346, but Fairfax 16 was assembled for a gentleman, John Stanley of Hooton, and Robinson assumes they emanate from similar elite milieux.

8 Derek Pearsall, 'The development of Middle English romance', *Medieval Studies*, 27 (1965), 91–116 (p. 92).

9 See A. McIntosh, M. Samuels and M. Benskin, *A Linguistic Atlas of Late Medieval England*, 4 vols (Aberdeen, 1986), vol. 4, LP 531.

10 This is a variant version of *The Child of Bristow*, which has been discussed by Barbara Hanawalt, '"The Childe of Bristowe" and the making of middle-class adolescence', in Barbara A. Hanawalt and David Wallace (eds), *Bodies and Disciplines: Intersections of Literature and History in Fifteenth-Century England* (Minneapolis,1996), pp. 155–78.

11 The Bolton Hours contains images and prayers relating specifically to York and Yorkshire, including St William of York and 'St' Richard Scrope, both archbishops of York, and St John of Beverley (in the East Riding), also archbishop.

12 William Langland, *The Vision of Piers Plowman*, B text, ed. A.V.C. Schmidt (London and New York, 1978), XII. 146–7: 'Ne in none beggers cote was that barn born, / But in a burgeises place, of Bethlem the beste'. For a vivid distinction between these two kinds of housing,

see Charles Phythian-Adams, *Desolation of a City: Coventry and the Urban Crisis of the Late Middle Ages* (Cambridge, 1979), pp. 80–1. On late-medieval housing types generally, see John Schofield, *Medieval London Houses* (New Haven, 1994); Jane Grenville, *Medieval Housing* (London, 1997).

13 John Collan, York, 1490: Borthwick Institute for Historical Research, Dean and Chapter of York, Probate Inventories, 1383–1499.

14 For this group, see Sylvia L. Thrupp, *The Merchant Class of Medieval London [1300–1500]* (Ann Arbor, 1948); Jenny Kermode, *Medieval Merchants: York, Beverley and Hull in the Later Middle Ages* (Cambridge, 1998); Sarah Rees Jones, 'The household and English urban government in the later middle ages', in M. Carlier and T. Soens (eds), *The Household in Later Medieval Europe* (Leuven, 2001). I am working on a fuller account of the idea of domesticity among urban elites in the fourteenth and fifteenth centuries.

15 The location of business or manufacture within the home marks off bourgeois domestic living from aristocratic life-styles.

16 *Le Bone Florence of Rome*, ed. Carol Falvo Heffernan (Manchester, 1976). All quotations are from this edition.

17 See *Florence de Rome: Chanson d'Aventure du Premier Quart du 13e Siècle*, ed. A. Wallensköld, SATF, 2 vols (Paris, 1909). A complete version (formerly owned by d'Arcy Hutton, Marske Hall, Richmond, Yorks.) was copied in the late thirteenth century by an English scribe, while two leaves of another version survive as endleaves in a copy of Hilton's *Speculum Contemplationis* (London, British Library, MS Lansdowne 362). The French poem was rewritten at least twice in French, and was translated into Spanish in the fourteenth century. The English translation in CUL Ff. 2. 38 was possibly made in the early fifteenth century. Its language is more northerly than that of the scribe.

18 J. Burke Severs (ed.), *A Manual of the Writings in Middle English 1050–1500, I, Romances* (New Haven, 1967), p. 120. See also Karen A. Winstead, 'Saints, wives, and other "hooly thynges": pious laywomen in Middle English romance', *Chaucer Yearbook: A Journal of Late Medieval Studies*, 2 (1995), 137–54 .

19 This paragraph and the next two are deeply indebted to conversations with Dr Cordelia Beattie of the Department of History, University of Edinburgh, and to her 'Meanings of singleness: the single woman in late medieval England', DPhil. dissertation, University of York, 2001.

20 Geoffrey Chaucer, *The Riverside Chaucer*, ed. Larry D. Benson *et al.* (Oxford, 1988), Parson's Tale, X. 867–8.

21 *Ibid., Knight's Tale*, I. 1169 and 1171.

22 For the sexualisation of virginity, see Kim Phillips, 'Maidenhood', in Katherine J. Lewis, Noel James Menuge and Kim Phillips (eds), *Young Medieval Women* (Stroud, 1999), pp. 1–24.

23 See Beattie, 'Meanings of singleness', pp. 24–6 and 45–54.

24 There are two occasions when Florence is called 'wyfe' by other charac-
    ters: the first is at line 1116, when Egravayne tells the Pope that in
    Emere's absence Mylys has tried to 'haue his wyfe'. At line 1301, when
    Mylys falsely tells Emere that Florence has imprisoned him during
    Emere's absence, he calls her 'thy wyfe'.

25 P. J. P. Goldberg, 'What was a servant?', in A. Curry and E. Matthew
    (eds), *Concepts and Patterns of Service in the Later Middle Ages* (Woodbridge,
    2000), pp. 1–20.

26 Shulamith Shahar, *Growing Old in the Middle Ages*, trans. Yael Lotan
    (London and New York, 1997), pp. 37–40.

27 See MED, tasten v. 2 (a), (b), (c). For maternal connotations, see the
    citation from Margery Kempe: 'Sche say owr Lady felyn and tastyn owr
    Lordys body … ȝyf þer wer ony sorhed'.

28 The best-known example of the *fabliau* version of the old man's body is
    in Chaucer's 'Merchant's Tale'; another is in Dunbar's 'The Two
    Married Women and the Widow', 89–119.

29 See *MED*, brisen v. 6; note the citation from ?Maidstone: 'Mercy, Lord
    … Heele me, for bresid be my bones'.

30 *Ibid.*, brisen v. 1, 2, 4, 5.

31 *Ibid.*, thing n. 4. (c). These senses survive in modern usage, e.g., 'dear
    thing', 'pretty little thing'.

32 *Ibid.*, thing n. 4. (a).

33 See my 'Looking closely: domestic authority in the late-medieval urban
    home', in Mary Erler and Maryann Kowaleski (eds), *Gendering the Master
    Narrative: Women and Power in the Middle Ages* (Ithaca and New York,
    2003), pp. 190–212.

34 There is an excellent discussion in *Hali Meiðhad*, ed. Bella Millett, EETS
    o.s. 284 (London, 1982), pp. xxx–xxxviii.

35 For edition, see previous note. There is a text and facing-page translation
    in *Medieval English Prose for Women from the Katherine Group and Ancrene
    Wisse*, eds Bella Millett and Jocelyn Wogan-Browne (Oxford, 1990), pp.
    2–41. My quotations are from this translation.

36 *Ibid.*, p. 33.

37 *Ibid.*, pp. 20–1.

38 For a brief and polemical account of medieval dualism, see Jacques le
    Goff, 'Body and ideology in the medieval West', in his *The Medieval
    Imagination*, trans. A. Goldhammer (Chicago and London, 1985), pp. 83–5.

39 See, e.g., Caroline Walker Bynum, '"And woman his humanity": female
    imagery in religious writings of the later Middle Ages', in her *Fragmen-
    tation and Redemption: Essays on Gender and the Human Body in Medieval
    Religion* (New York, 1991), pp. 151–79.

40 Sharon Farmer presents an interesting critique of the dominant scholarly
    tendency to equate women with the body in 'The beggar's body:
    intersections of gender and social status in high medieval Paris', in Sharon
    Farmer and Barbara Rosenwein (eds), *Monks and Nuns, Saints and Out-*

casts: Religion in Medieval Society (Ithaca and London, 2000), pp. 153–71. Using the records of miracles assembled for the inquest into the sanctity of St Louis, Farmer shows that poor men were particularly associated with the body by the clerical compilers of this evidence for the saint's miraculous powers.

41 See *Le Bone Florence*, ed. Heffernan, p. 24.

42 For women's role in the care of the sick, see Carol Rawcliffe, *Medicine and Society in Later Medieval England* (Stroud, 1995), chs 8 and 9.

10

Romancing the East: Greeks and Saracens in *Guy of Warwick*

Rebecca Wilcox

Guy's ties to the East

For decades, literary critics such as Frederic Jameson and Stephen Knight have argued that medieval romance, for the most part, unquestioningly reflects dominant ideologies of the ruling elite.[1] Far from conforming to this prescription, however, the fourteenth-century popular romance *Guy of Warwick* engages contemporary socio-political concerns in critical and transformative ways. *Guy*'s fantastic reworking of England's past through its titular hero both recognises England's historic culpabilities in its interactions with other countries and transforms these culpabilities into redeeming alternative possibilities for remembering the past and for performing the future. The historical events to which *Guy of Warwick* responds, above all others, took place during the first four – perhaps five – Crusades. Indeed, the earliest Anglo-Norman versions of *Guy*, which predate the oldest known English translations by more than half a century, followed closely on the Fourth Crusade.[2] While the Middle English *Guy* is clearly based on the Anglo-Norman romance, it emphasises with greater strength the Englishness of its material and its hero and intensifies the ideologically charged Crusade-like conflicts in which Guy participates.[3] The Middle English *Guy* reshapes England's historical relationships with the East in order to redress its English audience's anxieties regarding these relationships.

Recent criticism on *Guy of Warwick* has emphasised, above all else, the manuscript history of the romance. Critics such as L. Hibbard, A. J. Bliss, D. Pearsall, I. C. Cunningham, T. Shonk and J. Frankis explore the *Guy* manuscripts and their production, while M. Mills, J. Burton, P. Price, R. Dalrymple, T. Turville-Petre, S. Crane and V. B. Richmond elaborate *Guy*'s structure, its connections to hagiography and social politics, and its analogues in visual art and non-romance literature.[4] Yet, despite their interest in the romance, critics have almost entirely ignored one of the central themes in *Guy*: the hero's domination of Eastern empires, both Christian and Saracen. This neglect has limited criticism of *Guy* to fairly local concerns, in particular how the romance reinforces the socio-political ideals of its noble and upper bourgeois audience. Recognising the romance's Eastern emphasis reorients modern readings of *Guy* toward a broader historical framework: the romance engages wide chronological and geographical lenses that encompass several centuries of British history and most of the known medieval world. The importance of the East in *Guy of Warwick* reveals itself textually in three primary ways: the structure of the romance; its historical positioning; and the ideological conflicts that pit Guy against several different Eastern antagonists.

Structurally, Guy's adventures in the East comprise the centre of each half of the romance; in the first half, Guy falls in love with his lord's daughter, Felice; in order to win her affection he sets off to fight tournaments in Europe and repeatedly emerges the champion. Guy then travels to Constantinople to protect the Christian emperor Ernis from Saracen invaders. He is again victorious, successfully repulsing both the Saracens and Ernis' attempts to marry Guy to his daughter, Clarice. Guy returns to England where he defeats an Irish dragon who is ravaging Northumberland, after which he finally marries Felice. In the second half of the romance, Guy realises that he has neglected his heavenly duties in pursing only his desire for Felice. He once again travels through Europe to the East, this time to the Holy Land. There Guy defends Christian interests by defeating the Saracen giant Amoraunt, ensuring a balance of power more favourable to Christian dominance in the Holy Land. Guy finally returns to England and, as in the first half of the romance, reestablishes English sovereignty at home through one-to-one combat with Colbrond, champion of the Danish invaders. In the final scenes of the romance, Guy retires from public life and dies a hermit.

The structure of the romance, in two parallel cycles (a feature particularly marked in the early Auchinleck manuscript),[5] emphasises the centrality of the two long Eastern episodes.[6] This centrality is underlined by the importance of these episodes for Guy's development as a romance hero, for in each case he wins both military and moral battles in the East that could not have occurred elsewhere. In the first cycle, Guy triumphs over the Saracens who besiege Constantinople; he also overcomes the allure of the Emperor's daughter and his empire, which Guy would inherit as Clarice's husband. By conquering his foe and rejecting Clarice's temptations, Guy proves himself worthy of returning home and claiming Felice's love and her inheritance of Warwick. In the second cycle, Guy shifts from chivalric knight to knight of God, and again overcomes his foe, the giant Amoraunt. Guy also wins a moral victory for Christianity, not only in defeating a pagan, but also by ensuring safe passage for all Christians through the kingdom of Alexandria and by freeing the Christian defenders of Jerusalem (the Earl Jonas and his sons) from captivity. Thus each Eastern victory prepares Guy for a crucial transformation in his life: in the first, Guy returns from Constantinople ready to marry Felice and re-evaluate his purpose as a knight; in the second, the hero prepares himself to reject earthly values and to dedicate his life entirely to God. A doubling structure is also at work within each of the two cycles, emphasising the connection between Guy's triumphs in the East and those in England: in the first cycle, for instance, Guy fights two dragons (one near Constantinople and the other, later, in Northumberland), each of them threatening England or a symbolic representation thereof. Likewise, in the second cycle Guy takes on trials by battle with two giant African Saracens, one in Alexandria and one in England; by defeating each giant, Guy saves Christians (first Jonas and his family, then the English people) from the bonds of slavery. Each journey to the East spurs Guy to victory, both in arms and spiritually, but it also leads him back home to fulfil his duties to England. Guy's conquests in Constantinople and the Holy Land reinforce not only Western stereotypes of the East, but also the sense of Englishness against which these stereotyped images appear more alien.

While the double cycle that leads Guy from England to the East and back again emerges as a way of ordering and recognising coherence in this episodic romance, the Auchinleck version of *Guy of Warwick* offers the reader a visual clue as well: it changes from couplets to tail-rhyme stanzas between the two cycles and underlines this caesura with a short summary of part one before beginning part two. *Guy*'s place near the centre of the Auchinleck manuscript, both physically and thematically, replicates this sense of parallelism and continuation; each item in the codex complements *Guy*, either prefacing it or building upon it in ways too intricate to be explored here. As a whole, the collection suggests that the person or family who commissioned the book was interested in the East as a place for exploration, adventure, conquest, and Christian faith.[7] This context sharpens the focus of *Guy of Warwick* as a romance that is invested in Eastern identities and histories, especially when they are in conflict with Western Christianity. The rest of the contents of the Auchinleck manuscript support this claim: most of its other romances – notably, *Bevis of Hampton*, *Florice and Blauncheflour*, *King Richard* and *The King of Tars* – devote considerable attention to East–West conflict and, in some cases, fantastic resolution, while the religious material also tends to focus on Eastern figures and saints, like Margaret of Antioch and Catherine of Alexandria, who are imagined in these versions as openly in conflict with other Eastern religions. *Guy of Warwick* reworks these themes into a more immediate, historical framework. Indeed, *Guy* engages not only popular misconceptions of the East that we see so often in medieval romance – frequently centred on its religious and ethnic otherness, its perversity or licentiousness, and its violent threat to the West or Christianity – but also historical events whose implications for England and Western Europe remained unresolved well into the fourteenth century.

As its hero battles Eastern foes familiar to Crusade chronicles and legends, *Guy of Warwick* reveals the West's lingering anxieties about the questionable outcomes of the Crusades which, as a connected series of military and colonial endeavours, waxed and waned throughout England and Europe's later medieval period. The Crusades proved difficult for the medieval West to accept fully, particularly as success became more elusive and tales of the horrors wrought on Christians and non-Christians alike began to filter back to the homelands and enter popular knowledge and imagination.

The First Crusade (1096–99), although successful in capturing Jerusalem from the Muslims, was disastrous for relations between the West and the Byzantine East because it shattered the illusion, carefully maintained throughout decades of thinly veiled antagonism, that Eastern and Western Christianities still made up a single, unified entity called 'Christendom'. The Eastern Empire was important to the Christian West because it served as a geographical buffer zone between the West and its Muslim enemies. With Constantinople in the way, the Latin West was less vulnerable to invasion from the East. The Byzantine Empire also linked the West spiritually with the East and its major shrines. While Eastern and Western Christianity remained on reasonably amicable terms, Europe and England could assume a spiritual connection between themselves and their Eastern brethren.[8] Relations between Greeks and Latins had been strained for several decades before the First Crusade, but the distrust generated between Constantinople and the Latin Crusaders in the last years of the eleventh century would negatively influence East–West contact for centuries to come.

The utter failure of the Second Crusade (1147–49) and the ambiguous outcome of the Third Crusade (1189–92), led by Richard the Lionheart, increased Latin anxiety over Christianity's impotence to maintain control of the Holy Land. Richard's ruthlessness toward his prisoners of war, contrasted with Saladin's famous generosity toward Christians, may have caused the West to question the stereotypical monstrosity of its Muslim foe. The Fourth Crusade (1202–04) only confirmed the West's culpability: the Latin armies marched not against the infidel, but against their former Christian ally, the Byzantine Empire. Constantinople was burned and plundered of treasure and relics, and its citizens were raped and slaughtered.[9] The greed, arrogance, and poor judgement evidenced by such acts followed the Latin armies into the Fifth Crusade (1217–21), when they captured important Egyptian territories and were offered Jerusalem, but lost both due to immoderate demands and selfish leadership.

Guy's military triumphs compensate for the West's historical losses in the East, while his moral and spiritual superiority recuperates Latin atrocities against fellow Christians during the Crusades. Guy defeats his Eastern enemies manfully and cleanly; and, perhaps more importantly, he refrains from accepting compensation for his good deeds, much less demanding vast rewards as did his Crusading counterparts. Moreover, *Guy* rewrites the history of the Crusades obliquely rather than overtly; the romance does not simply embellish facts or modify major players, but instead places the echoes of these events into a distant past. *Guy of Warwick* ostensibly takes place not in the centuries of the historical Crusades, but in the mid tenth century, during the rule of King Athelstan. By making Guy a pre-conquest hero, the romance emphasises the purity of his Englishness – and thus his value as a representative of his people – and places the story within a much wider context of conflict, invasion, conversion, and resistance. By recalling historical events and people of the tenth century, notably toward the end of the romance when the Danes invade England, *Guy* plays on its audience's fears of external threats to national sovereignty and draws an implicit parallel between Guy's defence of his homeland and his defence of Western righteousness and Christianity while in the East. The romance thus legitimises Guy's Crusade-like efforts by linking them with England's past. The anachronistic setting of *Guy* in the tenth century also places the potentially troubling events of the Crusades into a long-finished and partly forgotten history, one that has taken on a quality of legend rather than recent, stark reality.

The argument of this essay, then, is that at the centre of each of

Guy's two cycles, the hero finds himself on a formative adventure in a fantastically imagined East; *Guy* devotes so much narrative attention to the East because the romance responds to and reimagines the West's conflicts with the East during the Crusades. *Guy* simultaneously asserts Latin dominance in both Christian and Muslim settings and rejects the most egregious moral error of the Crusades – the sack of Constantinople – by creating an alternative outcome in which the hero chooses not to seize control of the Byzantine Empire. In this way, *Guy* both affirms the project of the Crusades and rewrites those events that were unacceptable to the Latin West, allowing its audience to come to terms with its difficult past and to imagine a future of Crusading that will not repeat history's mistakes.

The Christian East: wily and womanly

The Byzantine Empire was the gateway to the East for the armies of the First Crusade and many of their later followers. In keeping with *Guy of Warwick*'s reworking of Crusade themes and events, Guy's first trip to the East leads him to Constantinople, the capital of Eastern Christendom. His stated motive: to help the Emperor Ernis repel the Saracens who have besieged the city. This Guy accomplishes successfully, but his adventures in Constantinople have only just begun; Guy's Byzantine beneficiaries, as I demonstrate below, prove more dangerous than the overt Saracen threat.

From the first news of the Emperor's distress, *Guy* establishes Constantinople's vulnerability and the potential rewards for the knight who will aid the city in its need. Guy hears of the siege of Constantinople through a group of merchants who have recently escaped the destruction of the Empire by the Sultan: 'In Costentyn þe noble emperour Ernis / Þai han strongliche bisett, y-wis. / Castel no cite nis him non bileued, / Þat altogider þai han to-dreued, / & for-brant, and strued, y-wis' (A 2819–23). The merchants continue by announcing in detail the riches they have brought with them from the noble city: 'Fowe & griis anouȝ lade we, / Gold and siluer, & riche stones, / Þat vertu bere mani for þe nones, / Gode cloþes of sikelatoun & Alisaundrinis, / Peloure of Matre, & purper & biis, / To ȝour wille as ȝe may se' (A 2832–7). These tidings echo popular justifications for the First Crusade by implying that the Byzantine Empire is not only in desperate straits, but that rich compensation will reward those willing to risk the trip eastward.[10]

The leaders of the First and Fourth Crusades were encouraged to take the cross using similar rationale. At the end of the eleventh century, a forged letter, purportedly from the Byzantine Emperor Alexius I to Count Robert of Flanders, circulated in Europe and was cited by the foremost instigator of the First Crusade, Pope Urban II.[11] According to Urban and the 'letter', Alexius had invited a Latin force to Constantinople in order to help the Greeks subdue Saracen infidels. Though the Emperor may indeed have hoped to lure Europeans for temporary military aid,[12] he undoubtedly did not intend to spark a large-scale invasion of the East. Europe, however, found it expedient to imagine that the Eastern Empire was on the brink of collapse;[13] the 'letter' was crafted to suggest this perspective:

> Nearly the entire territory from Jerusalem to Greece … and many other areas … have all been invaded by [the Turks], and hardly anything remains except Constantinople, which they threaten soon to take from us unless we are speedily relieved by the help of God and the faithful Latin Christians …. We therefore implore you to lead here to help us and all Greek Christians every faithful soldier of Christ you can obtain in your lands.[14]

In addition to this plea for 'every faithful soldier', the letter promises that the Emperor will place the city of Constantinople under the jurisdiction of the Latins. Contrary to the suggestions and promises in the 'letter', however, Alexius was reportedly alarmed to learn in 1096 that the armies of the First Crusade, a teeming horde of ill-disciplined folk of varying military abilities, had arrived at the shores of the Bosphorus and descended upon Byzantium.[15]

A century later, the armies of the Fourth Crusade were to receive a real request for relief from the Byzantine Empire. In 1202 Prince Alexius of Constantinople visited Philip of Germany, proposing that the Crusaders help him dethrone his uncle, the Emperor Alexius, who had in turn usurped it from Prince Alexius' father Isaac. To make the request more attractive, the young prince offered to submit the Eastern Church to the authority of Rome and to repay the Crusaders with large quantities of money and supplies as well as adding ten thousand of his own troops to the effort to conquer Egypt,[16] which was the explicit object of the Fourth Crusade. The Latins were eager to aid the supposedly helpless Eastern Empire and to gain valuable rewards and political influence in the region. But when Prince Alexius, now Alexius IV, failed to fulfil all the terms of his agreement, the Crusaders attacked Constantinople in retribution. Far from conquering Egypt and establishing a solid Christian dominance in the Near East, the Fourth Crusade did not advance beyond the borders of Christendom; it ended, instead, with the Latin conquest and pillage of Constantinople in 1204, when a Latin emperor, Count Baldwin of Flanders, was established for the first time on the throne of the Eastern Empire.

As in the historical Fourth Crusade, the enemy during Guy's sojourn in Constantinople quickly shifts from Saracen to Greek. Despite Emperor Ernis' warm welcome of Guy's help in destroying the Saracens, the Emperor's steward, Morgadour, is less friendly. Jealous of the attention (and the promise of the princess's hand in marriage) Guy receives from the Emperor, Morgadour treacherously plots against him. He encourages the hero to visit the princess, unsupervised, in her chambers, trying to incite the Emperor to turn on Guy; when the Emperor remains unconcerned for his daughter's chastity, Morgadour succeeds in convincing Guy that the Emperor plans to kill him. On the verge of leaving his host to join the Emperor's Saracen enemies, Guy encounters Ernis and resolves their misunderstanding; the fact remains, however, that Guy is prepared to defect to the infidel camp and attack Constantinople, the very city for which he had recently sacrificed the lives of many of his companions.

This incident recalls the tensions between historical Crusaders and Byzantine emperors, whose 'natural' Christian alliance against the Turks was undermined by mutual mistrust. Beginning with the First Crusade, many Crusade armies feared that the Eastern Christians would turn on them: stereotypes of the 'treacherous Greek' persisted throughout the centuries of chronicles and other literature written in response to the Crusades. One of the first events that seemed to support Latin suspicion of the Greeks occurred early in the campaigns of the First Crusade, when Alexius I, concerned for the stability of his Empire, negotiated a surrender of the city of Nicaea to the Greeks under the nose of the Latin army, who had hoped to plunder the city for its wealth.[17] Alexius' failure to aid the besieged and starving Crusaders after their capture of Antioch in 1098[18] and the Emperor's intercepted letters to the Egyptian Fatimids[19] further established the Crusaders' distrust of the Greeks.[20] Likewise, in the romance, Guy is easily persuaded of the Emperor's duplicity and his evil intentions. Thus the hero betrays the Greeks before he can, as he thinks, be betrayed by them. In this instance, however, Guy is mistaken in his mistrust of the Emperor; the real danger here is not that the Emperor plots against him, but that the Emperor has no control over his ranks, rendering him ineffective against internal as well as external threats. The Emperor's crime is incompetence rather than malevolence.

Though Christian knights fighting with Saracens against other Christians is not unheard of in medieval history, it is uncommon in Middle English literature; in *Guy*'s case, I would argue, Guy's near defection implies that the hero has been lured off course by the wily Greeks. As well as making the hasty and condemnable, though at last averted, decision to fight alongside Saracens and against Christians, Guy has been diverted from his service to Felice and his goal of returning to England victorious. The fact that Guy even considers changing his loyalties implies that he has lingered away from home for too long, allowing his primarily military role at Constantinople to blur into desire for power and leaving England vulnerable to foreign attack. Guy has, by this time, become contaminated by his lengthy stay at Constantinople; still developing into the mature knight he will become, Guy's contact with the Greeks poisons him with unorthodox ideas and values. Indeed, poisoning is an unmanly tactic for which the Greeks were notorious among Latin Christians. Greeks were thought to operate not through strength or skill, but through cunning. Anna Comnena, princess of Byzantium, recognises the Crusaders' suspicion of poisoning at the beginning of the First Crusade when Bohemond arrives at the Imperial court: served both raw and cooked meat, the Crusader chooses to have the raw food prepared for him by one of his own men, admitting that he 'was afraid [Alexius I] might arrange to kill [him] by putting a dose of poison in the food'.[21] Such a characterisation of Greeks is neatly represented in the romance by the figure of Morgadour, who, in fact, poisons Guy's reputation, threatening his honour and his life.

The history of the First and Fourth Crusades is particularly important to the present discussion because *Guy* incorporates elements of the historical events of the previous two centuries, reworking them to appeal to its contemporary audiences and revising historical outcomes into 'happy endings'. *Guy of Warwick*, like the architects of the Crusades, fantasises about rescuing a vulnerable Constantinople from the infidel and from the Byzantines' own internal moral corruption and incompetence. By echoing Alexius I's 'letter' and Alexius IV's plea to Germany, the romance creates the illusion of an Eastern Empire complicit in her own conquest by the West – a figurative damsel-in-distress who will marry and submit to her rescuer. Constantinople, however, is not the only vulnerable woman in this segment of the romance. By conjuring Clarice as a flesh-and-blood princess who must marry in order to secure the future of the Byzantine Empire, *Guy* reimagines the politics of conquering the rescued territories and establishing a Western emperor there – a solution that, in the romance, the Byzantine Emperor himself suggests. Ernis draws the audience's attention to the parallel positions of his daughter and his Empire by promising to reward Guy's defeat of the Saracens with Clarice's hand and half of his territory as a package deal: 'ʒif þou miʒt me of hem wreke, / & þe felouns out of mi lond do reke, / Mine feyr douhter þou schalt habbe, / & half mi lond, wiþ-outen gabbe' (A 2885–8).

The romance's conflation of Clarice and Constantinople plays once again on old Crusade imagery. Pope Urban, for instance, evoked the damsel-in-distress image during his crusading address at Clermont, in which he encouraged the West to embark on the First Crusade: 'Jerusalem is the navel of the world; the land is fruitful above all others, like another paradise of delights ... She seeks therefore and desires to be liberated, and does not cease to implore you to come to her aid.'[22] By portraying Clarice and Constantinople as two halves – the literal and the figurative – of the same feminine trope, *Guy* connects the hero's goal with that of the Crusades; furthermore, the romance replaces Jerusalem with Constantinople because, in the popular imagination as well as in Crusades literature, Constantinople is, much more than the Holy City, the land of milk and honey.[23]

By the thirteenth century, however, Constantinople had been ravished of her riches by the Fourth Crusade, leaving the Latins morally compromised by the destruction and carnage they left in their wake. *Guy* imagines Constantinople in all her glory, before her deflowering by the West, though the imminence of this deflowering may be alluded to by the sexual availability of Clarice, who could bring Guy all the riches of Byzantium through the more legitimate means of a conjugal union rather than military force.[24] Such a reimagining of the circumstances that led to the Western conquest of Constantinople invites the romance's audience to reconsider the terrible outcome of the historical Fourth Crusade, suggesting that the East was not only part of her own downfall, but even desirous of her conquest.

Honoured by Ernis' flattery and enticed by the lovely Clarice, Guy initially accepts the Emperor's invitation to marry his daughter and lingers in Constantinople for a time. He even goes to church to marry Clarice, but suddenly falls ill with a malady that signals the untenability of his acceptance of the Emperor's offer. Guy recognises that his illness is symbolic, sensing that his marriage to Clarice would make him culpable for deserting his true English love, Felice. Guy is thus threatened not only by the infamous treachery of the Greeks as figured in Morgadour, but also by their 'feminine wiles' in the character of Clarice.[25] The East's allure is a feminine, sexual presence – unsuspected, but all the more dangerous because of its subtle appeal to the hero's emotions and vanity rather than his honour and military skill.

The temptation to marry Clarice and inherit her father's empire nearly causes Guy to break his oath to Felice and desert his homeland, but the greater threat to Guy in this situation is the danger of re-enacting one of the greatest calamities of the Crusades: the Latin conquest of Constantinople. For the Crusaders who took Constantinople at the beginning of the thirteenth century, the rewards were clear: for the nobles, the possibility of lands and titles as well as reunification of the Eastern and Latin churches. More importantly, and for the majority of the Crusaders, the glory of Constantinople lay in its riches – monetary, cultural, and reliquary treasure. Of all the disasters committed by Crusaders during the Middle Ages, the sack of Constantinople in 1204 was most horrifying to Europe and to Rome because of the brutality it inflicted not on the infidel, but on fellow Christians. As it became clear that this conquest would not resolve the break between the Eastern and Latin churches or ensure the safety of overland routes to the Holy Land, initial justifications for it waned. *Guy of Warwick* replays the choice the Crusaders faced in 1204: to accept the losses of war and turn the other cheek on real or imagined acts of treason on the part of the Greeks, or to stay in Constantinople and take control of the richest city in Christendom. The Crusaders chose to capture the city; in order to recuperate the West, however, the romance hero must reject the obvious appeals of becoming, like Baldwin of Flanders, the first Latin Emperor of the East. Unlike Baldwin and the other Crusaders, Guy recognises that the Greeks would not accept him as their Emperor, even if Ernis would (A 4435–44).

If Guy's illness on his wedding day is not enough to convince him of the threat the East poses for him morally, another symbolic incident reveals to him the dangers of remaining in Constantinople. After defeating the Saracens, Guy goes out to explore the country, only to discover a dragon attacking a lion in the woods. In a scene that parallels Guy's victory over the Saracens, the hero saves the lion by stabbing the dragon through the throat and beheading it, much as he killed the Sultan besieging Constantinople. The lion, grateful for Guy's service, becomes the hero's faithful companion in a re-enactment of Chrétien de Troyes's *Yvain*, or *Le Chevalier au Lion*. In medieval European literature, lions traditionally symbolise Christ; in an English romance, they may be associated as well with Englishness, as are Richard the Lionheart and the three lions on the standard of England, Richard's battle flag. Indeed, Guy is compared to a 'lyoun' repeatedly throughout the romance, alluding to his Englishness and his inherent nobility through connection with England's favourite 'king of the beasts' as well as its favourite Crusader king. Guy and his lion become inseparable after the incident in the forest, but one day Guy becomes distracted by the entertainments offered by the Emperor's court – eating with the Emperor, sitting with him and 'pley[ing] in compeynie' (A 4299–302) – and allows his lion to wander off. Guy returns to his lodgings without the lion, who is attacked and mortally wounded by the treacherous Morgadour.[26] Guy's English identity and his Christian morality have thus been compromised through his dalliance at Constantinople.

When Guy forgets about his duties to his faith and his country, represented by the lion, preferring instead the luxuries of the Eastern court, he risks both loyal companionship and his own moral integrity. He also puts England at risk, depriving it of its best champion: while Guy lingers in Byzantium, Ireland (in the form of a dragon) threatens to ravish Northumbria. The subtle allure of the East, combined with its murderous treachery, threatens Guy's English identity and his very soul. Though Guy avenges the death of his lion by killing Morgadour, he cannot save the faithful beast; like his decision to side with the Saracens against Ernis and his temptation to marry Clarice, this incident implies a weakness on Guy's part, indicating that Guy's reputation and his faith have been poisoned by the attraction of the monetary, territorial, and sensual wealth the East has to offer. Guy tries to shift his guilt to Ernis by admonishing him, '"Seþþe þou no miȝt nouȝt waranti me, / Whar-to schuld y serui þe, / On oncouþe man in thi lond, / When þou no dost him bot schond?"' (A 4415–18); but the death of the lion forces Guy to realise that Constantinople is a dangerous place, spiritually as well as physically. '"Harm me is, & michel misdo; / þerfore ichil fram þe go, / & in oþer cuntres serue y wile, / Þer men wille ȝeld me mi while"' (A 4419–22), he decides, and takes leave of the Emperor, none too soon.

When Guy leaves Constantinople, refusing to marry Clarice and exposing the treachery within the Byzantine court, he enacts a fantasy of rejection in response to the East's invitations. Both Guy and the Latin leaders of the Fourth Crusade go to Constantinople, at least explicitly, to help a disempowered Emperor. But the romance responds to the West's ambivalence – even horror – about the conquest of Constantinople by rejecting the material and sensual rewards that both Alexius IV and Ernis offer in compensation.

Guy's experiences in Constantinople generate a clear set of traits that distinguish the Near East from the other lands he has visited. Together, these traits combine to form an identity that characterises the Eastern Empire and that infuses nearly everyone and every situation that Guy encounters there. The Christian East is ambiguous and friendly, but treacherous. It is feminine, sumptuous and luxurious; it has sexual appeal and the promise of great power and riches; it is vulnerable and desires Guy's protection, evoking the 'damsel in distress' trope of chivalric romance and making Guy's would-be marriage to Clarice appear, at least on the surface, a justifiable possibility. Despite all the East has to offer, however, Guy's sojourn there – like the conquest effected by the Fourth Crusade – is a diversion that threatens to lure him away from his goals and obligations in England as well as to the Roman Church. By purposefully and unnecessarily remaining on Eastern soil, Guy risks succumbing to the personality – that is, the representative characteristics that are developed through individuals rather than collectives in the romance – that the East engenders.

Impersonating the Muslim East: Saracens, giants and disguise

If the personality of the *Christian* East is seductive and subtle, the *Muslim* East is masculine: threatening, militaristic and physically overwhelming. In the second half of the romance, after he has left Felice, Guy makes his way to the Holy Land as a pilgrim-knight to seek God's forgiveness. Here the threat of treachery is present, but minimal; Guy must worry instead about the super-human physical force of the enemy. The Muslim East is also racialised in a way that the Christian East was not. In Constantinople, the Greeks are distinguished by their flawed morality, different because they do not share Guy's English sense of honour – a code that includes models for both knightly behaviour, exemplified by the trusty Herhaud, and female modesty, as we see in Felice. Even the Saracens at Constantinople, when we see them, perform not so much as racial or ideological others, but as a collective army against which Guy must wage battle because it has attacked his ally. When individuals are singled out of this army, usually because of their rank, Guy dispatches them quickly, with little dialogue that might suggest a conflict beyond the politics of the battlefield. The Saracens Guy encounters in the Christian East are a military enemy, not primarily a spiritual one, and they seem no more nor less honourable than the Greeks he meets there.

Once Guy becomes God's knight, however, his conflict with the Saracens gains deeper significance, and the enemy is portrayed as physically and ethnically as well as spiritually alien. Guy's primary adventure in the Holy Land occurs when he encounters Earl Jonas of Durras who, with his fifteen sons, has been captured while driving the Saracen enemy away from Jerusalem and into Alexandria, their 'owhen lond' (A 52: 3). Jonas' captor, King Triamour of Alexandria,[27] in turn displeases the Sultan, who requires that Triamour find a champion to fight for him against Amoraunt, the gigantic, black, fiendish Saracen of Egypt. Triamour delegates this task to Jonas, who, at the time Guy meets him, has spent the last year searching for the English hero. Guy has concealed his identity since becoming a poor pilgrim, but offers to fight Amoraunt in order to save Jonas and his family from certain death.

Though Guy technically fights for Triamour, the text explicitly qualifies his action by stating that Guy takes up the challenge for the sake of Jonas, a Christian and defender of Jerusalem. Moreover, Triamour promises to free all his Christian captives and grant safe passage through his lands for all Christians if Guy wins. Like the Emperor of Constantinople's invitation and his offer to make Guy his heir, this scenario echoes a widespread Crusader fantasy; ostensibly, the First Crusade was launched in part because pilgrims were being killed and robbed on their way to and from the Holy Land.[28] Later Crusades were aimed at capturing Egypt, which was a military stronghold of the Muslim world and considered crucial to the fate of Jerusalem from the Third Crusade onward.[29] Since, in the romance, the Christians already tenuously control Jerusalem,[30] a diplomatic alliance with the King of Alexandria would be a strategically brilliant move on Guy's part.

Before such an alliance is guaranteed, of course, Guy must defeat Amoraunt. The descriptions of the giant are vivid, and they are emphasised by repetition – the audience learns of Amoraunt's physical appearance both when Jonas tells Guy of his troubles, and again when Guy himself encounters his adversary. The first description, which introduces Amoraunt as a 'blac' Saracen, focuses on his intimidating physical presence: 'Michel & griselich was þat gome / Wiþ ani god man to duelle. / He is so michel & vnrede, / Of his siȝt a man may drede, / Wiþ tong as y þe telle. / As blac he is as brodes brend: / He semes as it were a fende, / þat comen were out of helle' (A 62: 5–12). When Guy comes face to face with his opponent, the giant no longer merely *seems* like a fiend; Guy's judgement is definitive: '"It is," seyd Gij, "no mannes sone: / It is a deuel fram helle is come"' (A 95: 10–11). The text focuses on three features that lead Guy to conclude that Amoraunt must be a devil: his religion ('Saracen'), his colour (black), and his impressive size.

Amoraunt, like Morgadour, does play an unfair trick on Guy – he convinces Guy to let him have respite to drink from the river, then refuses to allow Guy to do the same – but treachery is not the giant's dominant trait. Rather, he is dangerous because of his physical superiority and his sheer determination. He hates Guy not simply because the hero is on the other side of a military conflict, but also because he is *English* and *Christian*, a proven enemy of his Saracen clan.[31] This clash, then, is characterised not so much as a territorial dispute, but as an ideological battle between right and wrong, between Christian and Muslim. The fact that Amoraunt focuses on Guy's identity as an Englishman suggests that this episode tests Guy not only as an individual, but as a representative of England and English identity.

Unlike the Saracens whom Guy fought in the Christian East, Amoraunt is recognisably different. His size is abnormal, and the text repeatedly emphasises the blackness of his skin and eyes. Already alien because of his religion, Amoraunt's size and colour mark him as racially and ethnically *not English* in a physical way that religion alone can not.[32] Here we see a blurring of the boundaries among ethnic, racial, territorial and national identities that suggests that Amoraunt is a representative, if extreme, example of the non-English, non-Christian, Eastern 'race'.[33] His personality, like the people and place he represents, is aggressive and physically domineering.

My contention that Amoraunt is representative of an Eastern identity type is supported by the fact that he has a double – he reappears later in the romance as Colbrond – to whom the text links him through verbal repetition. Having defeated Amoraunt and helped a friend in need in Germany, Guy returns to England, hoping to end his days in peaceful asceticism. Before he retires from his public life, however, Guy must fight one last foe: Colbrond, champion of the invading Danes. Colbrond is like Amoraunt in almost every way: he is from Africa, part of the Muslim Empire (the Auchinleck text specifies that Amoraunt is from Egypt, while the Caius version agrees that both are from 'ynd', which was sometimes associated with the horn of Africa), a giant with black skin, and Saracen. The two episodes share structural similarities: Colbrond is described twice, once when Guy learns about the giant's existence and the need for a champion to fight him, and again when Guy faces him in battle: 'He was so michel & so vnrede, / Þat non hors miȝt him lede.../ Al his armour was blac as piche. / Wel foule he was & loþliche, / A grisely gom to fede' (A 255:

4–5, 257: 7–9). Between the two descriptions in each case, Guy is enlisted as the giant's opponent, and the leaders of each side agree to terms that will dictate what the winners will gain and the losers will lose. The battle between Guy and Colbrond develops parallel to the encounter with Amoraunt, including Guy's horse being struck from under him and the giant calling for Guy's surrender; Guy even kills the two heathens in much the same way, striking off the arm or arms of each opponent, then beheading him.

Amoraunt and Colbrond, then, are essentially the same foe; the significant difference between them is that Guy fights the former in the East, the latter on home turf. In the East, Amoraunt represents an Eastern identity that may threaten Guy personally, but which does not threaten his ethnic/racial/national identity. Guy can leave Amoraunt and the East behind and return to his homeland, the place of his ethnic roots. But as a representative of the East in England itself, Colbrond poses a greater threat. This episode of *Guy of Warwick* remembers, of course, the Danish invasion of King Athelstan's England in the tenth century, the temporal setting of the romance. Colbrond, along with the Danes for whom he fights, seek to replace English identity with another, foreign identity by making the English subjects of Denmark, a domination expressed by English king Athelstan as 'þraldom' (A 239: 11) or servitude. In Alexandria, Guy fought Amoraunt to preserve the most fundamental identity – life – of a group of captives, Jonas and his sons; in England, Guy likewise fights for a fundamental identity – the freedom of his people, threatened with becoming thralls in their own land.

In light of these struggles to preserve the right and the ability to maintain distinct proto-national identities and freedoms, the racial and ethnic affiliations that are contested or affirmed in the *Guy* texts become even more important. Unlike the squabbles for land one finds in a typical ancestral romance, the conflicts involved when Guy faces his Eastern opponents (especially Colbrond) are not internal skirmishes between Englishmen; they are the expressions of ethnic difference and the desire to maintain that difference, that spatial separation from the other. The author of the English *Guy* is careful to provide the audience with the imaginative tools to visualise and conceptualise Guy's adversaries as fundamentally different, both in appearance and in character, from the English hero. Colour is rarely evoked in the romance, yet Amoraunt and Colbrond are uniquely and repeatedly referred to as black;[34] their blackness is an external indicator of their difference from Guy, and of their fiendish moral status.

Because blackness has, in this romance, taken on such strong ideological overtones, I would like to retrace my steps, through Colbrond and Amoraunt, back to the first episode in which blackness becomes an identity marker in *Guy of Warwick*. I have delayed discussing this episode because its significance is most easily recognised in retrospect. The events to which I refer take place very soon after Guy returns to Europe from his stay in Constantinople, just before he returns to England to slay the Irish dragon. While making his way through Germany, Guy rescues a wounded knight, Tirri, who soon becomes a fast friend. They survive several adventures together, most of which involve defending themselves against Duke Otoun of Pavia, Guy's and Tirri's old nemesis. Eventually, the Duke manages to capture Tirri, and locks him away in a dungeon. As a faithful friend, Guy must save Tirri, but without alerting the Duke, for he also holds Tirri's beloved Oisel as his prisoner. Guy undertakes the rescue by disguising himself as 'Yon', dying his hair and face black, and presenting himself to the Duke bearing the gift of a swift steed raised by a Saracen, his 'owen cosyn' (A 6122). Conveniently, the Duke makes 'Yon' his jailer, allowing Guy to sneak Tirri away to safety without Otoun's knowledge. The hero then kills the Duke (who is on his way to church to marry Oisel), rescues the lady, and returns her to her lover, Tirri.

The episode reveals a side of Guy's personality that the audience has not yet observed: he is cunning, and operates not through force, but by manipulating the perceptions of those around him. I would suggest that this episode is, in fact, based on Guy's experiences in Constantinople, while foreshadowing his future conflicts with the black giants. Since Guy meets Tirri immediately after his sojourn in the Christian East, the obstacles he overcame there and the personalities with which he was in contact still exert an influence on him; thus, disguising himself as 'A man ... o fer cuntre' (A 6117) would seem a natural choice for penetrating Otoun's lair. Dying his face and hair black, Guy temporarily takes on an Eastern personality, ready to dissemble and deceive. Blackness here makes Guy difficult to identify, and gives him license to behave in a way that he has criticised in others. By intentionally taking on an Eastern identity for a short time, and for a noble purpose, Guy seems to absolve himself of any residual contamination that may linger in him as a result of the temptations he faced, and only partly overcame, in Constantinople.

The blackness of Guy's hair and skin, moreover, demonstrate visually for the Duke, as they will for the audience later, another identity marker he assumes in his disguise: Guy implicitly marks himself as a Saracen, or Muslim, by emphasising that the Saracen who raised his steed is his cousin. Thus Guy prepares the reader to associate blackness with Islam and with infiltration. After all, Guy invades the Duke's country – indeed, his home – paralleling Amoraunt's infringement upon the Holy Land and Colbrond's invasion of England toward the end of the romance. It is through some form of invasion, then, that Guy faces all of his significant enemies: Guy defeats the Saracens at Constantinople because they have invaded Eastern Christendom; he overthrows Otoun by invading the Duke's home in disguise; he kills the Irish dragon, who has invaded Northumberland; he then overcomes Amoraunt, who is thrust in Guy's path because Jonas invades Alexandria in response to the Muslim invasion of Jerusalem; and finally, Guy repulses the invading Danes on English soil by overpowering Colbrond. Such invasions are important symbolically because they violate the sacred space and corporate integrity of the invaded. In each case, the invasion threatens to overturn the native ruler and to disrupt national, ethnic, or religious identities.

Conclusion

Guy of Warwick engages with history through the transformative medium of fantasy, which allows the romance to reshape historical events its audiences found troubling and to provide satisfactory resolutions to historical errors committed during the Crusades. Equally importantly, the romance allows an exploration of both the hero's personal identity and England's national identity through Guy's contacts with the East. As suggested by the romance's diptych structure, the East becomes the locus of each of the two formative cycles in Guy's career as chivalric knight and knight of Christ.

I have suggested here that there are two Easts in *Guy of Warwick,* one Christian and the other Muslim, which the romance characterises differently through the personalities of archetypical individuals – on the one hand, the insidious Greeks represented by Morgadour the steward, Emperor Ernis, and his daughter Clarice; and on the other hand, the physically monstrous Saracen giants, Amoraunt and Colbrond. These 'personalities' of the East are in conflict with Guy and the English identity he represents. But Guy surmounts these conflicts through conquest of territories, individuals, and the temptations – power, riches, and sex – that the East offers him. I have only begun to indicate how these conflicts influence the romance's conceptualisation of English national identity, which still wants further study. This theme and others have, unfortunately, been largely neglected by scholars of Middle English romance who find *Guy*'s militarism and episodic structure unappealing. Through its fictional reworking of the Crusades, however, *Guy of Warwick* demonstrates that English identity in the late thirteenth and early fourteenth centuries – a period when Englishness was becoming an increasingly important aspect of England's national identity – was contingent on both England's domination of other territories and peoples and its vulnerability to external threat. Read from this perspective, the romance invites today's readers to take a closer look at the sometimes conflicting multiple layers of identities one recognises here: the feminine, the masculine, the monstrous, the religious, the national, the territorial, the individual. Because *Guy of Warwick* has been read and discussed so little since the rise of cultural studies in academia, the romance remains open to new readings that explore this complex work within the broad social, political and literary context of its inception.

Notes

I want to thank Geraldine Heng and Nicola McDonald for their feedback on this chapter throughout its development. I am also grateful to Elizabeth Scala and J. Patrick Bedell for suggestions on early drafts and to Marjorie Woods and Joan Holladay for encouragement as I researched the manuscript history of *Guy of Warwick*.

1 F. Jameson. 'Magical narratives: romance as genre', *New Literary History*, 7.1 (1975), 135–63; S. Knight, 'The social function of the Middle English romances', in David Aers (ed.), *Medieval Literature: Criticism, Ideology & History* (New York, 1986), pp. 99–122.

2 In *Chivalric Romances* (Bloomington, 1983), L. Ramsey suggests that the Anglo-Norman *Gui de Warewic* was composed between 1232 and 1242 (p. 48), while V. B. Richmond, following J. Wathelet-Willem, argues that the earliest *Guy* was written immediately after the Fourth Crusade; see Richmond, *The Legend of Guy of Warwick* (New York, 1996), p. 24.

3 V. B. Richmond and S. Crane each discuss in some detail the differences between the English *Guy* and its Anglo-Norman predecessors. See Crane, *Insular Romance: Politics, Faith, and Culture in Anglo-Norman and Middle English Literature* (Berkeley, 1986), pp. 1–17, 66–7, and Richmond, *The Legend of Guy*, pp. 37–49.

4 A few of the most important studies on the manuscript history of *Guy of Warwick* are L. A. Hibbard, *Mediaeval Romance in England* (New York, 1960), pp. 127–39; A. J. Bliss, 'Notes on the Auchinleck manuscript', *Speculum*, 26 (1951), 652–8; *The Auchinleck Manuscript, National Library of*

Scotland Advocates' MS. 19.2.1, eds D. Pearsall and I. C. Cunningham (London, 1977); T. Shonk, 'A study of the Auchinleck manuscript: bookmen and bookmaking in the early fourteenth century', *Speculum*, 60 *(1985)*, 71–91; J. Frankis, 'Taste and patronage in late medieval England as reflected in versions of *Guy of Warwick*', *Medium Aevum*, 66 (1997), 80–93. For more detailed analysis of the romance's structure, see M. Mills, 'Structure and meaning in *Guy of Warwick*', in John Simons (ed.), *From Medieval to Medievalism* (Basingstoke, 1992), pp. 54–68, who argues for a tripartite rather than a bipartite structure to the romance; and J. Burton, 'Narrative patterning and *Guy of Warwick*', *Yearbook of English Studies*, 22 (1992), 105–16. S. Crane in *Insular Romance* and V. B. Richmond in *The Legend of Guy* both elaborate on the romance's popular appeal, and Richmond catalogues Guy's appearance in other works and media. For hagiographic and biblical references, see P. Price in 'Confessions of a goddess-killer: Guy of Warwick and comprehensive entertainment', in J. Weiss, J. Fellows and M. Dickson (eds), *Medieval Insular Romance: Translation and Innovation* (Cambridge, 2000), pp. 93–110; R. Dalrymple, 'A liturgical allusion in "Guy of Warwick"', *Notes and Queries*, 45 (1998), 27–8; and Crane, *Insular Romance*, pp. 62–4, 92–117, 128–33. For discussions of *Guy*'s socio-political interests, see T. Turville-Petre, *England the Nation* (Oxford, 1996), particularly pp. 108–41, and Crane, *Insular Romance*, pp. 1–12, 62–91. This list is not exhaustive, but is reasonably representative of current work on *Guy*.

5   The version of *Guy* in the Auchinleck manuscript (Edinburgh, National Library of Scotland, MS Advocates' 19.2.1), compiled *c.* 1330 in or near London, has distinct advantages for the modern reader: it is the earliest extant version of the poem in Middle English, offers a relatively complete text, and is conveniently edited by J. Zupitza in *The Romance of Guy of Warwick*, EETS e.s. 42, 49, 59 (London, 1883–91). In addition, *Guy*'s inclusion in a large compilation manuscript allows us to study the romance in context (for a full list of the contents of the Auchinleck manuscript, see Bliss, 'Notes', pp. 652–3). The two most complete later versions of the romance in Middle English may be found in Cambridge, Gonville and Caius College, MS 107 and Cambridge University Library, MS Ff. 2. 38. The Auchinleck manuscript will be cited in this paper as 'A'.

6   I agree with Burton ('Narrative patterning') that the Auchinleck *Guy* is a single romance arranged as two parallel cycles. The break between the two parts is relatively insignificant: the second cycle continues on the same page and in the same column that complete the first cycle. There is no new item number, title, or illustration, all of which are common divisions between individual works in Auchinleck. *Reinbrun*, on the other hand, is marked as a separate romance in Auchinleck: it has a new original item number, its own title, and it begins with a large illustration.

7   Shonk suggests a bourgeois patron for the Auchinleck manuscript in 'A study of Auchinleck', p. 90, while Turville-Petre (*England the Nation*, p.

136) speculates that the book was commissioned by the Beauchamp family, who claimed to be descendants of Guy of Warwick.

8 Baldric of Dol's version of Urban's speech at Clermont highlights the 'brotherhood' of the Eastern and Western Churches by referring to Eastern Christians as 'fratrum nostrorum' and 'fratribus nostris'. See Baldrici, Episcopi Dolensis in *Recueil des historiens des croisades: historiens occidentaux*, 5 vols (Paris, 1841–95), vol. 4, p. 14.

9 Paradoxically, such behaviour is represented by both Pope Urban, instigator of the First Crusade, and a dubious letter supposedly written by Alexius I as characteristic of *Muslim* atrocities against Christians. For Urban's representation of the Muslims' behaviour toward Christians, see Baldric of Dol, Guibert of Nogent, and Robert of Rheims in E. Peters (ed.), *The First Crusade*, 2nd edn (Philadelphia, 1998), pp. 29–31, 36–7, and 27, respectively. For the Latin, see *Historiens occidentaux*, vol. 4, pp. 12–14 (Baldric) and 140 (Guibert), and vol. 3, pp. 727–8 (Robert). For the letter purportedly from Alexius I, see *Recueil des historiens des croisades: historiens grecs*, 2 vols (Paris, 1875–81), vol. 2, pp. 53–4.

10 Though the romance's focus on the merchants' riches *suggests*, rather than explicitly *promises*, compensation for acts of knightly prowess such as rescuing the Emperor of Constantinople, Felice has conditioned Guy to expect rewards for his knightly deeds by representing herself as the ultimate 'prize'; Guy rejects this dynamic in the second half of the romance. Not coincidentally, the depiction of the merchants echoes Fulcher of Chartres' enthusiastic description of Constantinople's riches in his Chronicle of the First Crusade: 'Oh, what an excellent and beautiful city! ... It is a great nuisance to recite what an opulence of all kinds of goods are found there; of gold, of silver, of many kinds of mantles, and of holy relics. In every season, merchants, in frequent sailings, bring to that place everything a man might need.' Peters (ed.), *The First Crusade*, p. 62. For the Latin, see *Historiens occidentaux*, vol. 3, p. 331.

11 In *Christianity, Social Tolerance, and Homosexuality* (Chicago, 1980), J. Boswell discusses this letter in terms of its depictions of the Muslim other as sexually and ethnically deviant (p. 279). He reproduces the letter in English translation as Appendix 2, pp. 367–9.

12 On Alexius' need for mercenary troops, see M. McGinty, *Fulcher of Chartres: Chronicle of the First Crusade* (Philadelphia, 1941), p. 15 (note 1) and S. Runciman, *A History of the Crusades*, 3 vols (Cambridge, 1951–4, reprinted Harmondsworth, 1965), vol. 1, pp. 104–5, 107.

13 For Urban's use of the 'call for help' from Constantinople, see the *Chronicle of Fulcher of Chartres*, I. 3 in Peters (ed.), *The First Crusade*, p. 52. For the Latin, see *Historiens occidentaux*, vol. 3, p. 323.

14 Boswell, *Christianity*, p. 368.

15 *The Alexiad of Anna Comnena*, trans. E. R. A. Sewter (Harmondsworth, 1969), pp. 308–9.

16 For the terms of Prince Alexius' agreement with the Fourth Crusaders,

see Joinville and Villehardouin, *Chronicles of the Crusades*, trans. M. R. B. Shaw (Harmondsworth, 1963), p. 50. For the French, see Villehardouin, *La Conquête de Constantinople*, ed. E. Faral (Paris, 1938), pp. 92, 94.

17 For a more detailed discussion of the capture of Nicaea and the so-called treachery of Alexius, see Runciman, *History of the Crusades*, vol. 1, pp. 175–82.

18 On Alexius' abandonment of the Crusaders at Antioch, see Runciman, *History of the Crusades*, vol. 1, pp. 239–40; *The Alexiad*, trans. Sewter, pp. 345, 349; D. Munro, *The Kingdom of the Crusaders* (New York, 1935), p. 51.

19 Runciman, *History of the Crusades*, vol. 1, pp. 272–3.

20 The motif of the 'treacherous Greek' is repeated in histories of the Crusades well beyond the end of the First Crusade. According to Runciman (*History of the Crusades* vol. 2, pp. 25, 28) the Latins blamed Alexius when they were attacked by the Turks and when they ran short of food and water during the Crusade of 1101. Over the course of the Second Crusade (1147–49), the Greeks were again accused of various treacheries, including killing Frederick Barbarossa and not following through on offers of monetary assistance (Munro, *Kingdom of the Crusaders*, pp. 136, 141, 198). In Ambroise's *Estoire de la Guerre Sainte*, ed. G. Paris (Paris, 1897), the Greeks are characterised as 'faus' (line 740), as 'gent colverte' and worse than Saracens (lines 1434–35), and they attempt to kill the titular hero, Richard, with poison arrows (lines 1925–26). References to the treachery of the Greeks in literature of the Fourth Crusade (1199–1204), during which Constantinople was taken by the Latins, are numerous; see, for example, Joinville and Villehardouin, *Chronicles*, pp. 80, 115, and p. 44 and 84 for internal treason (the French may be found in G. de Villehardouin, *La Conquête de Constantinople*, ed. Jean Dufournet (Paris, 1969), pp. 87, 127, 91 and 44, respectively); E. Peters, *Christian Society and the Crusades, 1198–1229* (Philadelphia, 1971), pp. 13–14, and p. 9 for treason within the Byzantine Empire; Robert of Clari, *The Conquest of Constantinople*, trans. Edgar Holmes McNeal (New York, 1936), pp. 83–6 (for the French, see Robert de Clari, *La Conquête de Constantinople*, ed. Philippe Lauer (Paris, 1956), pp. 59–62).

21 *The Alexiad*, trans. Sewter, p. 328.

22 The quote is taken from Robert of Rheims' version of Urban's Clermont address, translated by D. Munro, reprinted in Peters (ed.), *First Crusade*, p. 28. For the Latin, see *Historiens occidentaux*, vol. 3, p. 729.

23 Fulcher of Chartres, for instance, describes both Constantinople and Jerusalem in his Chronicle. His description of Constantinople corresponds nicely with Urban's descriptions of Jerusalem, an earthly paradise overflowing with riches and wonderful sights. Fulcher's impression of Jerusalem, however, is moderate, drawing the reader's attention to the rocky terrain, the lack of reliable natural water sources, and the modest size of the city. For Fulcher on Constantinople, see Peters (ed.), *The First Crusade*, p. 62. For the Latin, see *Historiens occidentaux*, vol. 3, pp. 331–2.

For Fulcher's description of Jerusalem, see Peters (ed.), *The First Crusade*, pp. 87–9. For the Latin, see *Historiens occidentaux*, vol. 3, pp. 355–7.

24 The deflowering metaphor used here applies not only to Clarice's sexual availability through marriage, but also to the crimes perpetrated upon the women of Constantinople when that city fell to the Latins in 1204. See Runciman, *History of the Crusades*, vol. 3, p. 123.

25 In 'Cannibalism, the First Crusade, and the genesis of medieval romance' (*differences: A Journal of Feminist Cultural Studies*, 10 (1998), 98–174), Geraldine Heng argues that the 'Romani' referred to as 'womanish' by Geoffrey of Monmouth are, in fact, Greeks. See *The Historia Regum Brittanie of Geoffrey of Monmouth I: Bern, Burgerbibliothek, MS 568*, ed. Neil Wright (Cambridge, 1985), pp. 128–9. Here Geoffrey explicitly links the Greeks with femininity or effeminacy. Implicitly, chroniclers of the Crusades often make this connection as well, frequently by citing the Greek aversion to hand-to-hand battle.

26 This episode, in which Guy's lion is killed by a Greek traitor, seems to invert a historical event of the Crusade of 1101. According to Runciman, the Crusaders killed Alexius I's pet lion during their brief riot in Constantinople (*History of the Crusades*, vol. 2, p. 20). If the killing of Guy's lion is symbolic of his temporary separation from Christ, the death of Alexius' lion may also be read as evidence of his problematic break with the Roman Church.

27 Triamour's name, which translates roughly as 'three loves', most probably refers to the trinity of gods attributed to Islam in many medieval romances: Apollo, Ternagant, and Mahoun (Mohammed).

28 Both Urban and the false letter of Alexius I cite the difficulty, even the horror, of the pilgrimage to the Holy Land as a reason for the West to venture East and 'liberate' Jerusalem as well as persecuted Christians, both Eastern and European. See, for instance, Guibert of Nogent's version of Urban's address in Peters (ed.), *First Crusade*, pp. 36–7. For the Latin, see *Historiens occidentaux*, vol. 4, pp. 139–40. See also Runciman, *History of the Crusades*, vol. 1, pp. 78–9, 98. Other contemporary romances also deal with this problem of waylaid pilgrims, including, for example, *Richard Coeur de Lion*, which shares many themes with *Guy*.

29 For the importance of Egypt in the Crusades, see Runciman, *History of the Crusades*, vol. 3, pp. 110–11, 151.

30 In reality, Christians had not held Jerusalem since Saladin recaptured the Holy City for the Muslims in 1187. Christians were never to regain direct control of the Holy City. In the tenth century, which is when, historically, the romance is set, Christians were still over a century away from taking Jerusalem for the first time.

31 Amoraunt presents himself as a relative of the Sultan whom Guy killed at Constantinople, thus associating himself explicitly with the threat against Eastern Christianity.

32 In *Guy of Warwick*, there are no examples in which religion itself acts as a

physical marker. There are rare instances in medieval English literature, however, for which this is not the case; in the *King of Tars*, which also appears in the Auchinleck manuscript, religious orientation determines the physical appearances of both the Sultan and his son.

33 For a discussion of 'ethnic nationalism' in medieval England, see Turville-Petre, *England the Nation*, pp. 16–17. Turville-Petre devotes an entire chapter to expressions of nationalism in the Auchinleck manuscript, including *Guy of Warwick*.

34 There are only two references to the colour black not discussed here: the Saracens Guy fights in Constantinople are briefly alluded to as black, but only when the discussion is about something else – the treasure that Guy took from them. The Irish dragon that Guy kills just before he marries Felice is also described as black. The thematic correlation between this dragon, which also invades England from a nearby country, and Colbrond / the Danes is probably not coincidental.

Index

This index aims to identify the key concepts and ideas that inform individual essays, to draw connections between the essays that otherwise might be missed, and to initiate a dialogue between the popular romances themselves.

All medieval texts and authors have been indexed, but modern medieval scholarship has not. End-of-chapter notes are only indexed when the information they contain is not easily apparent from reading the text.